# PICTURES INTO WORDS

*Stages*

SERIES EDITORS

# Pictures into Words

*Images in Contemporary French Fiction*

ARI J. BLATT

University of Nebraska Press · Lincoln and London

A portion of chapter 1, "Puzzling Pictures," was previously published as "Towards an Iconology of the Text: Art History and the Expanded Field in Claude Simon's *Triptyque*" in *Word & Image* 22, no. 1 (January–March 2006): 68–76. A section of chapter 4, "Remake," appeared in print as "Remake: Appropriating Film in Tanguy Viel's *Cinéma*" in *Contemporary French and Francophone Studies* 9, no. 4 (December 2005): 379–86. Both articles are reprinted with the permission of the Taylor & Francis Group (www.informaworld.com).



Funding for the completion of this project was provided by the Office of the Dean of the College of Arts and Sciences and the Office of the Vice President for Research and Graduate Studies at the University of Virginia.

∞

*Library of Congress Cataloging-in-Publication Data*

Blatt, Ari J.
Pictures into words: images in contemporary French fiction /
Ari J. Blatt.
p. cm. — (Stages) Includes bibliographical references and index.
ISBN 978-0-8032-3805-3 (cloth: alk. paper)
1. French fiction—20th century—History and criticism.
2. Art in literature. 3. Narration (Rhetoric). 4. Simon, Claude—Criticism and interpretation. 5. Perec, Georges—Criticism and interpretation. 6. Michon, Pierre—Criticism and interpretation. 7. Viel, Tanguy—Criticism and interpretation. I. Title.

PQ637.A77B53 2012 843'.91409357—dc23
2011037226

Set in Sabon by Kim Essman. Designed by A. Shahan.

For Solène

# Contents

# Illustrations

# Acknowledgments

A number of colleagues, institutions, and friends have helped make this book possible. At the University of Pennsylvania, where the idea for *Pictures into Words* first began to take shape, I am especially grateful to Gerald Prince, who served as a wonderful mentor. Gerry's intellectual rigor, generosity, and good humor will always be a model for me. Maurice Samuels was instrumental in helping me find my scholarly voice and remains a privileged interlocutor to this day. Christine Poggi from Penn's department of the History of Art shared much about her own field of expertise. More recently my colleagues at the University of Virginia have been stellar advocates of my work, and I thank them all for providing such a collegial and intellectually dynamic environment in which to research and teach. In particular, Claire Lyu, Amy Ogden, and John Lyons gave very thoughtful comments on various drafts. As chair of the Department of French Language and Literature, Cheryl Krueger came through on multiple occasions with resources necessary for the book's completion.

Further afield, I am indebted to Warren Motte, Derek Schilling, Carrie Noland, Jean Duffy, and Jan Baetens for their invaluable feedback on various portions of the manuscript. Kristen Elias Rowley at the University of Nebraska Press shepherded the project through the publication process with a great deal of professionalism and care. Comments and suggestions from the anonymous readers for the Press have made the final product more cohesive and clear. I learned a lot about the academic publishing business from Dick Holway. Andrew Sobanet, Melissa Friedman, Bettina Lerner, and Mark Oren cheered me on along the way. Larry Kritzman deserves special thanks for taking an early interest in this book, and for his guidance and encouragement over the years.

The Department of Romance Languages and Literatures and the Graduate School of Arts and Sciences at the University of Pennsylvania provided generous funding during the early stages of this project. A Chateaubriand Fellowship from the French Ministry of Foreign Affairs and a Jeanne Marandon Grant from the Société des Professeurs Français et Francophones d'Amérique allowed for research time in Paris. A summer stipend and Sesquicentennial Fellowship from the College of Arts and Sciences at the University of Virginia permitted me to finish the manuscript, while an additional award from the Dean of the College of Arts and Sciences and the Office of the Vice President for Research and Graduate Studies helped make publication of the illustrations possible. My sincerest thanks are due to the artists who granted me permission to reproduce their work in the following pages.

I have been humbled by the unwavering support of my family. Thank you to Jessica, Adam, and Ryan Agovino, Etan Blatt, Trish Hennessey, and Talya Blatt. In France, Jean-Pierre and Marie-Françoise Thomas, Benoit, Gwenaëlle, Arthur, Clément, and Victoire Jorion, and Alain Marlé welcomed me into their hearts and homes. My parents, Judy and Ken Blatt, are quite simply the most inspiring people I know.

My greatest gratitude goes to my wife, Solène Thomas-Blatt. Her understanding, patience, and love kept me going through even the most trying of times. I dedicate this book to her.

# PICTURES INTO WORDS

# Introduction

> Images for sale by the thousands, by the billions, by the millions of billions, ready to take the place of whatever is missing.
>
> LYDIE SALVAYRE, from *Contre*

> I never read, I just look at pictures.
>
> ANDY WARHOL, from *Andy Warhol: A Retrospective*

With the rise of modern forms of mechanical and, now, digital reproduction, contemporary culture has been subjected to an unstoppable invasion of visual signs that bombard us from all angles, emanating from numerous sources, at all hours of the day. Western society is "literally raining with images—whether pouring out of museums, channeled through television, video, software programs, and digital disks, or streaming from multimedia monitors and optical displays."[1] While traces of this ubiquitous iconic presence are evident in earlier periods—one might think, for example, of the public dissemination of royal iconography, of the king's "symbolic body," in *ancien régime* France, or of the exuberant commodification and consumption of image-based spectacles throughout the nineteenth century—the preponderance of graphic signs has proven to be a pervasive force in the post–World War II era, a period marked deeply by the advent of new means of exhibition and display and by the dominance of advertising, popular culture, and the mass media.[2]

Pictures are everywhere and people can't stop talking about them. To be sure, the last several decades have produced an abundance of discourses, commentaries, and theories about the status and power, and about the uses and abuses, of visual images. Keen observers of everyday life, in France and elsewhere, have spoken of a "cancerous growth of vision" throughout many parts of the developed world.[3] Inhabitants of advanced societies today are said to "consume pictures and no longer . . . beliefs."[4] Ours is a time characterized by a rampant form of "imagomania," an age marked by the gradual "videation" of culture, in which every individual risks being subjected to an unbridled and often anxiety-provoking "tyranny of the visual."[5] As Susan Sontag succinctly put it, the image "is at the very heart of our modernity."[6]

It is only natural that the modern flux of pictures, and the abundant critical thinking that aims to make sense of this proliferation, would have wide-ranging implications for the larger field of cultural production. *Pictures into Words* argues that the endemic traffic of images in the latter half of the twentieth century has profoundly affected the content, structure, and symbolic logic of contemporary French fiction in particular. To assess the implications of the "civilization of images"[7] for the writing of narrative, this book focuses on a distinctive corpus of texts that tell stories about pictures. These stories, in turn, address many of the most salient questions pertaining to the relationship between literature and visual culture today. What does late–twentieth-century French fiction have to say about the primacy of the visual in everyday life? How does literature—traditionally viewed as the image's semiotic "other"—cope with the chronic profusion of pictures? Where do literary texts stand with regard to ways of seeing? And finally, what might texts that are wholly invested in such issues ultimately reveal about the enterprise of writing during the most recent turn of the century, an age when the number of people reading works of literature suffered a marked decline?[8] Indeed, as this last question implies, the stakes are high. In a society overrun with visual signs, the fate of literature hangs in the balance: "either [literature] rises to the challenge," as Guy Scarpetta has remarked, "or it condemns itself to scarcity, exhaustion, and disappearance under the weight of society's screens."[9] *Pictures into Words* sets out to demonstrate how certain writers are not merely conscious of this alarming state of affairs, but have been actively grappling with these crucial questions, and with this enduring crisis of faith in literature, through narrative. The stories that they tell reevaluate and reinvigorate the position and future of fiction in a world where, as novelist Lydie Salvayre coolly (and sardonically) hints in the epigraph that opens this chapter, pictures claim to satisfy our every desire.[10]

## *Telling Pictures*

Derived from the Latin *pictura* (painting), a picture today has come to mean much more than a mass of colored pigment applied to a flat surface. According to traditional definitions, and depending on the context, the term may refer to a much wider variety of graphic representations, including drawings, statues and "monumental effigies," theatrical tableaux in which a group of people and objects are "picturesquely" arranged and posed, or a representation of something formed "by physical means, as by a lens," like photographs and films.[11] Regardless of the medium or support, a picture may signify a symbol or an illustration that denotes or elucidates a particular subject. The term might also refer to a number of less tangible, more figural and ephemeral visual representations, such as optical images (engendered by mirrors, prisms, and various technologies of projection), perceptual images (sense data, appearances), mental images (dreams, memories, ideas, or other pictures that form in the mind), and verbal images (like metaphors and descriptions).[12] Throughout this study I use the term "picture" (interchangeably with the term "image," though sometimes the latter is associated with those more disembodied visual objects that I enumerate above) to refer primarily to two-dimensional, graphic visual representations, which are to be understood in the most general, naturalistic, and concrete sense. That said, I privilege "picture" for its malleability, for its relative ambiguity, for the way it inherently encompasses the various other kinds of visual representations that appear in our line of sight and in the narratives under consideration here.[13]

Pictures of all kinds have intrigued the French for years. No wonder France has played such a vital role in the history of modern visual culture. France became the epicenter of modern painting during the second half of the nineteenth century, and its scientists and technicians paved the way for the invention of both photography and the cinema. The nation has an impressive record of sophisticated thinking about vision and visual representation and continues to exert its influence around the world. As historian and film scholar Antoine de Baecque notes, the question of the image "has always had in France its commentators, its historians, its own debates. . . . There is a uniqueness to the image in France, a French genius for images even, in how we produce, use, practice and, especially, interpret them."[14] The modern history of critical writing about images in France involves professional critics, poets, novelists, historians, sociologists, theologians, phenomenologists, anthropologists, and, of course, visual artists themselves. All of these groups regularly examine particular pictures to meditate on more perennial questions about power, vision, spectatorship, reality, and other ideological, aesthetic, and epistemological concerns. This legacy attests to a collective desire if not to institute a national standard of visual literacy, then at least to understand what images do and how they work. French culture's enthusiasm for reading images is evident in an array of intellectual signposts that marked the twentieth century: in the instrumental brand of visual semiology developed by essayists and critics in the 1950s and 1960s; in the turn toward painting, vision, and aesthetics by modern and contemporary philosophers; in the various reflections on photography that contributed to the medium's birth, in the 1970s and 1980s, as a legitimate object of theoretical inquiry; and in the impressive legacy of film criticism and theory that spans the twentieth century.[15] More mainstream figures like Daniel Schneiderman and the cast of "Arrêt sur images," a popular television program dedicated to the systematic close reading and demystification of some of France's most popular mass-media productions, also typify the nation's collective critical interest in the visible world. So, too, do other made-for-television programs like Agnès Varda's "Une minute pour une image," a series of 170 two-minute shorts from 1982 in which various subjects (from famous writers and artists to local business owners and functionaries) offer their own unique and often highly personal commentaries on select photographs. Another such program is "D'art d'art!," the weekly, rapid-fire art history lesson that airs on channel 2, which has recently emboldened viewers to decipher work as diverse as paintings by Zurburán, Raphael, and El Greco, installations by Sophie Calle and Piotr Kowalski, sculptures by Arman and Duchamp, and a Babylonian pillar (ca. 1750 BC) upon which the Code of Hammurabi has been engraved for eternity.

The enduring French admiration for images and ingenuity in understanding them is complemented by French literature's own longstanding passion for pictures. Historically, many of the most influential poets, playwrights, and novelists were also successful art critics.[16] A good number of them were also excellent practicing artists. Audiences worldwide continue to admire exhibitions of Victor Hugo's drawings, Emile Zola's photographs, and Henri Michaux's enigmatic "signs." Writers like Jean Cocteau, André Malraux, Alain Robbe-Grillet, and Marguerite Duras produced some of the last century's most enduring (and polemical) films. Throughout the history of French literature writers have often turned to images for inspiration, and have frequently incorporated descriptions of pictures, real or imagined, in their work.[17] Modern French fiction's gleaning of image culture is particularly significant in this regard. The nineteenth century, for example, proves rich in narrative works in which pictures of various kinds serve a variety of symbolic and diegetic purposes. Consider, for example, the mystifyingly hermetic tableau around which Honoré de Balzac's short story "Le chef d'œuvre inconnu" (1837) revolves, or the paintings attributed to Gustave Moreau that adorn the walls of Des Esseintes's salon in J-K Huysmans's *A Rebours* (1884).[18] Photographs and photographers are significantly present in stories by Champfleury ("La légende du daguerréotype," 1863), Alphonse Daudet ("Le photographe," 1873), and Emile Zola ("L'inondation," 1880), and descriptions of engravings, *affiches*, and other graphic images to see become, throughout the nineteenth century, a vast array of pictures to read.[19] The rampant development of visual technologies that created even more ways to exhibit graphic images to mass audiences—in newspapers, museums, dioramas, panoramas, postcards and *cartes de visite*, stereoscopes, zoopraxiscopes, magic lanterns, and cinemas—granted French culture a veritable stockpile of pictures with which to contend. Indeed, narratives that tap into what Charles Baudelaire called culture's "warehouse of images and signs" map the prominence of the visual on the larger cultural landscape of nineteenth-century France, a period that "seems to usher in a veritable impulse toward the image, a 'thrust of the gaze' (as Jean Starobinski called it) toward a world considered to be an inexhaustible reservoir of images and pictures for the eye."[20]

The motif of pictures, often complemented by a decidedly pictorial way of seeing, continues to appear in prose works throughout the first half of the twentieth century by a considerable number of French authors (in Marcel Proust, Victor Segalen, Louis Aragon, Julien Gracq, Jean-Paul Sartre, and Michel Butor, among others). The popularity of the cinema has also left an indelible mark on several literary texts from those days that take the moving image as theme.[21] It is not until the last few decades of the twentieth century, however, that French fiction's "impulse toward the visual" becomes more akin to an obsession. From Dominique Noguez's comic tale of a point-and-shoot vacation gone sour in *Les 36 photos que je croyais avoir prises à Séville* (1993) and Marguerite Duras's fetishistic meditation on a lover's photograph in *L'amant* (1984) to Didier Daeninckx's collection of fictions about television in *Zapping* (1994) and Michel Tournier's critique of various visual spectacles and simulacra of all kinds in *La goutte d'or* (1985), to give a few of the more notable examples, many texts have recently taken the exploration of the potential impact of pictures on fiction to new extremes. In doing so, they attest to, and often critique, the pervasiveness of images to which Western cultures have become so accustomed, all the while suggesting just how potent a narrative generator pictures can be.[22]

Exhibiting more than just a propensity toward the visual, however, the works by Claude Simon, Georges Perec, Pierre Michon, and Tanguy Viel that are studied in the following chapters are among the most direct, innovative, and constituent encounters with visual culture yet, mobilizing the images they tell as a principal thematic and diegetic force. Countless works of modern fiction include descriptions of, or allusions to, an image or a group of images as a self-reflexive prompt or symbolic marker. By contrast, the works that I examine here originate in, conjure up, and altogether concern pictures. They exemplify the text as "imagetext" or "iconotext" paradigm, to use the terminology developed by scholars of word and image studies. Rather than simply incorporating descriptions of images in an insubstantial or merely cosmetic way, these narratives engage "the place of visuality in language" through a manifest desire to "construct an entire text as an evocation, incorporation, or substitute for a visual object or experience."[23] Visuality, the visual arts, and visual culture, in turn, wholly condition the narrative and rhetorical effects of these texts. These are, in other words, books both *of* and *about* pictures. Claude Simon's *Triptyque* (1973), which will be studied in chapter 1, depends on a complex narrative web that weaves together three intercalated tales—each of which originates in a work by one of three modern painters —through a series of embedded descriptions of various lowbrow images that propel the novel forward and invite readers to imagine and envisage the story told within. Chapter 2, "Faking It (Phony Pictures)," analyzes George Perec's *Un cabinet d'amateur: Histoire d'un tableau* (1979), a carefully crafted literary ruse about a devious art market swindle. At the center of this story about an enthusiastic art collector and his prized collection of pictures lies a dizzying painting portrayed within a painting that represents all the works in the collection *en abyme*. Moving from a false painting and the tale of its fictional collector to a series of authentic images made by a real artist, Chapter 3 turns to Pierre Michon's *Vie de Joseph Roulin* (1988). In his own take on the time-honored tradition of the *Künstlerroman*, or artist's novel, Michon focuses his attention not on the painter (van Gogh, in this case), but on the model (the Provençal postman referred to in the book's title whose portrait van Gogh painted in 1888). This quasi-hagiographic, fictionalized biography of Roulin offers an oblique but telling look at the painter and his works, and contemplates the famous portraits and drawings of the postman in a new light. Finally, the last chapter takes readers from the galleries and modern museums to the movies with a study of Tanguy Viel's *Cinéma* (1999). In this breakthrough novel, a manic, pathologically cinephilic narrator obsessively "projects" Joseph Mankiewicz's classic 1972 film *Sleuth* from beginning through to "The End." Like each of the texts I study here, *Cinéma* demands a decidedly more visual way of reading, rousing readers to see the images on display not with their eyes but with the mind's eye.

To facilitate this cognitive envisioning of images in words, these texts not only explore the picture as theme, relying on the consistent evocation of visual representations to generate the stories they tell, they also exploit the world of visual culture as a prominent structuring metaphor. Aside from the obvious pictorial model to which its title refers, *Triptyque* is also arranged in much the same way as a jigsaw puzzle; *Un cabinet d'amateur* relies on a beguiling poetics of simulation rooted in the model of the trompe l'oeil; *Vie de Joseph Roulin* animates the still subject of a painting in a literary *tableau vivant* that brings the story of the postman's encounter with the famous painter to life; and *Cinéma* is explicitly conceived as a verbal film strip (what the narrator calls a "pellicule vocale").

Distinguishing themselves from texts that employ images in a less consequential or purely ornamental way, these narratives consider the possibility of a kind of writing modeled on graphic or plastic forms. They thus explore what is at stake when novelists choose to appropriate pictures in writing and, in doing so, let the pictures partake in the storytelling.

Telling, however, does not necessarily imply showing. From *Triptyque*'s archive of graphic images (which includes movie posters, photographs, postcards, film strips, and illustrated book covers) to the paintings at the center of *Un cabinet d'amateur* and *Vie de Joseph Roulin* and the film around which *Cinéma* revolves, none of the novels examined here reproduces the pictures they tell. Rather than occupy the visible space of the printed page—as they do in other influential word-image hybrids such as André Breton's *Nadja* (1928), the *ciné-romans* of Alain Robbe-Grillet, or other illustrated artists' books, photo-essays and photo-novellas, graphic novels, and collections of calligrammatic or concrete poetry that abound in the history of modern French literature—the images in these texts are rendered literally, but not visually, readable. Though optically invisible, the pictures that these narratives describe are nevertheless embodied by the literary sign that points "in the direction of the visible."[24] This dependence on a verbal description of a visual representation that idealistically endeavors to identify readers with beholders or spectators capable of discerning the image as if it were "before their own eyes" places these novels under the aegis of *ekphrasis*, which proves to be the most prominent discursive figure throughout.[25] Building on an ancient tradition that originates in Homer's famous description of Achilles's shield in *The Iliad* (ca. 800 BC), and in the verbal depictions of paintings in the *Imagines* of Philostratus the Elder (ca. third century AD), these texts are, in a sense, imagetexts, or ekphrastic narratives taken to the extreme. They not only represent the image in words, they consistently test the picturability of language and its capacity to make us "see."

Not inconsequentially, the literary turn toward its semiotic "other" that these texts reflect is more or less coterminous with a similar shift in Western thought away from problems rooted in linguistics and textuality toward questions motivated by more visual concerns. This pictorial or visual "turn," as critics refer to it, is evident in work by a number of writers, in both Europe and the United States, who since the 1960s have attempted to come to terms with the idea "that pictures form a point of peculiar friction and discomfort across a broad range of intellectual inquiry."[26] More recently, a number of thinkers, French thinkers in particular, have produced a wealth of scholarship that seeks to map a collective history of aesthetic philosophy from its origins in antiquity through the present. French presses have also recently published a number of more theoretically oriented writings that propose pioneering ways of understanding the nature of visual art, the conditions of its reception, and its connection to the other disciplines.[27] It is not altogether surprising that this inquiry into the wider theoretical and philosophical implications of pictures and vision (and the intellectual "friction" that looking at pictures often provokes) occurs in an age characterized by an inexorable circulation of visual signs. As W. J. T. Mitchell has argued, the problem of pictorial representations "presses inescapably now, and with unprecedented force, on every level of culture, from the most refined philosophical speculations to the most vulgar productions of mass media."[28] The four chapters that comprise *Pictures into Words* demonstrate fiction's recognition of this sense of urgency and suggest precisely how literature factors into the debate. One primary objective of this study, therefore, is to show how a particular brand of visually engaged, ekphrastic fiction that originates in and is energized by images can offer potent reflections on the nature of visual culture and bring literature to bear on the larger significance of pictures in society today.[29]

## *Reading for the Pictures*

The kind of intersemiotic crossbreeding that these narratives epitomize solicits readers to consider them within the context of other, extratextual signifying practices. It would be myopic, if not irresponsible, to study these works in isolation. Rather, these narratives deserve to be read for the pictures, so to speak. This is to say that the texts I study here elicit tacit links with a number of pictorial intertexts—namely, with visual artists and their work, much of which is produced at around the same time, and with the critics and theorists who seek to come to terms with this production—that serve as an indispensable hermeneutic tool. In a kind of "interpretive juxtaposition" that is modeled on—yet inverts—Mieke Bal's groundbreaking reading of Rembrandt's paintings through the lens of related verbal texts, part of each chapter in this book confronts literary narratives with a variety of works of visual art that prove to be integral to the exegesis.[30] Whether as a stimulus to the story or generator of description, as a thematic reference, cultural allusion, or theoretical subtext, these intertexts (quoted directly or hinted at indirectly in the narrative, mentioned by the authors in essays and interviews published elsewhere, or echoed in the larger nexus of associated artworks and ideas) allow for a more truly interdisciplinary understanding of the relationship between writing and the visual, and between these particular texts and their larger cultural contexts.

One of my aims in situating these narratives within the broader frame of contiguous trends in the history of art and visual-cultural studies is to correct the shortcomings of more traditional approaches to word and image relations by entering into the interdisciplinary fold between verbal and visual culture that these textual "imagetexts" necessarily engender.[31] For some time now, the field of visual studies, including art history, film studies, and visual-cultural studies more generally, has mobilized techniques usually associated with literary criticism and theory in order to better analyze the objects under consideration. Despite this cross-boundary borrowing, however, the impact of visual-cultural studies on literature remains spotty, to say the least. Art history, it would seem, has profited more from literary studies than literary studies has gained from art history.[32] As Mitchell notes, "The notion of an 'iconology of the text,' of a thorough rereading or reviewing of texts in the light of visual culture is still only a hypothetical possibility, though the emergence of studies in film, mass media, and of larger ambitions within art history make it seem more and more unavoidable."[33] Taking this challenge to heart, this book aspires to turn this "hypothetical possibility" into a reality by mobilizing the image as a prism through which to view texts that are explicitly engaged with the visual. The readings that follow elucidate certain shared tropes that reveal the underlying relationship between literature and the visual arts in the 1970s, 1980s, and 1990s. More specifically, narratives by Simon, Perec, Michon, and Viel incorporate images as part of a strategy that exposes how literature contributes to a larger transnational continuum of ideas, positions, and trends associated with much postwar artistic production. These include the emergence of an explicit kind of disciplinary boundary-crossing that constitutes a reaction against the hegemonic tenets of Modernism; the role of the false in the debate surrounding the "end of art"; the critique and, by contrast, the positive affirmation of the artwork as commodity; and debates about the continued pertinence of originality and authenticity in an age in which the recycling of culture has become the norm.

Simon's *Triptyque*, for example, explores the limits of its own medium (a text), while acting out an embryonic desire to assimilate some other, more visible form (like a picture). The novel thinks outside of the medium-specific box and experiments with the boundaries of writing not merely by modeling its three narrative strands on works by visual artists, but also by incorporating descriptions of (primarily lowbrow) images throughout. As it draws its energy from various types of extradisciplinary (and particularly visual) sources, *Triptyque* represents an equivalent to those works of contemporary art that forge a path into the "expanded field" of representation, mobilizing a strategy critical of, and resistant to, the modernist drive to purify form.

In its own writing of the image, Perec's *Un cabinet d'amateur* capitalizes on the author's interest in the subversively playful nature of trompe l'oeil. The text's harnessing of the powers of the false resonates with a series of contemporary or related visual-cultural intertexts that complicate the relationship between art and authenticity: these range from Andy Warhol's silkscreened *Brillo Boxes* and Arthur Danto's philosophical meditation on the larger implications of Warhol's work to the incredible story of Dutch forger Han van Meegeren and Orson Welles's 1974 filmic essay *F for Fake*. While equally seductive in its trickery, *Un cabinet d'amateur* nevertheless impels readers to recognize the potentially duplicitous nature of all forms of visual representation to which we are consistently—both optically as well as intellectually—subjected.

Michon's *Vie de Joseph Roulin* shares common interests with contemporary practices by a number of artists whose work aims to interrogate the institutions that collect, display, and exchange art. The text's particular exploration of the lives of van Gogh and his model, a simple postal clerk who remains dumbfounded by the painter's art, allows for a probing aesthetic and institutional critique. In consistently engaging one of modern art's most compelling quandaries—as the narrator ponders, "Who decides what is beautiful, and thus valuable?"—*Vie de Joseph Roulin* lays bare the inexorable conflation of modern art and economics.

Finally, Tanguy Viel's "remaking" of a film in words experiments with image appropriation in an allegorical kind of bricolage inherited from Marcel Duchamp's avant-garde logic of the readymade. In the final chapter I study *Cinéma* by way of a number of contemporary visual artists whose work also inherits Marcel Duchamp's appropriationist economy to suggest how Viel's novel constitutes a literary response to the innumerable "reverberations of the Readymade" in contemporary culture.

Such an "iconology" of French texts that refers to a number of artworks and critical writings produced outside of France (most particularly in the United States) is suggestive of the fluid international cultural exchange that has only continued to accelerate since the end of World War II. With the rise of advanced technologies of transportation and communication allowing for the liberal flow of individuals and information across an increasingly "flat" world, conventional geographic borders no longer pose a legitimate threat to cultural isolationism in the West.[34] Moreover, not only are the narratives studied here wholly conditioned by pictures, the connections between the writers and their visual-cultural environments are concrete, rendering the analyses that follow more nuanced than a merely comparative approach would allow. Simon, for example, was directly influenced in his writing by artwork that he saw firsthand while traveling in the United States; Perec was a film buff, and often mentioned his interest in contemporary art, most notably in the work of a number of American "hyperrealist" painters; Michon, a self-confessed iconolater, has commented explicitly on the vagaries of the international markets for both art and books, and is hardly immune to the effects of what he calls the encroachment of "non-literature" on literary space; and finally, not only is *Cinéma* a retelling of an American film, but Viel has written in more places than one about his admiration for Marcel Duchamp and the contemporary legacy of the readymade.

The truly interdisciplinary inquiry to which this type of reading aspires is, of course, tempered by an awareness of its author's own intellectual limitations. Although the analyses are, in part, informed by scholarship in art history, criticism, and theory, I remain wary of advancing claims about art per se, and make every attempt to avoid assuming the role or function of the art historian or critic. Instead, following the work of scholars who address the social history of art and literature, and providing the necessary interdisciplinary twist, parts of the readings that follow can be best described as art-historical or visual-cultural analyses of literature. These readings consider verbal representations in light of contemporaneous—but hardly arbitrary—developments in the practice and criticism of the various graphic and plastic arts. In this way this book seeks to reveal what literature has to tell readers about contemporary attitudes about art, and about representation more generally.

## *In Plato's Cave*

While narratives by Simon, Perec, Michon, and Viel intersect with the work of numerous postwar artists and their critics, the analyses in each chapter combine to underscore another central argument of this book: despite their seemingly jubilant raiding of image culture to generate, provide a structure for, and enrich their stories, many contemporary narratives that tell tales about pictures simultaneously evince a cautious skepticism and even anxiety about vision and visual representations. These writers, conscious of where they stand with respect to the broader field of cultural practices that include the visual arts, engage pictures in writing in a gesture that melds overt collaboration and lurking recalcitrance. Though the novels under consideration here intimate a certain complicity with the visual, and while many contemporary imagetexts implicitly acknowledge the potentially constructive potential of images for literature, I want to suggest that the tendency to tell pictures in contemporary French fiction simultaneously masks a fundamental tension with, indeed a latent imperviousness to, images and ways of seeing them.

Historically, although many societies, from ancient Greece to *ancien régime* France, generally esteemed the power of pictures and considered sight to be the most important of the senses, this did little to prevent a number of thinkers from vilifying the image and maligning our ability to see. Plato's politically conditioned iconophobia is only one of the earliest instances of a kind of antivisual position that would become more prominent over time, especially during the twentieth century. Yet what is particular to the more modern (and postmodern) theorizing about pictures is that proponents of the image's ubiquity have been consistently challenged, and rendered comparatively inert, by the plethora of detractors. Pictures today might be "everywhere transmitted" and "universally viewed," but the image as a category is commonly condemned. As Barbara Stafford writes, "[The image's] visionary role in speculating about the conduct of life is obliterated by a relentless discourse of voyeurism and trickery. . . .

Even as the din grows louder over plagiarism, misappropriation of written evidence, incomplete research, and errors in fact, images are perceived as more treacherous, requiring greater control, tougher proscriptions, than verbal modes."[35]

*Pictures into Words* detects a subtle but similarly iconoclastic position in the narratives it examines. The images that texts by Simon, Perec, Michon, and Viel portray are ambiguously deceptive and dangerously seductive, seen but not necessarily understood, fetishized, commercialized and, at times, downright fake, and decidedly more complex than they initially appear. It is only logical that the act of seeing should fare no better. Vision, as the most cynical iconophobes tell us, is defective and weak; our [unaided] eyes are hardly equipped to deal with the ever-increasing complexity of the visible world.[36] Thanks in part to the rampant development of increasingly popular "vision machines" throughout the nineteenth and twentieth centuries, a "crisis in perceptive faith" has become one of the enduring symptoms of modernity's legacy.[37] As intellectual historian Martin Jay has argued, for a number of modern thinkers sight is no longer the most noble, the most superior of senses. His analysis of discourses representative of a variety of fields—philosophy, social theory, psychoanalysis, cultural criticism, and post-structuralist theory—reveals a deeply rooted "negative obsession" with vision. What is perhaps most interesting for my purposes here is that Jay locates the most vocal, "most prevalent and multifarious" proponents of this "antiocularcentric" critique in thinkers who emerge from France. From Sartre's writings on the sadomasochism of the look and Foucault's critiques of panoptic surveillance and the abuses of a controlling institutional gaze to Debord's lament against the evils of spectacular society, "a great deal of recent French thought in a wide variety of fields," Jay writes, "is in one way or another imbued with a profound suspicion of vision and its hegemonic role in the modern era."[38] Keeping Jay's central thesis in mind, *Pictures into Words* ponders a distinctively literary take on this "antiocularcentric" attitude. More specifically, the chapters that follow collectively suggest how, and to what degree, the kind of antivisual discourse that Jay sees as a widespread phenomenon in contemporary French thought may be implicitly reflected in works of French fiction that are written at around the same time and that are themselves deeply invested in questions related to pictures and sight.

Although they do not give in to the kind of explicit and pernicious iconophobia that Jay's study traces—in other words, they do not entirely deny the idea that "good looking" is still possible—those novels that tell pictures do nevertheless tacitly convey a lingering sense of resistance toward vision and visual representations.[39] Though readers never actually see with their own eyes any of the pictures described or alluded to in these texts—though, as some of the images reproduced on the pages that follow suggest, with a bit of effort they easily could—each novel nevertheless raises a significant number of questions regarding ways the virtually seamless permeation of images has affected modern visual subjectivity, ultimately challenging certain assumptions associated with the act and sensation of vision and our perception of the visible world. More specifically, these texts offer a critical reflection on the various epistemological and political implications of sight. They interrogate the tenuous relationship between vision and understanding, suggesting that to see (*voir*) is not necessarily to know (*savoir*). They also test our beliefs about the uses and abuses of the gaze. They seek to ascertain truth and beauty in pictures, and question the institutions responsible for endowing both aesthetic and financial value. And they investigate the dangerously seductive powers of images, exposing what can be best described as their nefarious transparency. The narratives studied here thus collectively suggest that even though we are consistently hounded by visual representations and generally tend to regard them with a certain degree of suspicion, we tend all the same to underestimate vastly their complexity and to neglect the potentially harmful consequences of their omnipresence. Conscious of this paradox, these texts stage a critical excavation of the relationship between vision and intellection, highlighting the inevitable inconsistencies between the two and implicitly warning us of society's generalized visual naïveté. Looking in these novels is suspect: vision is blurry, voyeuristic and, at times, violent in Simon, misleading in Perec, mystified by deficiencies in both cultural and economic capital in Michon, and associated with frenzied, obsessive-compulsive behavior in Viel. Lost in the shadows of Plato's cave, these narratives project an unexpected vision of the world; they warn us against trusting in the immediacy and the innocence of the image, promote our ambivalence about how we see, and ultimately question the ethical and epistemological implications behind the commonplace conceit that "seeing is believing." Beware, these texts seem to say, for what you see is not necessarily what you get. Exploring what we say about pictures and how we make sense of them—or, more importantly, how we do not—these fictions invite readers to recognize the modern subject's complex position with regard to images today.

## *Reviving the* Paragone, *or the Text Writes Back*

I have focused my attention thus far almost exclusively on the relationship certain texts entertain with pictures and picturing, with art, art history, and the theory of art, with images, visual culture, and discourses about vision. What remains to be seen, however, is what the telling of pictures in fiction brings to bear, precisely, on writing itself. How might the literary incorporation of images in these stories impact the ways we think not only about pictures and perception, but also about *texts*, *reading*, and the role that *literature* occupies in society today?

When literature engages other forms of representation it indirectly acknowledges and reinforces its own priorities. "The impulse to move beyond the novel's own medium, words, and to appropriate the effects and media of the visual arts ends in not only superimposing the model of another (visual) art on the novel, but also in affirming the very powers and capacities of the original art and medium."[40] The pleonastic strategy of writing the image effectively creates a screen onto which the powers of the text can be projected. The picture in narrative is an excellent "barometer for literature's views on itself, on representation, and on the power of writing" because the image's relative "otherness" permits the text to become more conscious of its textuality.[41] No matter how extensive its engagement with pictures might be, moments in which a literary text represents a visual object inevitably call attention to the fact that literature—unlike painting, sculpture, or even film (which, of course, is not entirely visual)—does things explicitly with words.

The texts studied in this book thus revive the Renaissance notion of the *paragone*, or competition between the sister arts, and stage the larger struggle for power between literature and its visual others.[42] To write the image in fiction is, in essence, an attempt to control it, to tame it, and to reassert the crucial role that language plays in our appreciation, understanding, and interpretation of pictures. Ultimately, the cautious skepticism of visual representations and the optical experience that these texts elicit is part of a larger compulsion in which the work of literary fiction mounts a defense in face of the onslaught of images. These texts, in other words, make a case for fiction's continued relevance and "write back" in an attempt to reclaim some of the ground lost after almost a century of gradual cultural colonization by commodified visual forms. This phenomenon has slowly exiled literature to the margins, and has led some critics of contemporary culture like Mark Poster to rank the "disintegration of bourgeois, literate culture and its replacement by massified visual culture" as one of the most significant social changes of the last half-century. It is as significant, he argues, as the gradual disappearance of Communist political regimes, the rise of Asia as an economic and political superpower, and the growth of multinational corporate control.[43] As a result of this epistemic shift from what French mediologists call the regime of the "readable" to that of the "seeable," the outlook for literary culture appears altogether dismal.[44] "Nowadays," Gilbert Adair writes, "absolutely everything is channeled through the 'image'; it is no longer the word but the image that has become, or seems destined to become, the basic unit of media communication; and at last, with the advent and dizzyingly expanding popularity of personal computers, words themselves (thoughts, rather) are being transformed into images."[45] Indeed, active literacy in the West has seemingly been displaced, and replaced, by the passive consumption of pictures: "Reading skills—as the educationalists say—continue to decline with each new generation. Novel reading is not a pastime of the young now being educated, nor, for that matter, is it a preoccupation of any but a very few of those who came of age in the last warm years of linear type's hegemony."[46]

According to the dreariest of critical discourses, most people, it seems safe to say, are more comfortable with the immediacy and ready availability of pictures than with the more time-consuming investment required to fully experience literary texts. When Andy Warhol famously quipped, "I never read, I just look at pictures,"[47] he encapsulated a trend that continues to this day to replace one's craving for narratives not with stories on a page—let alone as oral storytelling—but with images embedded in frames or projected onto a variety of screens.[48] All of which leads one to ponder the fate of the fictions we tell in words in a world where, to cite Jonathan Franzen's sinister metaphor, "Barney has murdered Mother Goose."[49]

This book, then, reveals a pictorial paradox in contemporary fiction. In a culture dominated by the presence of visual signs, those texts that enthusiastically tell pictures also often seek to rival them in an act of self-preservation and revalorization since, no matter how much they engage the image and strive to be seen, they ultimately, and quite simply, do things with words. It is only in literature, through literature, that Mother Goose can make her stand. Recasting Archdeacon Frollo's defeatist premonition, in Victor Hugo's *Notre Dame de Paris* (1831), about the fate of architecture in a world of printed books, these texts collectively seem to say, "This will *not* kill That." Image culture, in all its various forms, might not completely displace the printed word after all.[50] Resisting gloomy pronouncements by critics that lament the recent "rise of the image" and subsequent "fall of the word," these narratives testify to the continued aspirations of literature to measure up to the visual.[51] The mix of wonder and anxiety about images enacted in these texts is ultimately part of a strategy to vivify and bolster the status of language in general and of fiction in particular. As each of the chapters that follow aims to demonstrate, telling pictures in fiction has the potential to re-enchant the text so that it may show readers living in a world of images what narratives are still worth.

# 1

# Puzzling Pictures

> My task which I am trying to achieve is, by the power of the written word, to make you hear, to make you feel—it is, before all, to make you *see*. That—and no more, and it is everything.
>
> JOSEPH CONRAD, *The Nigger of the Narcissus*

What does it mean to write the visible? Compared to its sister arts (save, perhaps, film, the hybrid form par excellence), the specificity of the literary text lies in the particular way it communicates its message. The relationship between words and the objects they designate is neither one of direct demonstration nor even of resemblance. Rather, language conjures up ideas of things on the basis of its belonging to a particular system of signification, a system that governs a word's meaning in accordance with certain accepted conventions. Words cannot mirror or imitate reality in the way that, say, painting does; they refer to it instead. No matter how hard it tries, narrative does not show, it tells.[1] If certain media are thought of as better equipped to engage the viewer optically, literary fiction is fundamentally more attuned to stimulating the mind's eye.

Consistent with these remarks is novelist Claude Simon's contention that when one is reading a work of literature there is never exactly vision, but intellection. Though he acknowledges the inherent inability of writing to summon *in praesentia* what we see in the world, Simon, perhaps more than any other French writer of the last half-century, also seeks to drive his writing as close to the edge of sight as possible. Like the other works explored elsewhere in this study, many of his novels seek to "move toward the visible,"[2] to measure up to the image, without ever literally attaining the status of a work of visual art capable of being seen. Consequently, Simon occasionally invokes an allegory that thematizes visuality and the desire to see: namely, that of Orion blinded. According to Greek mythology, the sightless giant, wounded by the king of Chios for illicitly courting his daughter, was destined to roam the planet in search of the rising sun, hopeful that its rays might somehow restore his sight. Masterfully depicted in Nicolas Poussin's celebrated canvas,[3] and reproduced emblematically on the cover of Simon's illustrated book *Orion aveugle* (1970), Orion's quest stands as a metaphor for "the writer advancing blindly in his language, groping in the midst of a forest of signs toward something he will never attain."[4] The scrupulous word-by-word construction of an elusive narrative that will ultimately contain neither a definitive beginning nor end (Simon's novels are all quite similar in this regard), a narrative that therefore consistently turns in upon itself "like a traveler lost in the woods,"[5] constitutes for its author the principal adventure of writing. Yet if the analogy invokes the author who proceeds blindly, unable to predict precisely where his story will lead, the Simonian text also yearns, like Orion, for sight. The expansive corpus of texts—especially from the period between the publication of *Le vent* (1957) and *Les géorgiques* (1981)—can be characterized as a sustained reflection on vision and visual representation. Many of these novels hinge on an unresolved tension between speech and vision, between readability and visibility. As much as Simon's works explore the vast associative networks of language and celebrate their inherent textuality, they are equally "obsessed" with vision and visual representations.[6]

The narrative drive to explore and approximate the image, to overcome the inherent limitations of language and invite readers to envision the world described in words, is especially palpable in what is arguably Simon's most visually engaged work: *Triptyque* (1973).[7] The novel is structured around two visual metaphors: the obvious model, the triptych, gives way near the end to the picture puzzle. Its primary narrative sequences, while broken into disparate fragments, are pieced together like a collage. The vivid descriptions of characters, landscapes, and events depicted in each of the novel's three intercalated strands are generated, respectively, from works of three well-known painters.[8] Moreover, each of these narrative series contains multiple descriptions of various visual representations, most of which are mass-produced, imperfect, and decidedly lowbrow: from cheap postcards and aging film stock to torn posters, dusty engravings, and faulty projections of damaged films. Almost all of these descriptions depict elements that figure in the three primary sequences.[9] As such, each of the seemingly distinct narrative strands is embedded within the others, an effect that initiates a surprisingly fluid and phantasmatic kind of narrative disequilibrium induced by images that appear to come alive. At the same time elements of the diegesis are persistently exposed as the stuff of pictures. This phenomenon, emblematic of certain contemporary texts that tell tales about pictures—and operative on a number of different levels in the works by Georges Perec, Pierre Michon, and Tanguy Viel that will be studied in subsequent chapters—short-circuits the novel's mimetic function, creating in the process a "fuzzy" kind of fiction in which things are never quite what they appear to be.[10]

Consistently negotiating its fascination with the visual, *Triptyque* is also, in many ways, a novel in spite of itself. In exploring the limits of its representational status (as a text), the narrative simultaneously conveys an embryonic desire to live up to and assimilate something other and decidedly more visible (like a painting, photograph, or collage). This tendency for the various artistic media to engage one another so thoroughly is typical of the period in which *Triptyque* was published. Beginning in the mid-1950s and continuing throughout the 1970s, most of the various artistic disciplines began to accept and open up to other forms of creative expression, each medium engaging its ontological "others" in innovative and exciting ways. Although earlier traces of this kind of interartistic crossbreeding can be located in work emblematic of Horace's classic kinship between painting and poetry (*ut pictura poesis*) or Richard Wagner's later theorization of the *Gesamtkunstwerk*, or "total work of art," the rampant kind of artistic synthesis that occurs during the latter half of the twentieth century is far more complex and complete than during any preceding period. A typically postmodern resistance toward the master narratives most usually associated with modern artistic sensibility may help to explain why this is so.[11] Notions of artistic purity, autonomy, beauty, originality, and genius—pillars of Enlightenment modernity that Emmanuel Kant so vigorously promoted in his third *Critique*—were destined to be recalibrated and ultimately repudiated during the second half of the twentieth century by a collective force of writers and thinkers who favored a much less exclusive conception of culture, one that stressed the importance of pluralism, multiplicities, and tolerance. A wide variety of artists contributed to this critique in kind.[12] A number of painters, for example, began searching elsewhere for content, materially incorporating photographic techniques and everyday materials in their work, often looking to mass-media images—in television, advertising, and film, in particular—for inspiration. Sculpture became more painterly, more architectural, and, for some, more "theatrical." Performance art looked to theater, installation art often incorporated elements of design, and the birth of new media comprised an amalgam of all of the above. Many successful artists were also well versed in the latest and most fashionable theoretical modes, and some chose to publish their own treatises alongside the work of their critics. As the history of art has shown, throughout these years fields that were once considered traditionally distinct would seek to merge onto a vast plane of transitory images, techniques, and ideas, each discipline looking for inspiration in, and feeding off, the other.

As I suggest throughout this chapter, *Triptyque* enacts this proclivity for a work of literature to explore the potential impact of the other arts in an age when the constraints of medium specificity could no longer keep each distinct discipline fenced in. Drawing its energy from various types of extradisciplinary and particularly visual sources, the novel mobilizes a strategy that examines, and challenges, the hegemony of purified forms. *Triptyque* can thus be read as a potent sign of its times, as a historically conditioned text that enacts the complex relationship between text and image, and between the verbal and the visual, during a period marked by a comprehensive turn toward heterogeneity and interdisciplinarity in the arts.

## *Pictorial Poetics*

Claude Simon frequently acknowledged his desire to write like a painter. His interest in and familiarity with the visual arts is also well known. Various interviews, essays, and public presentations attest to his finely tuned appreciation of the history of art and expert understanding of painterly technique.[13] Although he was absorbed by the practice of writing for more than half a century, throughout his career Simon continued to engage the visual arts hands-on in a variety of ways: his skill as a draftsman is discernible in the various drawings that serve as inside covers for two of his books (*Orion aveugle* and *Album d'un amateur*); a number of critical studies have made public a few figurative sketches from the manuscripts that help illustrate Simon's creative practice;[14] he remained until his death an avid practitioner of collage; and two books of photographs attest to an equally impressive competence behind the lens.[15] Simon also envisaged cinematic adaptations of two of his novels. While he wrote a screenplay for *La route des Flandres*, the film was never made. A short version of *Triptyque*, however, was produced by a German television company in 1974–75. Despite some minor gripes about the final product, Simon's participation in the production is another lasting testimony to his enthusiasm for bringing visual culture to bear on his larger literary project.[16]

With such a discerning eye and great proficiency for the arts, one wonders what might have led Simon to choose writing as his primary vocation. Was it just a matter of preference? Was he simply more comfortable working with words? Or could his interest in photography, painting, and even film have been, as Lucien Dällenbach proposes, "dethroned" by the text, one-upped by literature, which was "too jealous to tolerate any competition from another art?"[17] However rhetorical it may be, Dällenbach's hypothesis is predicated on the idea that each mode of expression, graphic or otherwise, is mutually exclusive, and that one activity must necessarily take precedence over the others. However, the kind of hierarchy that pits one art form directly against another is vitiated, precisely, by Simon's prose. The author's particularly visual way of writing not only "tolerates" the other arts, it welcomes them with open arms.

Perhaps one way of understanding this propensity toward the variety of visual forms that so influence his work lies in Simon's admitting to an almost photographic way of perceiving the world around him: "I do not see things so much in movement, but rather as a sequence of fixed images. Add to that an idiosyncrasy, perhaps a visual deficiency: images linger on my retina. At the race track, for example, the horses will have already jumped, yet I can still see their bodies suspended over the hurdle. I reconstitute what happened before and after on the basis of this image."[18] Given the emphasis on perception and mechanically reproduced images in Simon's fiction it is not so implausible to imagine the author as a fusion of man and image-generating machine, capable of capturing and replicating the details of the visible world like a camera.[19] These "fixed images," stockpiled in the writer's imagination, are reconfigured during the writing process and combined with other images to create a dynamic narrative composed almost entirely of descriptive literary snapshots.[20] In *Triptyque*, for example, the image of a trout swimming upstream is frozen the moment it is perceived by the anonymous and objective narrative "eye": "Passing abruptly from its lazy state of immobility to motion, the trout darts away like an arrow and disappears upstream in the zone hidden from view by the blinding reflection of the sky, allowing the trace of its rigid, elongated form, propelled solely by the rapid wrigglings of its tail, to persist on the retina"(9). Much like Simon's particular way of seeing, the text captures and records a passing moment as if mechanically, framing it first as a static image and reconstituting it in words on the page. Here the retina is effectively transformed into a machinelike sensorial apparatus capable of storing the picture it composes from reality for future reference. The detached nature of the narrative voice that is mobilized throughout *Triptyque*, a voice that speaks primarily in the present tense and in a uniform tone, is starkly mechanical in nature and objective in the sense of an *objectif*, an optical lens that mediates between the things we see and their representations.

Numerous images like this one accumulate throughout Simon's novels. Detailed descriptions consistently blend together and impress upon the reader the effect of a conscious, observing subject, or in some cases one remembering its past. Citing Tolstoy, Simon has remarked, "a healthy man routinely thinks, feels, and remembers an untold number of things at once."[21] The challenge with which the writer is faced is to call to mind a similar sensation of simultaneity in words. The linear nature of narrative complicates this task since it requires the novel to reconcile two essential yet famously opposed categories: space, historically associated with the work of visual artists, and time, which traditionally governs the work of the poet or novelist.[22] The distinction between the inherently spatial nature of painting and the temporal status of narrative began to falter with the rise of modernism. As Joseph Frank argues, one of the primary features of modern literature is its attempt to spatialize the temporal flow (what he refers to as the "time-logic") of language.[23] Simon's prose seeks to do precisely that. Harnessing the power of language to act as a "signifying knot,"[24] *Triptyque* mobilizes the capacity of words to allude to a variety of images and references at once. The result ultimately allows for a more dynamic reading experience, since, as the author notes, "all the elements of the text (and this is where I disagree with Leonardo da Vinci) are always *present*. Even if they are not obvious, they are still there, just below the surface of, or behind, what is immediately readable."[25] In most of his novels, many of the principal narrative elements and events are linked together by a constellation of words that consistently echo and reference one another through a variety of stylistic devices (metaphors, metonymies, assonances and alliterations, as well as the rhythm and the cadence of particular sentences). In this way the text seemingly superimposes certain narrative elements over others, fostering the illusion of synchronicity in the process. In *Triptyque*, to cite a rather startling example among many, the description of a young woman fellating a man in a barn ("her cheeks forming hollows as she sucks" [121]) resonates again, two pages later, with the weathered face of an old woman ("the absence of teeth causing the cheeks to form hollows, as though she were sucking on something" [123]). Thanks to the mediation of these ubiquitous and eminently suggestive "junction words,"[26] Simon's prose explores the expansive referential nature of language and its capacity to resist the inherent linearity and temporality of literature.

At the same time Simon also employs a more visual logic to overcome the spatial constraints of language. Frequently approaching the composition of his narratives in terms of a picture, Simon relies on the idea that the arrangement of a fixed graphic image allows for the presentation of all of its parts, however diverse and disparate they might be, at once: "I work like a painter on the surface of a canvas where all the components of the image are present at the same time. I alter one area in relation to another to ensure that the whole composition comes together evenly."[27] Traditionally, painting has been considered the art form most well suited to expressing simultaneity, even in narrative paintings where a series of actions that occur contiguously appear on the canvas frozen in a single instant. Simon's decidedly more "figural" project often borrows certain procedures associated with painting to complicate the boundary between visual and verbal forms of expression.[28]

Of course, as art historian Michael Baxandall has remarked, there is an inherent awkwardness in the motivation to write like a painter. Dealing with a simultaneously available field like painting from within a medium more traditionally associated with temporal unfolding is an intrinsically thorny issue. Yet our experience of painting, on a perceptual level, does not necessarily occur in a moment's time. As Baxandall argues, "if a picture is simultaneously available in its entirety, *looking* at a picture is as temporally linear as language."[29] Baxandall's point is an important one that helps to explain how Simon's painterly poetics ultimately manages to overcome this spatiotemporal inconsistency. *Triptyque*, in particular, does not constitute an attempt to relate objects and events literally as they might appear simultaneously in memory, or, for that matter, in a painting. Instead, the text aims to capture subtly our perceptual experience of the objects and events represented therein, which is an ineluctably temporal affair.[30] The various descriptions of pictures, landscapes, people, and things that permeate Simon's novels must not be considered objective accounts of how these things exist in the world, even in Simon's most "impersonal" works of the 1970s where the narrative is recounted from the perspective of a mechanical, camera-like "eye." Rather, they relate someone's or something's subjective encounter with the world. Although the text attempts to reduce as much as possible the psychologizing, personal presence of a more subjective narrative position that might influence the reader's own experience, *Triptyque*, while it comes close, never manages to attain fully the level of objectivity that this would require. The "failure" to do so is precisely the point. The "eye" may be anonymous and invisible, but it is always present to frame and order the narrative and designate the language and syntax employed in its descriptions. This is true of every novel, even those written in the most neutral of third-person voices. *Triptyque* simply renders this truth more "visible" by suggesting that the very idea of a wholly disinterested, objective work of literature is an illusion.[31] Simon himself has said as much: "One can never tell everything, just as one can never tell everything at once. All writing (like all painting) is firstly the result of choice, then of an ordering process, a selection of priorities . . . without mentioning the weight of unforeseen meanings that words bear with them."[32] As a result, then, *Triptyque* simulates an objective experience of the world in order to suggest that all narratives, no matter how impartial they might seem, necessarily evoke the processes of their own construction.

## *The Image Effect*

Simon frequently conceives of the creative process in pictorial terms, and often refers to the visual arts as a model for his writing that goes beyond the simulation of simultaneity discussed above.[33] The author's reflections on the work of a wide variety of artists also provide evidence of the extent to which the visual arts help generate ideas. From Poussin, Cézanne, and Dubuffet to Piero della Francesca and Louise Nevelson, the list of influences is extensive and spans hundreds of years of art history. Jean Duffy has, to date, offered the most comprehensive analysis of the ways works by Jean Dubuffet, Paul Delvaux, and Francis Bacon act as thematic stimuli in *Triptyque*. Each of the three primary narrative sequences originates in the work of one of these painters, and Simon has admitted to using them as the basis for some of the novel's principal motifs. The sinuous black lines and undulating shapes that characterize Dubuffet's series of *Hourloupe* paintings from the 1960s, for example, suggest elements that are part of the novel's countryside strand.[34] Paul Delvaux's paintings of somber neighborhoods on the outskirts of Belgian cities evoke the gloomy, after-hours atmosphere of the urban sequence. And, as Duffy observes, the starkly decorated hotel room by the sea corresponds to the "anonymous and minimalist decors that Bacon's figures inhabit," while the various positions adopted by the naked woman "recall forcefully the very awkward and unlikely poses adopted by Bacon's nudes."[35]

Along with these various visual generators, the novel's overtly iconographic style contributes to the text's painterly effect. *Triptyque*'s anonymous narrator describes the world as if it existed in an image, often fixated on shape and line: "The bar is lit by two frosted glass globes hanging from the ceiling that cast a dim light on the walls covered with yellow wallpaper with vertical stripes enclosing a repeated pattern of little bouquets in dull colors" (99). Sometimes the text describes scenes as if they were composed by the hand of an artist: "two profiles of it are visible at the same time . . . as though the space between the two profiles had been swept with the stroke of a brush whose bristles were unevenly coated with paint" (20). Other pictorial metaphors abound. A cloudless blue sky, for example, appears "of a uniform color, as though applied by a house painter on a canvas situated several yards behind the window" (59), and a skinned rabbit "seems to be painted in a pink monochrome, darkening to a brick red in the shadows" (62). Elsewhere the sidewalks, massive concrete walls, and smoky chimneys that populate the industrial cityscape recall "watercolors in dull hues" (128) in which objects "appear to be made of one and the same substance diluted by water" (129).

Although these metaphors resonate with discourses most

readily associated with painting, other comparisons are based on more mechanical forms of reproduction. At times the novel fosters a filmic effect, or, more generally, an "image effect."[36] Readers spy a cat, for example, as she slowly approaches a pair of unsuspecting chickens, aping the birds' gestures and halting her movement as they do, "in the middle of a step at times, with one paw motionless in the air, then resuming its forward motion and completing the step it has started taking, like a movie actor when a film that has jammed in the projector begins to move again" (68). Elsewhere, in a movie poster adorned with three distinct groups of figures—two men standing at the edge of a forest, a couple leaning against a brick wall, and a pair of faces that appear in the poster's foreground—the distinct "compositions" seem "as though they were being simultaneously projected by three machines onto the screen of smoke and black clouds that cause the title of the film, in red letters, to stand out clearly" (71). And, later, "a long traveling shot follows two boys walking along, as behind them the background of foliage, of a fresh green color, dotted with black shadows and little round patches gleaming in the sunlight, glides along from right to left" (112). Ultimately, all of these graphically oriented descriptions, painterly or cinematic, convey Simon's particular brand of visuality, a narrative optics—a "textual eye"—that perceives the world as a collection of images.[37]

Several of the passages cited above also attest to another unmistakably visual aspect of *Triptyque*: namely, the affluence of colors. The novel's palette is rich and varied. Colors are often the defining characteristic of certain objects and characters: a mattress, for example, is "of a yellowish-brown color with narrow parallel stripes in groups of three" (24), and a rainbow that forms over the mist by a waterfall contains all the requisite hues: "The concentric bands, violet, indigo, blue, pale green, yellow-orange, and red hang suspended, iridescent and transparent, in the fine, luminous mist" (82). This vibrant color scheme is yet another demonstration of Simon's drive to write "like a painter." It also enhances the effect of simultaneity the text strives to perform. Each distinct sequence of the narrative resonates with the next through the consistent blending of colors, light, and shadow that one would expect to see in a painted triptych where, for example, "a certain red at the top of the left panel echoes so well with another red or even a certain green on the bottom right such that the three paintings compose a cohesive whole."[38] The compositional unity of *Triptyque* is therefore not only linguistic in nature, but is also significantly pictorial. Simon looks to the visual arts to justify the seemingly abrupt shifts from one scene to the next, basing this justification on a particular theory of harmony that he remarks most notably in painting. The sudden shift from a description of a skinned rabbit hanging outside the house in the countryside to the portrait of a woman lying on the bed in her hotel room by the seaside seems an apparent non sequitur of great proportions: "Half of the rabbit's body is now bared, so that the pink muscles of the thighs, the hindquarters, and the belly are visible, as in an anatomical plate. Brusquely stretching out the leg whose foot has been resting flat on the bed, the woman causes the door of the wardrobe to pivot round, whereupon it slams against the door frame, bounds backward, and then ceases to move, as the objects reflected in the mirror hung on it are successively swept up in a rapid horizontal movement followed by two briefer ones before they cease to move"(25). On the level of the plot, there is little to explain what these two images have to do with one other, if anything. Nor is there any evidence of explicit linguistic or semantic echoes. Nevertheless, the juxtaposition manages to maintain an internal harmony.

The text conflates the rabbit's posture with that of the nude woman, both bodies prostrate on a flat surface, their respective anatomies entirely exposed. A subtle sense of unity in this seemingly awkward composition lessens the shock of the association—the eviscerated hare is described as an object of fascination and pleasure rather than disgust—all the while affirming the violence of the narrator's voyeuristic (indeed, misogynistic) gaze.

For Simon, the parallelism that these two incongruent descriptions achieve when configured in this way is "credible" because their juxtaposition makes sense in the context of the narrative.[39] Like the famous scene in Marcel Proust's *À la recherche du temps perdu* that suddenly transports readers from the courtyard of the Hôtel de Guermantes, in which the narrator stumbles on two uneven cobblestones, to a memory of St. Mark's cathedral in Venice, Simon's own narrative leaps correspond to the novel's internal logic. Much like two eyes painted onto the same profile in a Picasso canvas, a sight that defies the laws of biology yet functions altogether naturally when considered in the context of Picasso's cubist practice, these combinations of elements remain credible because they function as part of a system (a text, a painting) that constitutes a cogent ensemble. As Simon's comments suggest, unlike a typically realist work in which such a juxtaposition would put into question the credibility of the description, the conjunction of similarly disparate events and descriptions in a novel like *Triptyque* (from the flayed rabbit to the nude woman, for example) does not elicit the same concerns.

Given its decidedly visual composition, the importance the novel places on vision is hardly surprising. The various modes of perception deserve particular attention. At times the viewing apparatus is akin to an impartial, objective camera. The urban scene, for example, is also often depicted as if it were shot on film: "Doubtless the camera has been hoisted up to the very top of either a church steeple or one of those scaffoldings . . . but in any case along the axis of a long artery, for one sees this latter from a steep plunging angle" (94). At other times the world is described with such precision that the camera "eye" takes on x-ray proportions. The depiction of the flayed, blood-soaked rabbit penetrates the animal's skin and reads much like a biology textbook: "Below the rib cage with its scalloped edge, the belly, emptied of its viscera, forms a hollow. On the limbs and the various parts of the skinned body one can see, as in an anatomical plate, the long muscles, swelling out in the form of a spindle, crisscrossing, interlacing, stretching out parallel, or overlapping each other. They are attached to the bones by their sinewy, whitish ends" (62). Contrary to the cinematic survey that captures the topographical relief of the world from above, here the description comes down to earth and permeates its surfaces. For Claude Gandelman, this "haptic" vision—exemplified in the visceral paintings of skinned animals by artists such as Rembrandt, Soutine, and Bacon—attributes a tactile quality to sight.[40] The text's vision is almost medical in its precision: the eye follows and discerns an object's visible contours only to subsequently dissect and examine those layers that lie under its skin. The effect is surprisingly democratic. Few details escape the penetrating lens of Simon's vision machine. From the flayed rabbit to descriptions of clothing, facial expressions, roads, rivers, chimneys, sexual encounters, and, of course, pictures, the text views all of its diverse components with an astonishing fairness, as if to say that everything that exists in the world is made up of the same basic matter. The narrative thus dismantles any pre-established hierarchies that would render certain objects more worthy of a reader's attentions than others.

This attention to details raises a crucial paradox, since no matter how meticulous the narrative's vision, what actually "happens" in *Triptyque*, what readers actually "see," ultimately remains a mystery. *Tryptique*'s superimposition of multiple diegetic layers onto one another mixes and matches the various plot strands in a complex literary collage of images within images that disregard narrative order. Its focus constantly shifts from one setting and situation to the next and back again in a rhizomatic criss-crossing of elements, a literary "Persian rug" that has neither discernible beginning nor definitive end.[41] Even the most diligent of readers risks losing track.[42] Consider the following attempt at a synopsis: The first of the novel's three primary narrative sequences—the first of three panels of the textual triptych, as it were—takes place in a nonspecific, hilly countryside hamlet (in the Vosges? in the Jura?), where two young boys spend their time swimming in the local stream and lounging on the grass. Peeping through a small hole in a dilapidated barn wall, the boys catch a glimpse of a passionate couple in flagrante delicto on a pile of hay. Apart from these juvenile voyeurs, we read of another boy (one of the peepers?) torn between his geometry homework and some racy film stock that he keeps in his desk drawer, hidden away from the prying eyes of a woman (his mother? grandmother? the maid?) who is busy outside skinning a rabbit, which is presumably to be that night's dinner. A trio of young girls is playing outside. One of them (entrusted to the boys? to the other girls?) ostensibly drowns (perhaps not?) in the stream near the novel's conclusion (this is *Triptyque*'s most crucial prevarication).[43] The second sequence depicts another pair of lovers together in a dank alleyway in a nondescript urban area (in the Parisian suburbs? in Northern France?). The man, drunk and wearing a soiled tuxedo, has presumably left a wedding (his own?) to seduce the local cocktail waitress (his mistress all along?) into accompanying him out behind her place of work for an impromptu late-night tryst. As they grapple under the rain in the alleyway, a film (pornographic?) is being shown, despite a series of recurring mechanical difficulties (few images in Simon's work are flawless) to a group of patient spectators in the cinema behind them. At one point another man (the waitress's boyfriend? A local from the bar? The groom's best man? Is one of them Polish? Are both?) enters the alley, clearly incensed, and an altercation ensues. The third narrative strand takes place in a coastal resort (signs point to the Riviera). A half-naked woman who speaks with a foreign accent (American?) lies on a bed in a hotel room overlooking the sea. At times she seems to be talking to (pleading with?) a man (a police officer? A wealthy paramour? Both?) who can presumably help her save a boy (her son?) from a possible prison sentence (drug bust?).

As I hope my parenthetical queries have made clear, the novel is awash in narrative ambiguity. Though some critics have gamely attempted to fill in the blanks and provide a definitive summary of the novel's plot, the end results are often falsely transparent.[44] Like the broken films and the torn movie posters that populate its pages, *Triptyque* is loath to provide its readers with a totally coherent vision of the world. The numerous pictures that move the narrative forward contribute to the novel's diegetic haziness, since these various representations are consistently conflated with a narrative "reality" that the text purportedly represents. This confusion is a direct result of the embedding of each narrative strand within a picture of another. For example, the seaside scene is evoked in a description of a postcard that depicts the ocean and the palatial residences and hotels that line the coast. This postcard lies on the table in the house in the countryside scene (1).

Both the seaside scene and the countryside scene are inlaid within the urban sequence, again, as posters affixed to the wall of the cinema (46). This urban scene, in which a man (the groom?) and a woman (the waitress?) are enlaced behind this same (or so it seems) cinema, is itself placed *en abyme* in the seaside scene. Here the same couple (or two people who look exceedingly similar) is described on the cover of a book that lies on the floor next to the nude woman (164). Another film that is playing, this time in the barn in the countryside scene (and not in the urban cinema), is set in a coastal city (Nice, probably) that greatly resembles the resort area depicted on the postcard mentioned above (104). And these are just a few of the many "frame shifts" that make *Triptyque* one of the most puzzling novels of the last half-century.[45] Each sequence is consistently revealed to be a picture that turns up elsewhere in the text. The narrative consistently exposes itself to have been a representation of a representation all along.

The effects of this consistent *mise en abyme* of one diegetic sequence within the fabric of another, through the mediation of pictures, are dizzying, to say the least. Not unlike the network of linguistic associations that echo each other throughout, the pictures that saturate the novel and add to its complexity persistently incite a double take, causing the reader to search (ultimately in vain) for stable ground. *Triptyque*'s vertiginous pictorial poetics mobilize the image to erase the frontier between the first and second degrees of representation. The mirror onto the world that the novel ostensibly represents is a mirror held up to a series of constantly revolving visual representations of that world. *Triptyque* thus breaks with the realist illusion and acknowledges its status as a simulation.

The constant conflation of *Triptyque*'s diegetic "reality" with a series of multimedia representations is a crucial first step in understanding the novel's relationship to the larger cultural context. The kind of world that *Triptyque* depicts, a world in which reality is consistently reduced to a pictorial representation, exemplifies a new way of thinking about subjectivity and perception that certain thinkers would begin to explore at around the time of its publication. In a number of essays that would mark the cultural landscape of the 1970s, Jean Baudrillard famously lamented the gradual implosion of the real in a society dominated more and more by the virtual. The propagation of images, information technology, and the mass media, he maintained, led to the subject's total loss of control over what had become an unchecked circulation of visual signs. As a consequence everyday life became flooded with representations to such a point that one's experience of the world is progressively replaced by an experience of signs mistaken for "real." Enter the realm of the "hyperreal." Reconfiguring Mallarmé's celebrated dictum for a postmodern age, Baudrillard's decidedly more Cimmerian kind of theorizing claimed instead that everything is ultimately destined to end up not in a book, but in a picture (and a mass-produced, highly commodified one at that).[46]

The "hyperrealistic" nature of representation in *Triptyque* is essential to a reappraisal of Simon's seemingly formalist poetics. As certain critics have remarked, Simon's output from the early 1970s is primarily one of purely textual experimentation.[47] The novels written during this period—the trio consisting of *Les corps conducteurs* (1971), *Triptyque*, and *Leçon de choses* (1975) most notably—ostensibly lack any explicit connection to larger historical phenomena.[48] Unlike a number of Simon's earlier novels, here there are no narrative recollections of participation in wars and revolutionary conflicts. Their stories "no longer relate to the fortuitous adventures of arbitrary characters."[49] Nor do we read the hazy mnemonic reconstructions of amorous scandals involving long-lost family members from centuries ago. As most critics assert, these texts exhibit more self-reflexive and "objective" tendencies that correspond more readily to the formalist ideology espoused by practitioners of the *nouveau roman* (Alain Robbe-Grillet, in particular) and their closest readers (Jean Ricardou, most famously). Much less rooted in Simon's autobiographical and intertextual project, developed more extensively in works like *La route des Flandres* (1960), *Histoire* (1967), and *Le jardin des Plantes* (1997), the novels from the early 1970s by contrast are by and large read as "less and less anchored in the representation of a psychologically coherent subject's perceptions, memories, or imagination of a diegetically coherent world."[50] For some *Triptyque* would appear to be an essentially ahistorical enterprise.

The novel, however, does not altogether evacuate the notion of history or collective memory. Although it leaves behind a recognizable historical past, preferring to locate its narrative in a more indeterminate temporal and spatial setting, the novel's engagement with visual forms and the institutions of which they are a part suggests a latent identification with a more familiar historical present. As Fredric Jameson has argued, simulacral moments in literature, instances in which the diegetic "real" is exposed to have been an image all along effectively "lift us from the realm of linguistic problematics and linguistic philosophy into that of image society and the media."[51] In this context, *Triptyque* must not simply be read as a novel about the art and adventure of writing itself, as many of Simon's critics have done.[52] Rather, the text demands critical readers who will consider how it also corresponds with the concerns of a world colonized by pictures.

Like *Triptyque*, much of the visual art produced on both sides of the Atlantic during the 1960s and early 1970s exhibits characteristics of modern culture's frenetic traffic of images. From situationist *détournement* and the photo-based *nouvelle figuration* of painters like Gérard Fromanger and Jacques Monoroy to Andy Warhol's silk-screened recalibrations of popular icons and James Rosenquist's politically charged collages, preexisting representations of reality begin to replace reality itself as one of the prime subjects of art. The trend to picture pictures is symptomatic of the growing resistance to the rhetoric of purity integral to theories of modern art. According to Clement Greenberg, one of the most influential and outspoken of modernist critics, for much of the first half of the twentieth century the visual arts were dominated by artists' explorations into the very nature of the medium within which they were working. Modern art, he claimed, is a primarily self-critical enterprise in which "characteristic methods of a discipline" are used to "criticize" the discipline itself. The only works that deserve to be judged favorably are those that fully evacuate traces of other forms, characteristics that might contaminate the purity of the medium in question. The goal, in other words, is to "eliminate from the specific effects of each art any and every effect that might be conceivably borrowed from or by the medium of any other art."[53] In the case of painting, whose area of competence is defined by those characteristics unique to it—elements that include the shape of the support, the pigment, and, above all, the flatness of the picture plane—Greenberg's directive deemed the presence of traits such as literariness, theatricality, realism, and subject matter undesirable.

In its insistence on the "entrenchment" of medium specificity, Greenberg's conception of modernism proposes a teleological reading of the history of art. Advances in painterly technique gradually lead toward the creation of a "pure" picture whose sole aim is to engage the viewer optically and provide a totally disinterested kind of aesthetic pleasure. This aim is achieved through the progressive drive toward an increasingly abstract, content-free, and relatively "flat" picture plane. Beginning in the latter half of the nineteenth century, and corresponding with a shift in sensibility that Greenberg attributes to the viewer's desire to experience the world more literally and immediately, modern paintings began to make fewer and fewer attempts to mask the medium with which they were created. Impressionist canvases, for example, were among the first to expose the material nature of painting itself and frankly declare "what painting has always been but has for long tried to dissemble: colors placed on a two-dimensional surface."[54] They also began to lay bare the illusion of depth, formerly provided by the representation of a third dimension, that was so important to the Old Masters. According to Greenberg's narrative, as modernism developed, many artists began to work less and less in three-dimensional perspective and tended toward flatness and two-dimensionality, toward "lines and surfaces that define or enclose space but hardly occupy it."[55] Ever since the advent, in the fifteenth century, of single-point perspective and related techniques that offer the illusion of depth, figurative paintings implicated the body of the observer. They created the impression that viewers could figuratively walk into the work and explore the world it represented.[56] Works of abstract modern art that Greenberg championed, on the other hand, altered this more corporal relationship to the viewer by concentrating on a planar surface to be explored solely by the eye. For Greenberg, the apotheosis of this drive toward opticality was manifest in many works by abstract expressionist painters working throughout the 1940s and 1950s—artists like Jackson Pollock and, later, Kenneth Noland and Helen Frankenthaler—who produced a body of work that was devoid of figurative subject matter and those elements, like narrative and theatricality, associated with the sister arts. Their work tapped directly into the very nature of what makes painting unique, and, for Greenberg, managed to appeal strictly to the optical imagination. These works are, in a sense, purified works of art.

Greenberg's formalist teleology would remain very influential up until the early 1960s.[57] With the arrival on the scene of minimalist works that blurred the purified boundary lines between painting and sculpture, and with pop art's spectacular return to figuration and subject matter, the restrictive spirit of Greenberg's modernist dogma was made all too apparent. Despite his impressive critical influence, the optical and disciplinary purity that he supported was slowly being contaminated. The qualities that had been repressed by modernist orthodoxy—content, drama, mimesis—began to return to the center of the art world's attention. As Brian Wallis put it, "the central purpose of art and art criticism since the early 1960s has been the dismantling of the monolithic myth of modernism and the dissolution of its oppressive progression of great ideas and great masters."[58]

One of the foremost advocates for the reactionary resistance to the "myth" of modernism was art historian Rosalind Krauss. Throughout the 1970s Krauss dedicated her efforts to recuperating those artists and movements that Greenberg's exclusionary logic had repressed. As she assessed the situation, the new forms that began to develop in the late 1950s and continued to evolve into the 1970s effectively began to break down the medium-specific boundaries that Greenberg sought to uphold. In her seminal essay from 1979, "Sculpture in the Expanded Field," Krauss examines how contemporary sculptural practice transgresses conventional disciplinary frontiers. With the advent of site-specific pieces—earthworks and complex multimedia installations primarily—the modernist category of "sculpture," she assessed, was becoming more difficult to define. Artists during this period began to think of that particular medium in terms of an "expanded field" that embraced other traditionally distinct categories like architecture and landscape. These developments led Krauss to theorize a situation in which artistic practice, in direct opposition to Greenberg, "is not defined in relation to a given medium . . . but rather in relation to the logical operations on a set of cultural terms for which any medium—photography, books, lines on walls, mirrors, or sculpture itself—might be used."[59] During the 1980s Krauss became an uncompromising apologist for artistic heterogeneity and the critique of the history of artistic principles that this heterogeneity fostered, working to recover earlier artists, like Marcel Duchamp and the Surrealists, who were all but ignored by Greenberg's restrictive paradigm of purity.

Krauss found in the work of Robert Rauschenberg the perfect antidote to Greenberg's militant purism. For Krauss, Rauschenberg's "combine" paintings and oil and silkscreen hybrids of the 1950s and 1960s represented a major shift in artistic practice away from pure abstraction toward a more liberal playing with images, figuration, and reproducibility. The heterogeneous nature of the combines in particular represented a revolutionary disregard for medium specificity during a time when "single-image art" was all the rage.[60] Indeed, Rauschenberg's art from this period is ultimately so significant, as history has proven, because it masterfully led the tradition of painting into new and unexplored spaces of visual culture that Greenberg's stringent criteria for aesthetic judgment could no longer assimilate.

Given his own interest in the formal properties and creative processes associated with collage, it is not surprising that Claude Simon found a kindred spirit in Rauschenberg as well. In a variety of published interviews from the 1970s Simon makes frequent reference to the painter, and two of the artist's combine paintings figure among the twenty-one images reproduced in *Orion aveugle*.[61] Additionally, in a key essay presented at a 1971 conference on the *nouveau roman*, Simon notes the influence of another Rauschenberg piece (*Charlene*, 1954) on *Les corps conducteurs*, the novel that directly precedes the publication of *Triptyque*.[62] A close comparative reading of both image and text ultimately reveals the extent to which Rauschenberg's painting acts as a principal generator not only of that narrative's themes and principal motifs, but also of its formal structure.[63]

To be sure, Rauschenberg's influence is not only manifest in work from the early 1970s. Another combine also makes its mark on a piece that Simon published more than a decade later in the *Revue de la Bibliothèque Nationale*.[64] Entitled "Parenthèse," this text was printed alongside two reproductions of Rauschenberg's *Odalisk* (1955–58), an eclectic work that is part painting, part sculpture, and part collage (image 1). The piece, whose central box, open on two sides, is covered with various reproductions of works of art, including a number of classic "erotic" paintings, is mounted on a white post that rests on a pillow. A stuffed rooster is affixed proudly on top. Here, again, the artwork's status as stimulus to the text of "Parenthèse" is clear, as Simon notes: "There was, in my text, the story of a character who frequents brothels: the Rauschenberg rested on a pillow, one could see on the

Image 1. Robert Rauschenberg, *Odalisk*, 1955–58. Freestanding combine, 210.8 x 64.1 x 68.8 cm. Museum Ludwig, Cologne. © Estate of Robert Rauschenberg/Licensed by VAGA, New York NY. Photo courtesy Rheinisches Bildarchiv, Cologne.

sides of this cube unstudied photos of nude women, the reproduction of a classic painting (*Cupid and Psyche*) was integrated within ('intertextuality'). . . . And not only that: a certain, generalized color scheme . . . I would say that I felt something analogous to what I was trying to do."[65] Given the publication date of "Parenthèse," fourteen years after the appearance of *Les corps conducteurs*, we can maintain that Simon's interest in Rauschenberg was not simply a passing fancy. Once again Simon admits the importance of the kind of painting that Rauschenberg called the "combine" for providing a paradigm that would help shape the thematic and compositional elements within his own work. His comments also hint at an interest in the painter that goes beyond the generative potential of the artwork, pointing to a more epistemological type of kinship that is crucial to understanding Simon's relationship to contemporary artistic practices, and to contemporary cultural production in general.

Like *Triptyque*, a work that demands that dexterous readers make sense of disparate narrative strands, Rauschenberg's combines are like visual puzzles whose elements need to be considered together in order for the ensemble to take shape. Although each part of an artwork like *Odalisk* is charged with its own unique significance, when it is considered in its entirety each of these elements functions together to form a new matrix of signification. The spectator confronted with a combine painting is therefore challenged to wade through a multitude of possibilities and construct a reading that will "resolve the 'puzzle' and bring together the various levels of commercial material, art-historical reproductions, and handmade additions."[66]

Similarly, the puzzle is a potent analogy for the way readers experience meaning in Simon's novel. *Triptyque* renders this analogy explicit when "one of those enormous jigsaw puzzles that Anglo-Saxons are so fond of, measuring approximately twenty by thirty inches" (168) appears on a table in the hotel room by the sea. Like the novel, at this point five pages from the end, "the puzzle is almost completely put together" (168). As readers conditioned by *Triptyque*'s labyrinthine structure might expect, another narrative sequence is embedded within. Here, despite a few missing pieces, an Arcadian valley hamlet clearly resonates with the novel's descriptions of the rustic scene. The unidentified man in the hotel room aims to reconstruct a picture similar to the one so vividly described throughout the novel. Moments later, however, irritation sets in. Although he manages to complete the picture, coolly fixing its last piece in place, he then inexplicably destroys the fruits of his labor: "suddenly his right hand violently sweeps back and forth across the surface of the table, breaking up the puzzle and scattering the little pieces all about" (171). His reaction points to the reader, who, despite finishing the novel, is still faced with a variety of vague conclusions. Does the little girl in the rustic sequence drown in the creek? What, exactly, is the relationship between the woman in the hotel room and the man who intends to help her with her son? What film have the spectators who leave the movie theater at the end of the novel been watching, if not the filmic version of *Triptyque* itself? Here, like Simon's imagined reader, the spectators exit the theater befogged, but none the worse for wear: "Blinking their eyes, a bit dazzled and confused, like someone just awakening from a sound sleep" (171). If, for Simon, perception (like memory) is flawed, if "any attempt to record or reconstruct reality accurately and fully is condemned to failure,"[67] then our experience of the world—and of every text that aims to represent that world—is necessarily incomplete. *Triptyque* uses unstable plot lines to challenge the notion of a totalizing and totally cohesive narrative whole, as if to say that in life, as in art, pieces of the puzzle are always prone to go missing. *Triptyque* ultimately highlights this unavoidable epistemological impasse.[68]

Moreover, throughout the narrative, *Triptyque* consistently references devices responsible for the production of various representations in order to stress its own status as a construct. A film projector, for example, is made all too evident, as the spectators in the urban theater are consistently upset by the incessant "crackling noise" (22) of the machine that emanates from the booth behind them. Later we read of a mirror in the hotel room by the seaside that reveals "in a brown monotone, the dark shape of the camera which the multiple lenses, its film reels, its base, its cables, and the attentive though blurred faces of the film crew standing in a group behind it" (97). A poster that is described in detail—in which "chiaroscuro effects make the two bodies appear to be molded together in a single mass"—has been fabricated "thanks to another trick on the part of the painter" (30). And in another scene, the voice of a film director yelling "Cut!" suddenly interrupts the narrative flow (98).

Whereas the already fragile mimetic illusion in *Triptyque* is subverted by the constant presence of these self-reflexive metaphors, the similarly anti-illusionistic nature of Rauschenberg's combines derives, in particular, from the artist's direct incorporation of found objects, mass-produced pictures, and raw materials. His images of images, along with his work's absorption of the detritus of daily life, highlight the fact that his creations are, at base, assemblages. Rauschenberg works as a *bricoleur*, wading through a mass of discarded objects in order to bring them together to create something new. For his part, Simon has remarked that he appreciates the unrefined nature of the objects that Rauschenberg brings together in his work: "the composition, the combination of these 'raw' materials, bits of fabric, dripping paint, photos or commercial reproductions of artworks, sometimes layers of glaze, pieces of wood, etc."[69] This shared interest in the concrete materiality of objects corresponds with a more widespread, postwar attack on humanism and a generalized turn toward the material substance of the world. Eschewing the traditional value of "high" art, many postwar artists looked for inspiration, quite literally, at their feet, seeking out objects and materials that were most readily available to them. Many artists working in the 1950s and thereafter felt the urge to consider art as an open field where nontraditional forms could play a decisive role. Rosalind Krauss refers to this as art's capacity to materialize the image. Although she locates the origins of this tendency in the work of Marcel Duchamp, Rauschenberg goes even further in treating the pictorial surface itself like a "species of material," rather than a mere support, that literally absorbs the objects embedded, like a "splinter under the skin," from within. As a result, representation is understood "as though it were a corporal thing."[70]

In the work of Claude Simon, this tendency manifests itself both in the author's experimentation with language as a kind of material, as well as in his interest in the essence of things. Simon conceives of his writing as a process of fabrication, of the construction of a similarly material object: "My only goal in writing (and I think that it's every writer's goal—Novalis said it years ago) has always been simple: to write. To write for writing's sake, as a painter paints for painting's sake. To *fabricate* a text, or rather a textual object that responds to a certain 'feeling' that I have about the work, and particularly about the novel."[71] Simon's association of the novel with a "textual object" that is clearly produced and crafted attests to his desire to create a work of literature that can perhaps be experienced in a more plastic, more visual way.

Although several recent studies have suggested the complex thematic and structural matrix linking Rauschenberg to Simon,[72] the consideration of the impact of Rauschenberg's work on the novelist from an art-historical and cultural-historical perspective has been altogether neglected. Rauschenberg's skepticism with regard to the myth of modernist purity —"what's a pure medium?" he once asked—similarly marks Simon's own project.[73] The painter, especially if one considers his reinvention of collage techniques first popularized by the cubists, was one of the first contemporary artists to have participated in the expansion of traditional artistic categories that would allow for a more fruitful kind of cross-pollination between media like painting, sculpture, photography, film, and literature. As one of the first artists whose work was so materially and intellectually heterogeneous that it typifies what Rosalind Krauss would ultimately come to term the age of the "post-medium condition,"[74] Rauschenberg occupies a crucial position in the historical shift from a culture of (Greenbergian) modernism to a more variegated and porous kind of cultural production that was developing during the latter half of the twentieth century.

What *Triptyque* shares most with Rauschenberg's work is a particular kind of ontological crisis, typical of much visual art produced during that period, in which the work of art refuses to come to terms with its own specific "area of competence." In the process, these works defy any definitive categorical affiliation. In much the same way that the combine paintings contaminate the purified space between painting and sculpture, Simon's novel manifests a desire to break free from the material and genetic constraints of literature in an attempt to become something other, something more concrete and concretely visual. Consequently, *Triptyque* represents a literary counterpart to those works of art that forge a path into the expanded field. For Krauss, the moment a particular artistic category opens itself up to the other arts and becomes "only one term on the periphery of a field in which there are other, differently structured possibilities," then this category, whether it be painting, sculpture, photography or some other art form, "gain[s] the 'permission' to think these other forms."[75] As part of its inherent drive to "move toward the visible," Simon's puzzling imagetext exemplifies this kind of interdisciplinary "thinking." In much the same way that Rauschenberg's combines "think" painting, photography, and sculpture simultaneously, or in the way that minimalist sculpture "thinks" painting or photo-realist painting "thinks" photography, *Triptyque* aims to occupy a similarly ambiguous space between disciplines.

Of course, this assertion implies one inevitable caveat. Simon's project is, after all, a literary one. No matter how much *Triptyque* "thinks" painting, photography, and film, no matter how much it experiments with and aspires to live up to the effects of various kinds of visual media, it remains resolutely a novel, which is to say a text whose "matter" is unmistakably "written in language."[76] Unlike certain textual imagetexts that reproduce pictures on their pages and invest them with significant narrative potential, *Triptyque*, no matter how hard it tries, does not show its pictures; it tells them instead. Despite the writer's drive to harness the power of language and make readers hear, feel, and "before all, to make [them] see!"[77] *Triptyque*, like each of the other narratives examined in the chapters to follow, consistently exercises its inherent textuality to affirm what ultimately sets literature apart.

# 2

# Faking It (Phony Pictures)

> In fact, he will doubt whether a philosopher could even *have* "final and actual" opinions, whether for a philosopher every cave does not have, *must* not have, an even deeper cave behind it—a more extensive, stranger, richer world above the surface, an abyss behind every ground, beneath every "groundwork".
>
> FRIEDRICH NIETZSCHE, *Beyond Good and Evil*

> These things, because they are fake, are infinitely more real.
>
> CHARLES BAUDELAIRE, *Salon de 1859*

*Un cabinet d'amateur: Histoire d'un tableau* (1979) is a fitting monument to many of its author's most important preoccupations.[1] The last literary narrative that Georges Perec published in its entirety before his untimely death in 1982, the text doubles as an imaginary archive that encrypts from within elements associated with the writer's present and his past, with people and things linked to his life and work. Like much of Perec's writing, the narrative masks an intricate layering of dissimulated allusions.[2] Hidden beneath its complex surface structure lies a multifaceted network of references, both explicit and implicit, obvious and oblique, to the author's private affairs (parents, friends) and public history (the Occupation, Ellis Island), to high culture (Cranach, Chardin,

Cézanne) and the lowbrow ("Jonathan Cheap" [177]), to a library full of books read and adored (Poe, Verne, Mann, Roussel, Robbe-Grillet), and to those Perec wrote himself (especially *La vie mode d'emploi*).[3] Although the narrative catalogues many aspects of the author's life and times, it is no less representative of his mystifyingly illusionist poetics. For in *Un cabinet d'amateur*, a deceptively straightforward account of a collector and his cherished collection of paintings, appearances are consciously designed to deceive. Like Simon's *Triptyque*, Perec's text responds to the increasing ubiquity of the visual in contemporary culture by crafting a tale saturated with pictures that are never quite what they seem.[4]

*Un cabinet d'amateur* introduces readers to German-born brewery magnate Hermann Raffke, a millionaire collector of some of the world's finest works of art, whose acquisitions range from masterpieces by Gérôme, Holbein, Poussin, Greuze, and Rubens to a number of more modest paintings by American artists of lesser renown (Bernie Bickford's *Charles M. Murphy Attempting the Mile Record on June 30th 1899* [146]). In a gesture reminiscent of the *Kunstkabinett* or *Kunstkammer* paintings made popular in Europe during the seventeenth century, Raffke, like those Dutch princes centuries earlier, commissions a canvas in which he is depicted magisterially surveying the almost one hundred paintings in his private gallery, each image meticulously recreated, to scale, on the canvas.[5] The novel opens during a cultural festival in Pittsburgh where the painting, itself entitled *Un cabinet d'amateur*, is prominently on display. There it succeeds in attracting the attention of a number of critics who praise its "Poe-like" strangeness and the way it probes larger aesthetic questions, "what received opinion considers to constitute Beauty in Art" (132). After a slow start, the painting also becomes exceedingly popular with visitors intrigued by its distinct representational structure. Unlike traditional *Kunstkabinett* paintings, Raffke's commission not only represents the works amassed in his collection, it depicts itself *en abyme*, "for the artist has put his painting in the painting, so that the art collector, sitting in his gallery, has in his line of sight, on the far wall, the paintings which represent himself looking at his collection of paintings" (137). The painting, embedded within itself, appears embedded again in the next, smaller generation of the image, and so on ad infinitum. Extraordinarily, its creator Heinrich Kürz did not simply replicate the paintings in each of the original's subsequent reflections. Rather, with every ensuing layer each image appears to be, in some way or another, different from the model that precedes it. From one copy to the next objects represented on the canvas change color, figures disappear, new compositional elements reveal themselves, and, in one especially compelling case, the consecutive images construct—as in a flip book or a film—a narrative over time: "a boxing champion, still in fine fettle in the first copy, was receiving a terrible uppercut in the second, and was lying flat-out in the third" (139). Given the spatial constraints of the picture, every subsequent generation of this gallery portrait is exponentially smaller than the one in which it figures, a fact that obliges the most curious of spectators to arm themselves with a magnifying glass and a steady hand.[6]

The visual archive of Raffke's collection that Kürz's painting represents reveals itself to be a fabrication that is carefully designed to fool the public into thinking that the images it depicts are authentic works of art. As readers learn near the novel's conclusion, some years prior to the exhibition of *Un cabinet d'amateur*, Raffke was informed that the paintings that he had spent years amassing were fakes. Infuriated by the news, the victimized collector decided to avenge himself on the movers and shakers of the art world who had proven incapable of preventing such a scandal yet who, at the same time, had traditionally prided themselves on their so-called expertise. Hiring his nephew, alias Heinrich Kürz, and a particularly astute critic, Lester Nowak, to help him carry out his duplicitous scheme, Raffke consequently elected to saturate the market with a new series of deliberately forged paintings. The creation of the *Kunstkabinett* picture was simply part of the larger plan, the "keystone to this patient plot" in which the paintings within the painting would naturally appear to be miniaturized replicas of "*genuine*" works of art (187).

In an ingeniously reflexive twist, the structure of the text echoes the inherent falsity of the pictures it describes, self-consciously exposing itself as a simulation of a curious event that never actually happened. Perec's "story of painting" mirrors the pictures it tells in that it, too, is not entirely what it claims to be. The ultimate moment of narrative demystification occurs in the text's last lines: "The careful inspections that were carried out soon showed that most of the paintings from the Raffke Collection were indeed fakes, as fake as most of the details in this fictional tale, invented solely for the pleasure—and the thrill—of deception" (188). From the very beginning, *Un cabinet d'amateur* (the narrative, like the painting) relies upon a tautly wound tension between reality and make believe. Although the book's French subtitle ("*histoire d'un tableau*") evokes the reality of a "chronicle," a "record," or a "history," readers cannot entirely rule out the possibility that it refers merely to the (fictional) "story" of a painting.[7] Then again, two discursive footnotes (155–56) lend an air of historical authority and authenticity that grounds the text in an extradiegetic reality of which the "author" is a part. The novel's accumulation of verifiable details (real place names, real people, real paintings), examples of false erudition, and a variety of reality effects, also work momentarily to mask its fictional status. In the end, however, the text's ontological scale definitively tips in favor of the false. Pretending, at times, to be a work of investigative reportage, the narrative of events comprising the purported "Raffke affair"—which also includes citations from Nowak's sophisticated thesis on Kürz's artwork, and a reprint of the two seemingly authentic catalogues documenting the sale of Raffke's fakes at auction—is a complex work of verbal trickery calculated to suspend disbelief and dupe its readers into (mis)taking a carefully crafted illusion for a historically valid human interest story.

"It's all fake," Perec said of his earlier novel, *La vie mode d'emploi*, "but it needed to seem real."[8] *Un cabinet d'amateur*, constructed around a similar logic of simulation, takes this devious representational strategy and amplifies it to the next degree. The text adopts a logic inherited from the tradition of trompe l'oeil art in which the beholder is taken under the spell of an image that purports to be the thing that it represents, only to be shaken out from under that spell moments later by a cognitive shock that every trompe l'oeil image, at one point or another, triggers. For what the beholder perceives in the trompe l'oeil only appears to materialize for a brief while since, in a movement that some critics consider its defining feature, every illusion of this kind ultimately affirms its inherent difference from the object that it represents.[9] Perec's tale, like the trompe l'oeil images that it emulates, blurs the tenuous boundary between appearing and being, seeing and believing, between real things and their faithfully rendered copies.

The constant tension and vacillation between the virtual and the "real" is a common trope of much contemporary fiction. Unlike more traditionally realist forms of representation that aim to "mirror" the world in all its complexity, *Un cabinet d'amateur* constitutes a decidedly warped reflection of that world, warning readers to take a text's (and an image's) purported relationship to reality with a grain of salt. The author exploits this textual wariness by incorporating images designed to lead readers down a path strewn with a variety of pseudorealist, *trompe-lecteur* traps. "Warning! This book is dangerous," as one critic exhorted.[10] The text effectively harnesses the power of the false, exalting the counterfeiter in the process, and manipulates the very foundations of realist representation in order to destabilize it from within. As part of a strategy that bears the mark of the leftist political leanings that motivated its author's earliest forays into cultural criticism, while at the same time capitalizing on an interest in the complex aesthetic function of trompe l'oeil visual art that Perec also explored in earlier writings, *Un cabinet d'amateur* signals the potentially duplicitous nature of all forms of representation to which we are consistently—optically as well as intellectually—subjected.

## *This Is Not a Wall*

In a lengthy meditation from 1974 on the various kinds of spaces, or the "species of spaces," that we inhabit from day to day, an essay that expands from the inside out, from a bed in a room in an apartment in a building in a country located somewhere in "the world," Perec ruminates on those places one might frequent over the course of a lifetime, yet often take for granted. Tucked into a chapter extolling the not so ordinary details of "the apartment," complementing a discussion of stairways and doors, readers come across a short passage on "walls" in which the author lays the groundwork for a veritable theory of the trompe l'oeil that he will continue to develop over the years.

The chapter begins rather modestly: "I put a picture up

on a wall." Yet this seemingly straightforward act of home decoration triggers a more complex philosophical quandary that raises a variety of questions about the power of images. A painting hung on a wall serves a transformative function as well: "The wall is no longer what delimits and defines the place where I live . . . it is nothing more than a support for the picture." The painting, as it were, alters the very functionality of the wall. No longer a structure that delineates a space, the wall becomes a mere background for the image. At the same time, however, the wall takes precedence over the work of art: "But I also forget the picture, I no longer look at it, I no longer know how to look at it."[11] Once the tableau is in place, its status is relegated to that of a mere ornament, which is to say that the wall, in turn, "kills" the painting. This is an echo of Jacques Derrida's reading of the *parergon*, or frame, which is at once internal and external to the work of art. In Perec's quasi-deconstructionist paradigm, paintings are as likely to serve as "backgrounds" as the walls upon which they hang.[12]

Several years later, in his preface to *L'œil ébloui*, a book of photographs of trompe l'oeil murals from around the world taken by Cuchi White, Perec reconsiders this puzzling optical and epistemological impasse.[13] What if the wall were not a wall after all? What if the painting were not really a painting? Why not, he proposes, reduce each of the elements of the equation to the other's terms? In other words, transform the wall into a painting and the painting into a wall. Cover the wall with a trompe l'oeil image that proudly proclaims "This is not a wall," yet which, at the same time, denies its status as a painting since, for a brief moment at least, the trompe l'oeil creates the illusion of an actual space to be explored and occupied like any other.

Unlike Magritte's infamous pipe—which, as the image

about *The Treachery of Images* (1929) rightly claims, is "not a pipe" but a painted representation of a pipe—"the wall painted in trompe l'oeil is, indeed, a wall." At the same time, however, paint and surface collaborate in a trompe l'oeil mural to create an illusion, a visual and intellectual ruse in which "the simulacrum of painting yearns to pass for something that it is not."[14] The key to the trompe l'oeil, therefore, lies in this curious movement between trickery and disbelief when, for an instant, we are fooled. Impelled by the power of the illusion, the trompe l'oeil beholder is invited to reach out and touch the painted object or the space it represents in order to verify that it is, in fact, real.

The viewer's desire to question the relation between vision and the truth—"But the real? Where does it begin? And how can one ever verify the credibility of the message transmitted to our optical systems?"[15]—is crucial to Perec's interest in the spurious nature of the trompe l'oeil. It is also an integral part of what motivates the structure of *Un cabinet d'amateur*, published two years prior to *L'œil ébloui*. The trompe l'oeil is such a vital part of Perec's poetic project not simply because it wields its powers to entice and entrap, but because a secondary movement also empowers the subject to interrogate the very reality that the image so effectively simulates. This movement, which allows the viewing subject the distance and perspective necessary to exit the world of make-believe, is triggered the instant he is made aware of this entrapment with a shiver, as if roused from a dreamlike state with a pinch.

This kind of experience is epitomized for Perec in what he considers the pinnacle of trompe l'oeil easel painting: Cornelius Norbertus Gijsbrechts's *Trompe l'oeil: The Reverse of a Framed Painting*, ca. 1670 (image 2). This picture, created by one of the masters of the form, depicts, as the title suggests, the back of a painting. Here the wooden

Image 2. Cornelius Norbertus Gijsbrechts, *Trompe l'oeil: The Reverse of a Framed Painting*, 1670. Oil on canvas, 66.4 x 87 cm. National Gallery of Denmark, Copenhagen. © SMK Photo.

frame and stark underbelly of a small, stretched canvas are rendered so genuinely that the image seems three-dimensional, inviting viewers to wonder what might be painted on the other side. Perec can only imagine the scene that must have played out occasionally in the artist's studio where the painting was originally stored, propped against the back wall to entice curious visitors. "Sooner or later, an eventual client would pick it up and turn it around to see what was painted behind; the impression must have been like holding both sides of a mirror at once."[16]

Gijsbrechts's painting is as intentionally frustrating and vertiginous as any well-executed simulacrum that "subverts the cherished dichotomy of model and copy, original and reproduction, image and likeness."[17] Not merely a copy of the hidden structure that supports a painting on a canvas, the reversed painting is designed to simulate, rather than imitate, what it represents. Whereas an imitation simply re-presents the thing upon which it is modeled, linked to the object by a set of "internal, essential relations of resemblance to [that] model," the simulacrum "bears a deceptive resemblance to its putative model."[18] A painting that merely resembles an object does not need to declare its difference since there is no risk that the viewer will privilege the object over the image itself. The birds, fish, cured meats, and other delicacies that populate Chardin's lush, gastronomic still lifes, for example, do not self-reflexively maintain that they are not, in truth, real. Even though Chardin's images depict objects that appear delightfully "realistic," the paintings recognize that most viewers are unlikely to mistake them for real things. On the other hand, Gijsbrechts's trompe l'oeil more self-assuredly proclaims that while it may appear to resemble the back of a painting, it most definitely is *not*.

The beholder of a realist image might accept the illusion of reality but is ultimately certain of the image's status as a representation. Before a trompe l'oeil, on the other hand, the spectator is, by design, initially incapable of acknowledging that the work in question is actually a representation, convinced by his perception that what he sees is part and parcel of the surrounding environment.[19] The difference between a realistically painted object and a trompe l'oeil detail therefore lies less in "what" we see than in "how" we see it. The body, in particular, is much less implicated in our response to a realistic painting than it is before a well-crafted trompe l'oeil since the latter suggests the veritable presence of the object in space and may compel the beholder to reach out and touch it. Not simply "just a picture," the simulacrum—"mimesis in excess"[20]—is an "enlightened" image, explicitly calling attention to its own powers of persuasion. Like Magritte's painting of a pipe, which prominently announces what every trompe l'oeil image, were it not mute, would say, Gijsbrechts's painting seems to whisper a quiet injunction: "This is not the backside of a painting."

Like Gijsbrechts's image, *Un cabinet d'amateur* experiments with this self-conscious awareness and takes the trompe l'oeil as a privileged structuring metaphor. The novel "affirms its difference" in the end, and it does so quite literally. Near the conclusion the narrator intervenes to reveal that "most of the details in this fictional tale" are, indeed, false (188). So too are the paintings that comprise it: "most of the paintings from the Raffke Collection were indeed fakes" (188). Not only do the images from Raffke's collection, sold off at auction to the highest bidder as part of the collector's vengeful scheme, manage to dupe even the sharpest appraiser, they are also designed to fool readers of Perec's text. Whereas some of the painters, paintings, and references to the art world that might sound familiar actually do exist—even though a certain "R. Mutt" (139) never painted a thing—most of the "real" painters mentioned are not responsible for the works attributed to them. One would be hard pressed, for example, to locate *Cigarette Salesgirl* (179) in any catalogue raisonné listing the collected work of Pierre-Auguste Renoir, even though the artist did produce a picture called *The Apple Seller* (1890) and his son, famed filmmaker Jean Renoir, directed a silent 1928 fantasy picture called *The Little Match Girl*. Readers who are not familiar with the history of art—and, in some cases, even those who are—might be led to think that certain painters or paintings do exist, even when they do not. The picture at the center of Perec's narrative that represents these misleading pictures *en abyme* exists in word only. One couldn't hope to paint *Un cabinet d'amateur*. One can only, as Perec has done, describe it.[21] The narrative therefore functions as an uncanny intellectual trap triggered by words on the page that seek to rival the kind of visual ruse deployed by artists like Gijsbrechts or Magritte. Like every image painted in the tradition of Zeuxis's famously convincing grapes, or Parrhasios's even more persuasive curtain, the mimetic mirror onto the world that the novel traditionally represents becomes lost in Perec's narrative funhouse, reflecting a series of bogus figures and trick images in a dizzying abyss of false appearances.[22]

### *Mining the Powers of the Simulacrum*

I want to suggest that Perec's manipulation of these false appearances is motivated, in *Un cabinet d'amateur* and elsewhere,[23] by a particularly pragmatic tactic. The text deploys the fake—phony pictures, fake painters, false erudition—in order to remind readers of the potential dangers of representation and warn them of its limitations. Not simply designed to lure readers into a series of vertiginous, albeit stimulating traps, Perec's stylistic and thematic play with the false is a didactic tool. If *Un cabinet d'amateur* explores the aesthetic potential of the trompe l'oeil simulacrum, it also recognizes the simulacrum's capacity for social critique.

As part of a generalized critical strategy to enlighten readers to the ubiquity of certain hegemonic social, cultural, and political practices, Perec's use of the false originates in his earlier interest in the kind of Marxist aesthetics that was widely debated in Parisian intellectual circles after World War II. Perec's writings from the late 1950s and early 1960s for *La ligne générale*—a short-lived journal of cultural criticism devoted to a revolutionary critique of bourgeois, capitalist ideology and the kind of thinking that fosters "a counterfeit image of the world and of man"—was a turning point in his career as a writer.[24] A decade later Perec would go on to collaborate with radical philosopher Paul Virilio and sociologist Jean Duvignaud on another contemporary journal of social and ideological critique, *Cause commune*, which set out to "call into question the ideas and beliefs that form the bedrock of our civilization."[25] This critical spirit is also clearly manifest in Perec's early novels, *Les choses* (1965) and *Un homme qui dort* (1967) particularly, which testify to the tension that the author confronted throughout his career between the aesthetic and the political, or what he called "the lyric drive and the conviction to investigate."[26] When asked in 1965 to comment on the "myth of happiness" propagated by a consumer-based society, an ideology that his novel *Les choses* aims to demystify, Perec acknowledges that part of his task as a writer is to equip readers with a critical sociology necessary to challenge the most dominant institutions and ideals: "Our world offers in its 'things' various goods, not only objects to consume but values . . . I simply wonder about these values. The response—and political engagement is one—lies with the reader who, after having read this book, will react according to his own experience."[27] Although Perec went on to concentrate on other modes and genres of writing, taking great pride in the stylistic versatility of the texts that he produced,[28] the heightened critical consciousness of these initial stages of his career undoubtedly left a trace on what was to follow.

Notions like the fake, the copy, the simulacrum, and the trompe l'oeil are crucial to modes of social critique prevalent during the 1960s and 1970s precisely because they engage, and target, the contested area of mediation that exists between the subject and the truth. According to the kind of committed theorizing around which Perec and his fellow essayists mobilized, the very notion of (bourgeois) ideology that the editors of *La ligne générale* attempted to expose as a manipulative and alienating force was itself understood as a distortion of the real. For the Marxist critic, ideology is not simply a system of beliefs belonging to a particular community or group but a dominant doctrine rooted in society to such a point that it surreptitiously affects an individual's capacity to make conscious, subjective decisions. Ideology can thus be understood as a fundamental perversion of the link between appearances and essences. For Marx, one of the metaphors that most effectively illustrates the effects of false consciousness fostered by the prevailing ideology is, literally, a false image, a kind of trompe l'oeil that inhibits the subject, who thus becomes alienated from the truth and incapable of distinguishing between veracity and artifice. To be caught up in a system dominated by the ideological myths of modern life is akin to being trapped in a "camera obscura" whose field of vision is taken over by a distorted image of the world, one that appears upside down.[29]

If ideology is construed as false consciousness, as a false appearance, as a "refusal of the real"—in other words, as fake—could it not also, if turned inwards, reveal that which it conceals?[30] If one could channel the power of the false to call attention to itself, then one might be able to deconstruct the principles on which the illusion is founded, thereby triggering a critical response. Part of the general philosophical project in France during the 1960s and 1970s was dedicated to this task, as other liberal thinkers such as Gilles Deleuze, coterminous with Perec, sought to recuperate the positive, pragmatic potential inherent in the fake and the simulacrum. As Deleuze suggests, the power of the simulacrum to undermine the very foundations and organizational structures that govern representation is a way to empower the public. By bringing critical thinking "to the streets," the simulacrum "not only provides a means of resistance to the dominant powers but also permits an emergent collective . . . to express its own power to create a new sensibility and form of life no longer legitimated by or grounded in the dominant truths."[31] For Deleuze, therefore, consciousness of the limits of representation is the first step in building momentum toward a revolutionary social event.

In a similarly provocative way, the trompe l'oeil allows Perec to promote a redemptive mode of thinking, one that would critique those surface appearances that mask the true nature of things. Perec's earlier writings on the need to rethink the false claims promoted by modern forms of literary realism are a more explicitly politicized manifestation of ideas that resonate in his later work: "We live in a world that is seemingly incomprehensible: bourgeois ideology clouds the issues and shuffles the cards. We read newspapers that lie, we see films that mean nothing to us, we read books that conceal the essential. . . . But all of this is mere appearance: we do not have to live up to the image of a society that, because it is running out of steam, is driving us toward an abyss. Under the agonizing of the bourgeoisie a new world is born, a new force. It's hidden from view; we do not see it easily."[32] For Perec, ideology is blinding. Even worse, it is as ubiquitous as those texts and images through which it proliferates. What matters, therefore, is that we perceive—or at least attempt to perceive—what lies beneath it all, and that we teach ourselves to unmask the hegemonic structures that enshroud the truth.

Perec's championing of the simulacrum's capacity to threaten the established hierarchy marks a direct affront to the kind of thinking, originating in Plato's *Republic*, which relies on a similarly hierarchical system, one that discriminates between appearances and essences. This theory of representation proposes a rigid ordering of things and their copies that scorns representations, both verbal and visual, in favor of true things, themselves embodied by an Idea (*eidos*): "So the art of imitation is surely far removed from the truth, it seems, and that is why it produces everything, because it only touches some small element of each thing, and that an image."[33] The imitative artist—the maker of "appearances, not realities"[34]—is like a mirror that reflects all that it sees. Reflections, however, represent merely the appearance of things, not the essence of the thing itself. Plato conceives of the potential for the propagation of imitations—doubles, copies, and replicas—as a risk. His iconoclastic logic is thus motivated not simply by aesthetic concerns, but also by an acute political anxiety. Painters (and poets), imitators and creators of mere appearances—as opposed to, say, carpenters and other artisans whose work requires knowledge of the essence of the thing that they produce—are a liability to the proper functioning of the state. Consequently, they should be stripped of their *droit de cité* and banished from the republic.[35] According to the philosopher's exclusionary paradigm, images and their creators represent a legitimate sociopolitical threat.

Centuries later Gilles Deleuze would recuperate the simulacrum in a revolutionary "reversal of Platonism": "So 'to reverse Platonism' means to make the simulacra rise and to affirm their rights among icons and copies. The problem no longer has to do with the distinction Essence-Appearance or Model-Copy. This distinction operates completely within the world of representation. Rather, it has to do with undertaking the subversion of this world."[36] Whereas other theorists like Guy Debord and Jean Baudrillard were, at around the same time, lamenting the dystopic consequences of an uncontrollable surge of simulacra in contemporary culture, here Deleuze champions the potentially positive outcome of such a proliferation. For Deleuze, the subversion of the foundational terms that allow ideology to exist in the first place is a constructive gesture in the long run. The power and propagation of the false renders all hierarchies null and void: "it engulfs all foundations, it assures a universal breakdown (*effondrement*), but as a joyful and positive event, as an un-founding (*effondement*)."[37] Gijsbrechts's *Trompe l'œil* is precisely the kind of image that disrupts the mimetic order and fosters this kind of joyous "un-founding" of appearances and essences that Deleuze sees as necessary for the experience of a new, more liberated experience of the world. Indeed, for centuries before thinkers such as Deleuze began to sing its praises, the simulacrum was generally denigrated because it represented an unsettling negation of mimesis.[38] The *Reverse of a Framed Painting* is a potent manifestation of this negation since it manages to, quite literally, turn the Platonic hierarchy inside out.

It is no wonder that Perec, who believed that artistic brilliance could be characterized as an "error in the system," should have appreciated the disruptive effects that paintings like Gijsbrechts's brought about not only in viewers but also on the history of art. Originating in the Lucretian theory of the *clinamen*, Perec's desire to avoid a totalizing application of any one faultless system to his work led him to introduce frequently that "minor error" which would allow the text to function with more liberty than it would have were it wholly free of imperfections.[39] In *La vie mode d'emploi*, the most prominent error in the machine is the famous missing chapter.[40] Perec plays with this concept in a more obvious manner in *Un cabinet d'amateur*, in which each painting as it appears in its subsequent embedded reflection is slightly different from its model. From one copy to the next, the painter has imposed a series of startling modifications that destabilize the painting's infinite duplication in miniature: "the shepherd bringing home his sheep (*The Painting Lesson*, Dutch school) could count ten of them in the first copy, twenty in the second, and none at all in the third" (139–40). By altering a detail in each generation of the image, tripping up the mimetic impulse inherent in all replication, the *clinamen* as it is deployed in *Un cabinet d'amateur* allows for the novel's consistent perversion of the systematic hierarchy established between original and copy.

Perec's narrative also concretizes the desire to upset that hierarchy in the discourse of Raffke's enlisted critic, Lester Nowak, hired to help carry out his diabolical counterfeiting scheme. In a series of comments published in his doctoral thesis, "Heinrich Kürz, an American artist, 1884–1914," Nowak echoes the faith in the power of the simulacrum to destabilize the hegemony of the model and test the mimetic foundation upon which all representation relies. As Nowak argues, each successive reflection embedded within Kürz's *Kunstkabinett* privileges "an inventiveness transcending enumeration, a flash of inspiration transcending citation and a freedom transcending memory" (144). The picture within the picture is not simply a serial reproduction that subsumes the copy to the model. Rather, the copy surpasses its model. With each generation of the painting within the painting Kürz "invents" new images that might resemble the images that precede them, yet which are not entirely modeled after them. Nowak's explanation of the "enigma" behind these minuscule variations is telling in this regard, since he reads Kürz's practice of "infinite regression" as a way for the work to become "conscious of its limitations," to "be able to turn itself, when necessary, into derision and denounce itself as an illusion, as a mere exacerbation of that form of perception which can produce only *trompe l'oeil*" (169).

Nowak appreciates Kürz's painting because it consciously denounces itself as an illusion, proving the power of the trompe l'oeil to upset the "established order" of art (144). His critical reading of Kürz's tableau is therefore not so much a treatise on "Art and Reflection," as his first article was entitled, but would perhaps best be referred to as part of a larger history of what Michael Camille has called "art and delusion." Whereas Ernst Gombrich's celebrated examination of the perceptualist impulse in his landmark study *Art and Illusion* (1960) constructs a history of images that progressively seek to render visual appearances, the particular history in which Kürz's painting is located considers "art that could not claim to be about objects at all but about strategies of their simulation."[41] Privileging the false and seducing viewers with its vertiginous reflections, Kürz's painting, in other words, is Plato's worst nightmare.

Like those trompe l'oeil murals that inspire Perec to question the artificiality of their own illusion, *Un cabinet d'amateur* ponders the "fidelity of the message transmitted to our optical systems."[42] Although the text incorporates images to entrap readers initially with its illusory tricks, it consequently deploys them as a tool to warn of the dangers of false appearance and to expose the kind of duplicitous *tromperie* that often entraps us. Trompe l'oeil, then, in order to *détromper l'œil*.[43]

### *Welcome to Hoaxville*

Like the other novels in this study, *Un cabinet d'amateur* can be read as symptomatic of the vast cultural—not to mention visual-cultural—network within which it was produced. That Perec's narrative not only thematizes the production, circulation, and reception of pictures but is also structured around an antimimetic logic of simulation is not surprising considering the advent of a specifically simulacral style of painting and sculpture that flourished throughout the 1960s and into the 1970s in both France and abroad. While hardly an expert, Perec was certainly familiar with the kind of pop-influenced, photo-based photo-realism that artists such as Malcolm Morley, Richard Estes, Chuck Close, and their French counterparts (Jacques Bodin, Pierre Barraya, and Gérard Fromanger) were practicing at the time.[44] A number of critics and thinkers in France were also exploring the same interstices between reality and illusion in a series of works that sought to understand the causes and effects of a new, particularly hyperrealist kind of postmodern subjectivity.[45] Moreover, the period surrounding the publication of Perec's text witnessed a number of intriguing counterfeiting scandals that revolved around the production and exchange of carefully crafted forgeries. The decade during which *Un cabinet d'amateur* was conceived and written happens to be a defining moment in the storied cultural history of the false. Perec's engagement with this larger cultural phenomenon reveals some of the more potent historical nuances of his multifaceted tale.

The twentieth century saw its fair share of forgers. Take Eric Hebborn, for example, a British draughtsman of remarkable talent who made a life's work out of fooling some of the world's most prestigious institutions of art, from the most esteemed auction houses to the halls of the Getty and Metropolitan museums. His meticulously crafted forgeries have been circulating on the art market ever since the fifties, and some of his fakes still reside in museum collections, unbeknownst to staff whose job it is to prevent this very thing from happening. Not unlike the team of protagonists who construct their own counterfeiting con in Perec's novel, Hebborn's fakes respond, in part, to a personal vendetta maliciously directed toward the art world's experts.[46]

A few decades before Hebborn began honing his skills, Dutchman Han van Meegeren became embroiled in another infamous scandal that captured much of Europe's attention. Directly after the fall of Hitler's regime, a previously unknown

Vermeer canvas was found among the collection of art owned by Luftwaffe commander Hermann Goering. The painting was traced to van Meegeren who, in order to avoid being prosecuted for collaboration with the enemy, admitted having sold Goering the Vermeer. As he went on to explain, however, the crime was not as serious as the authorities had expected. The painting he sold was a fake.[47] In an effort to save himself, van Meegeren asserted that he was not in cahoots with the Nazis, but had managed to manipulate and fool one of their most visible figureheads. His fake, he claimed, sided with the allies. After having consulted with a series of specialists, the courts were convinced that the fake was, in fact, "authentic," and subsequently sentenced the "collaborator" to prison. In a last-ditch attempt to prove his innocence, van Meegeren responded in spectacular fashion by producing another perfect forgery—another "real fake"—from within the confines of his prison cell.[48]

Public reaction to these and similar scandals is often mired in ambivalence. Although the blatant lack of professional scruples and respect for venerable institutions is often shocking, we must also contend with an undeniable sense of fascination for those who manage to concoct such elaborate hoaxes and dupe such a large and often well-informed audience. The level of deceit can be downright repulsive, especially when these cons jeopardize the careers, finances, or reputations of innocent people or the organizations for which they work. The fact remains that this type of trickery is a truly spectacular, and spectacularly entertaining, act. Our distaste for this sort of blatant dishonesty is at once tempered by the illicit sense of pleasure we take in considering that such a heroic subversion of these powerful institutions is in fact possible.

One of the greatest public scandals of this kind to have occurred during the last half-century, a compelling story that brought together an art forger, a literary faker, and a jet-setting film director, was the infamous Clifford Irving hoax of 1971. Irving, an American novelist, was thrust onto the public stage in the year after he announced the imminent publication of a supposedly authorized biography of the billionaire hermit Howard Hughes. To write such a book was no small feat, especially considering that gaining access to Hughes, who had been cloistered in Las Vegas for over a decade, was next to impossible. Claiming that he had met with the elusive recluse more than a hundred times over several years in secret locations scattered throughout Mexico and the Bahamas, amassing hundreds of recorded interviews, letters, and private documents along the way, Irving and his editors publicized the release of the book as a groundbreaking literary event. Hughes, after all, was an exceptionally mysterious figure whose self-imposed exile rendered the possibility of such a public disclosure of his personal life all the more intriguing. The media was rightly loath to believe that Irving had ever spoken with Hughes, and a group of graphologists was quickly called upon to verify the handwriting in the documents that Irving presented as proof. These skilled analysts corroborated the biographer's claim. Irving, it seemed, was for real.

The story began to unravel, however, less than a year later, when Hughes came out of hiding (over the telephone) and publicly denounced Irving as a fake. In time another journalist familiar with Hughes came forward and added fuel to the fire, alleging that Irving had stolen information from his own files on the tycoon. After a highly publicized trial Irving, his wife, and another co-conspirator were sentenced to jail in June 1972. After serving fourteen months in federal prison Irving was released and was ready to reembark on his literary career. He has since published an array of popular novels.

A personal account of the Hughes con, in which the author admits to his wrongdoings, was published in 1981 as *The Hoax*.

Several years prior to the Hughes scandal, Irving became involved with another equally shady figure living in exile on the Spanish island of Ibiza: the cultivated Hungarian polyglot Elmyr de Hory. In the years prior to their meeting, De Hory was busy making a name for himself as one of the world's most renowned art forgers. Irving was so intrigued that he wrote and published (shortly before he became involved in his own public affair) a biography documenting the trials and tribulations of de Hory's unique career on the periphery of the international art market.[49] Not long after the publication of this volume, both de Hory and Irving would become the subject of a documentary film by François Reichenbach, commissioned by the BBC yet never completed. Reichenbach's unused footage wound up in the hands of his esteemed colleague and friend, Orson Welles. Welles, captivated by the mystique of the fake, decided to recuperate the Frenchman's efforts and resuscitate the dormant film in his own way. While Welles was working on the de Hory story, however, news of the Irving-Hughes scandal broke, and the acclaimed director, recognizing the opportunity, decided to expand the scope of his project to include the reflexive dimension that Irving's own forgery scandal brought to the picture. The coincidental timing of the Irving trial allowed Welles to engage the current state of artful deception from within: de Hory the forger, and Irving, the faker who wrote about him, both appear in a film by another world-famous trickster, Welles, in a motion picture that itself can hardly be trusted. *F for Fake*, as it was called, was released in the United States in 1973 and in France two years later.

A cinematic essay on various forms of forgery, *F for Fake*

Image 3. Screen capture from *F for Fake*, 1972, directed by Orson Welles. Janus Film/Les Films de l'Astrophore.

not only documents the scandals in which its protagonists were involved but also acts as a potent exploration of the nature of authorship, expertise, and deception. De Hory, Irving, and even Reichenbach all appear, their stories woven together by the director who is shown, on several occasions, working his technical magic at the helm of an elaborate editing machine and performing parlor tricks to the delight of an excited young boy (image 3).

Indeed, the director consistently refers to himself as a conjurer of sorts, and compares the art of filmmaking to a cunning magician's ruse. Welles, whose work was of "critical importance" for Perec, is a self-proclaimed "charlatan," an conjurer of sorts who has made a career out of movie-making trickery.[50]

*F for Fake*, not unlike *Un cabinet d'amateur*, is a defense and illustration of trompe l'oeil aesthetics. In the cinema, as the film warns us, seeing does not necessarily mean believing. The enactment of this elaborate iconoclastic gesture is prepared during the first few minutes of the film, when Welles relays the following disclaimer: "This is a promise. During the next hour everything you'll hear from us is really true and based on solid fact." *F for Fake* thus begins by officially declaring its status as a documentary. However, the film's claims to the kind of veracity one would expect from a work of *cinéma vérité* is merely a false front designed to lure the unsuspecting members of its audience.

As it so happens, the film does not end an hour later. Rather, its duration exceeds Welles's self-declared limit by more than fifteen minutes. The director, having anticipated that most spectators would not actually go to the trouble of keeping track of time, ends his film with a tale involving Welles's girlfriend and another series of forged paintings, Picassos this time. Although designed to look as though it actually occurred, the anecdote is a figment of the director's imagination. This "reenactment of recent history" at first seems plausible, especially given Welles's adroit editing of his footage. "Why not?" the film seems to say: "Stranger things have happened." The truth, however, is revealed moments later when the director giddily exposes the nature of his ruse: "That hour, ladies and gentlemen, is over. For the past seventeen minutes, I've been lying my head off." The director's final avowal strikingly brings to mind the conclusion of *Un cabinet d'amateur*, at which point the narrator intervenes to divulge that most everything we have read up to this point is fake, "invented solely for the pleasure—and the thrill—of deception" (85). Not unlike Welles's film, Perec's novel—fiction in disguise—presents itself as a legitimate depiction of the truth.

Moreover, both novel and film present their audiences with a trio of like-minded fakers: the painter, the writer, and the mastermind. Elmyr de Hory and Heinrich Kürz, the genius counterfeiters that figure, respectively, in Welles's film and Perec's novel, are equally mysterious characters. De Hory is supposedly Hungarian, but his hard-to-place accent and fluency in five languages makes this difficult to verify. Welles admits that he does not know much about him, and even if he did he would prefer not to reveal too many secrets. Kürz, in comparison, is an American of German origin (11), yet his name, like De Hory's, is also a cover. As the narrator of *Un cabinet d'amateur* will eventually disclose, Kürz is actually Humbert Raffke, the collector's nephew. As history has shown, many of this century's most successful counterfeiting schemes do not necessarily require the perpetrator to work under an alias: van Meegeren and Hebborn are, after all, authentic surnames. Welles and Perec, on the other hand, present characters who mirror the text in which they play a role: like *F for Fake* and *Un cabinet d'amateur*, de Hory and Kürz are not who they claim to be.[51]

Clifford Irving and Perec's scholar-accomplice Lester Nowak are also alike in their success at fooling the masses with their duplicitous writings. Indeed, like the letters and manuscripts supposedly penned by Howard Hughes that Irving tenders to prove the authenticity of his biographical endeavors, Nowak's seemingly erudite critique of Kürz's visual pastiche also revolves around an empty center. Although Nowak's critical reading of the painting is a valid one—it is undeniable, for example, that Kürz's canvas deploys a complex logic of *mise en abyme* to suggest, as Nowak writes, the "vertiginous spirituality of the Eternal Return" (138)—the genius of his thesis lies in its ability to misinform. In the end, thanks in part to Nowak's exaltation of the image in which they figure, all the paintings in Raffke's collection sell, and sell well. The experts charged with the sale of the collection cannot help but be taken in by the discourse of a "colleague" whose analysis is as comprehensive as it is admirable. Nowak typifies Welles's conception of the expert, the "new oracle," who can, with one judgment, transform an insignificant object into a priceless work of art.

Although de Hory, Kürz, Irving, and Nowak are themselves fine examples of disreputable genius, Welles and Raffke are the principal masterminds behind the ruse.[52] Both effectively construct an ingenious scenario designed to deceive. This is not the first time that Welles has dabbled in this kind of trickery. The director began his career as a fake. As he notes in the film, his own clever duplicity guaranteed him his first acting job: as a young upstart in Dublin, claiming that he was a star back in New York, he quickly landed his first theatrical roles. Welles would continue to build a reputation with a more elaborate kind of trickery, and it is only fitting that his last completed film should focus on his finely tuned talents of deception. One only has to think of his most triumphant hoax on October 30, 1938: the young actor, working in radio at the time, terrified millions of Americans by duping them into believing that hostile Martian forces had invaded the planet. The success of Welles's adaptation of H. G. Wells's "The War of the Worlds" can be attributed primarily to the program's simulation of a live news broadcast, positioning genuine reality effects—broadcasters reporting "live from the field" and authentic sounding studio updates ("this just in")—within a carefully constructed fictional world. *F for Fake* relies on a similar combination of reality, simulation, and pure fiction, fusing interview footage and real documents—such as newspaper headlines popularizing the Irving scandal from the *New York Daily News*—to authenticate a film that perverts the documentary mode to which it initially claims to subscribe. The decidedly more Nietzchean French title of the film, *Vérités et mensonges*, more effectively evokes what is at stake, for

*F for Fake* not only explores the creation and reception of a series of artful deceptions, but also interrogates the complex rift between reality and illusion.[53] As the director comments near the end of his film, "The truth, and please forgive us for it, is that we've been forging an art story. As a charlatan, of course, my job was to try to make it real. Not that reality has anything to do with it. Reality? It's the toothbrush waiting at home for you in its glass, a bus ticket, a paycheck, and the grave. . . . What we professional liars hope to serve is truth. I'm afraid the pompous word for that is art. Picasso, himself, said it. 'Art,' he said, 'is a lie. A lie that makes us realize the truth.'" The artist, above all, is a purveyor of the truth. For Welles, art is closer to the truth than reality, which is superficial in its everydayness, since it gives form to the world. His film embraces the false to suggest that fiction can often more easily render the truth than those forms that claim to relate reality objectively. The paradox is that art is fundamentally a "lie." The purveyor of truth about the world and the way we live is in essence a "professional liar." In its support of the idea that the truth is often "the most profound fiction," *F for Fake* "blurs the differences" between the cinema of fiction and the cinema of reality.[54]

Similarly, Perec explores this tension between fiction and documentation in *Un cabinet d'amateur*. Although the narrative deploys techniques that foster the impression of verisimilitude—situating the action in recognizable places (Pittsburgh, Boston), referencing real painters (Holbein, Bosch, Greuze, Tiepolo), reprinting brief descriptions of images as they might appear in an auction catalogue, and invoking authentic works of art (Joseph Vernet's *La tempête*, for example)—as Leonard Koos has pointed out, a substantial number of overtly fictional "cracks" appear on the surface of the text that allow the imaginary to peek through.[55] We read, for example, of nonexistent germanophone newspapers with such names as the "Chicago Tagblatt" and the "New York Zeitung," and are invited to consider descriptions of invented paintings such as *Les ensorcelés du lac Ontario*, which is attributed to Kürz himself. Furthermore, the narrative is populated by characters whose names attest to Perec's nimble onomastic gymnastics: from "the steel magnate Kellogg O'Brien" and "the millionaire Barry O. Fugger" (132) to the Cleveland-based German painter "Adolphus Kleidröst" (137).[56] These moments of pure fictionality cramp the text's illusion of reality. Like those "fissures" in a trompe l'oeil that reveal that the object of the beholder's gaze is not "real" at all, they point to the ephemeral nature of the illusion. In the end we are only momentarily fooled. As Perec notes, the "will" of the trompe l'oeil is to "trick or enchant the beholder *for an instant*."[57] The effects of the trompe l'oeil are short-lived. Discovery of the painter's trap is in fact necessary for the proper functioning of the illusion, since viewers need to be visually shocked and intellectually stimulated: "the goal of the artist is not to encourage the viewer to say 'This is so beautiful!' but 'What! This isn't real?'"[58] Like the beholder of a trompe l'oeil image who is quickly made aware of the optical trick, alert readers of Perec's text are made complicit with the ruse from the beginning.

Koos therefore locates a series of "cracks" in places where the fictional nature of the story becomes transparent. But the narrative intervention at the novel's conclusion, designed to expose emphatically the text's true motives, paradoxically allows for the potential return of the "real." The narrator's admission of the novel's status as pure prevarication only verifies what Koos's "cracks" have already exposed: that *Un cabinet d'amateur* is a work of fiction. Yet his statement does not altogether evacuate the possibility that part of the narrative is, in fact, true. As the narrator notes, after all of the paintings in his collection were sold Raffke sent a letter to each buyer explaining that "*most* of the works they had bought were fakes, and that he had painted them" (187, emphasis mine). Shortly thereafter, the narrator informs the reader that the same trick has been played on the level of the text's reception and that "*most* of the paintings from the Raffke Collection were indeed fakes, as fake as *most* of the details in this fictional tale" (188, emphasis mine). In the end, not everything in the novel is false. "Most" of it is. Much like those photographs by Cuchi White that are reprinted in *L'œil ébloui*, images that occasionally reveal a physical crack on the surface of a trompe l'oeil mural where the paint that has been worn down by the passage of time exposes the "real" surface (brick, wood, stucco, and so forth) that lies underneath, the inconclusive ending of *Un cabinet d'amateur* creates a space in which "reality reasserts its rights."[59] The "history of a painting" that purportedly looks back to the earlier part of the century and objectively traces the events motivating the "Raffke affair" turns out to be "mostly" just a story, a work of pure fiction that straddles the ambiguous threshold between reality and illusion.

### *It's Pretty, But Is It Art?*

The concomitant cultural prominence of the fake that I have been discussing here—witnessed in art practices like photorealist painting, in the theoretical writings of thinkers such as Deleuze and Foucault, and materialized in figures like de Hory and Irving—signals the potential for a more historically determined reading of Perec's text. *Un cabinet d'amateur* is symptomatic of the contemporary resurgence, critical interrogation, and ultimate privileging of the false in art and theory around the time of the text's publication. More specifically, in engaging the hierarchy between appearances and essences in a text in which things are not necessarily what they seem—and, more importantly, in a text both of and about pictures that are not necessarily what they claim to be—*Un cabinet d'amateur* contributes to a particular debate that began in the late 1960s in which critics and philosophers from a variety of disciplines sought to understand precisely what it is that allows for the distinction between an object and its representation. This is especially important with a counterfeit work of art, when that representation is indistinguishable from the object upon which it is modeled. Why, as the novel asks, are Raffke's fakes—some of which sell for over $100,000 at auction—deemed worthless kitsch if they are virtually indistinguishable from the "real" paintings upon which they are modeled? What, after all, is the difference between a work of art and its replica? If the critics and connoisseurs are unable to distinguish an original from its copy, why should these doubles be considered less valuable? In his film, Orson Welles gets straight to the crux of the issue at hand when he refers to all representations, authentic and fake alike, and wonders, "It's pretty, but is it Art?"[60]

When it was first exhibited in New York in 1964, critic Arthur Danto asked a similar question of Andy Warhol's *Brillo Box* (image 4), ultimately concluding that, yes, Warhol's replica was decidedly more than a simple copy of an industrially produced container. Rather than concentrate on the conflation of art and commerce that the work so clearly suggests—all of Warhol's work, as critic Benjamin Buchloch maintains, accepts the inevitable impact of capitalism and market forces on artistic production, thereby reinforcing "the erosion of the high art-mass culture dialectic"[61]—Danto, an analytic philosopher by trade, concentrates on what the *Brillo Box* reveals about the philosophical implications of art. For

Image 4. Andy Warhol, *Brillo Box*, 1964. Plywood boxes with serigraph and acrylic. Location: The Museum of Modern Art, New York NY. Digital image © The Museum of Modern Art/Licensed by SCALA/Art Resource, New York. © 2010 The Andy Warhol Foundation for the Visual Arts, Inc./Artists Rights Society (ARS), New York.

Danto, the *Brillo Box* contributes significantly to our understanding of art's ontology because it seems to embody fully in its very nature the definition of art itself, to exemplify the work of art become idea, and to enact "the consciousness of art *being* art in a reflexive way that bears comparison with philosophy."[62] Warhol's box reifies what he sees as one of the questions most crucial to philosophical inquiry, since it asks how "two outwardly indiscernible things can belong to different, indeed to momentously different, philosophical categories." From Descartes to Kant, and Hegel to Heidegger, thinking philosophically includes searching for deep differences between things that appear identical.[63]

As fundamental as it is to his aesthetic theory, this idea (variants of which reappear throughout many of his books) does nevertheless raise what some feel is a curious inconsistency or blind spot in Danto's thinking. Although when viewed from afar, or in a photographic reproduction for that matter, Warhol's *Brillo Box* may seem indistinguishable from a true Brillo box, a number of differences are, in fact, visible to the naked eye. Unlike the cardboard box upon which it is modeled, Warhol's version is an oversized, plywood construction onto which the Brillo logo has been manually applied in a silkscreen process. The *Brillo Box* is also relatively smooth on all sides, lacking the seams and packing flaps found on the kind of industrially produced packages in which Brillo pads are usually shipped. Although this is not necessarily an "outwardly" visible difference, one can also assume that Warhol's *Brillo Box* is empty. Danto's use of the *Brillo Box* as an illustration of his philosophy represses the possibility that viewers might be able to see these differences. Some would therefore argue that his philosophy is predicated on the viewer's (and ostensibly on Danto's own) perceptual naïveté.

For most art historians, this frankly myopic kind of observation and inattentiveness to the details that contribute to a work's meaning is inexcusable. It is not surprising that certain critics object to Danto's reading of Warhol and accuse him of proffering an interpretation that, quite simply, misses the point.[64] Two objections are nevertheless possible in defense of Danto's claims. For one, it seems that critics of his particular reading of Warhol rely on the idea—or the misconception, depending on one's point of view—that vision is an objective act. The differences between a real Brillo box and a Warhol simulacrum may be visible, but only to those who choose to look for them. Danto, like the more easily fooled readers of Perec's novel, was himself duped by the illusion, at least for a while. It is precisely at this moment, when those distinctions between the art object and the "real thing" it represents are indiscernible, that what Danto would refer to as the deeper philosophical implications of Warhol's work begin to crystallize. Although he elides the inevitable differences between the industrial boxes and Warhol's copy, he does acknowledge that differences exist. He admits, albeit sheepishly, that certain viewers might see through the trompe l'oeil illusion and notice that, although it may look like it, Warhol's *Brillo Box* is not a "real" Brillo box after all. But "the differences surely cannot constitute the difference between art and reality."[65]

Like Deleuze, who also regarded the advent of pop simulation as the cultural embodiment of this "reversal of Platonism,"[66] Danto's particular approach to the *Brillo Box* allows for the systematic subversion of Plato's insistence on the difference between essences and appearances. Philosophers had always thought that a work of art and the reality that it represents could be told apart "on purely visual terms." Not so, he claims, with the *Brillo Box*: "So Warhol, and the pop artists in general, rendered almost worthless everything written by philosophers of art, or at best rendered it of local significance. For me, through pop, art showed what the proper philosophical question about itself really was. It was this: What makes the difference between an artwork and something which is not an artwork if in fact they look exactly alike?"[67]

The theory of the trompe l'oeil that Perec first engages in his writing resonates with much of Danto's thinking. In his preface to Cuchi White's photographs, for example, Perec ponders the institutional theory of art, wondering why certain things are deemed more appropriate to be represented in painting than others: "How is a picture representing a reversed painting a painting, a work of art? How is it less worthy to be represented by the means of painting than an apple, a bottle, a little patch of yellow wall, Charles I hunting?"[68] He goes on to ask, more generally, why such objects, in and of themselves, are not considered works of art, whereas others have been designated as such: "How is Marcel Duchamp's sugar cube a work of art? Or the piece of a sweater worn by Christian Boltanski in 1949?"[69] Finally, as a last example of what he refers to as these "simulacra" that challenge art's traditional ontology, the author refers to a forged postage stamp that is made to look like the real thing. Here Perec invokes the very same question that Danto finds so crucial to the philosophy of art, since the work in question arranges the two seemingly identical stamps and challenges viewers to decide "which is which?"

Danto's particular theory of art relies on an inherently posthistorical reading of contemporary culture, since he claims that art's becoming conscious of the history of the institution (and, more particularly, of the history of its critical discourses) that constitutes it as art is only really possible after the "end of art." Invoking an idea originating in Hegel, Danto remarks, "with the disclosure or discovery of its true philosophical nature, art attains the end of its history."[70] When a work of art is capable of questioning its identity as a work of art, yet proves unable to answer that question itself, it turns to philosophy for help. It is at this moment that art effectively comes to an end. This seemingly devastating point is not as nihilistic as it might sound. Danto is by no means asserting that we have entered into a period when art is no longer possible. Rather, his theory proposes that, beginning in the 1960s, the criteria to which an object must conform in order to be considered a work of art were rendered invalid—which is to say that it is not exactly "art" that has actually come to an "end," but the "narratives"—and more importantly the modernist narrative—that chart its historical progress.[71] The reevaluation of the definitional schemata in art signals a shift away from what he considers the two main "episodes" of the history of Western art as espoused in the writing of Giorgio Vasari and Clement Greenberg. Art is dissolved as a historically determined concept as soon as it "recognized that there was no special way a work of art had to be," an assertion that laughs in the face of Greenberg's strict standards for quality.[72] According to Danto's paradigm, the period marked by the reaction against the dominant mode of abstract expressionism in the mid-1960s—a period that witnessed the rise of pop art in the United States and *nouveau réalisme* in France—signaled the beginning, as it were, of the end. The effects, if the cultural production of the 1960s are any indication, were remarkably liberating, paving the way for a kind of artistic production that looked nothing like what was previously expected. From conceptual practices and performance to land art and appropriationism, "everything was permitted, since nothing any longer was historically mandated."[73]

*Un cabinet d'amateur* engages the "end of art" as a particular object of inquiry. Consider Nowak's reading of the tableau at the center of the narrative: "What had aroused the almost morbid fascination which had surrounded the work was not so much the artist's technical skill, but this spatial, and at the same time temporal, perspective. For, Lester Nowak concluded, there could be no mistake about it. This work was an image of the death of art, a mirror-reflection on this world which is condemned to an infinite reproduction of its own models" (143). As with the *Brillo Box*, Kürz's painting incites viewers to reconsider the world as one in which images upon images are doomed to repeat themselves in an endless series of replicas.[74]

Considered together, then, *L'œil ébloui* and *Un cabinet d'amateur* do not merely elaborate and enact Perec's theory of the trompe l'oeil. Like the other literary narratives I study here, they also contribute a particularly literary perspective to debates crucial to contemporary cultural production. Though Welles was decidedly less vocal when it came to the nonfilmic, and Perec adamantly downplayed his knowledge of painting, both *F for Fake* and *Un cabinet d'amateur* testify nevertheless to their creators' interest in questions concerning art's ontology. In rescuing the fake from its exile on the margins of culture, in recuperating the simulacrum and considering its value as a viable cultural artifact, *Un cabinet d'amateur* offers a decidedly literary take on the discussion concerning the nature and future of art "after the end of art." Even if Perec was not a confirmed critic of art—as he states, "I would clarify right away that I am absolutely not an art critic, which is to say that I never wrote about a painter from the perspective of his painting"—his work, like Welles's, nevertheless stages questions crucial to its philosophy.[75]

# 3

# *Tableau vivant*

Now I'm working with another model, a postman in a
blue uniform with gold trimmings, a big, bearded
face, very Socratic. A more interesting man than many people.

VINCENT VAN GOGH, from a letter to his brother, Theo

When I hear the word culture, I take out my checkbook.

Character in JEAN-LUC GODARD's film *Le mépris*

Playing with the literary tradition of the *Künstlerroman*—traditionally a work of fiction that probes the life of the artist, fictional or otherwise, in an attempt to unlock the mysteries of aesthetic creation—Pierre Michon's *Vie de Joseph Roulin* (1988) chooses to focus its attentions not on the creator of the work of art, but on its model.[1] The subject in question, Joseph-Étienne Roulin, is the simple Provençal postal worker whose "big, bearded face" Vincent van Gogh famously memorialized in a series of drawings and oil paintings that are housed today in some of the world's most prestigious museums and private collections.[2] Michon's acclaimed novella, published in France exactly a century after the portraits were produced, seamlessly blends fact and fiction to build on van Gogh's own painterly renderings and bring a relatively exciting period from the postman's mostly banal life to light.[3]

Homing in on the year 1888—when the struggling artist, having relocated to the Mediterranean city of Arles in search of sun, came to befriend and then paint the heavy-drinking civil servant—the narrative imagines the relationship between these two apparently dissimilar men and projects onto the page what Roulin might have been thinking about van Gogh, and about his art, all along. Although occasional references to the painter's own eccentric behavior provide an oblique biography of a figure whose peripatetic life and tortured last days have been documented time and time again—the notorious cutting of the ear figures several times, but only in passing (*JR* 21, 28, 42)—here the more speculative portrait of the unassuming postal clerk truly takes center stage.

With a literary-historical nod to the hagiographic narratives of the Middle Ages, Michon's fictionalized biography casts its scruffy working-class protagonist as van Gogh might have truly seen him: as a saintly prince, depicted in the series of portraits like a "pope" (*JR* 5) or a king on a throne, his well-worn postal cap "a crown amongst all others" (*JR* 14) (image 5).[4] To be sure, Roulin was not only an acquaintance of the artist, but became a dear and trusted friend over time. The postman and his family cared for van Gogh, watched over his affairs, and kept his worried brother abreast of his condition during a difficult period in early 1889 when the painter was interned at a mental hospital in Saint-Rémy.

When it is compared to the decidedly more venerable legacy of the unconventional Dutch genius—a man whose life and work would be mythologized and canonized posthumously—the significance of Roulin's place in history has been virtually ignored.[5] All that we know of him are "a few trifles" (*JR* 5), thanks primarily to several brief references that van Gogh makes to the postman in his correspondence. In a move not unlike the one Pierre Michon made in his earlier pseudo-

Image 5. Vincent van Gogh, *Postman Joseph Roulin*, 1888. Oil on canvas, 81.3 x 65.4 cm (32 x 25¾ in.). Museum of Fine Arts, Boston. Gift of Robert Treat Paine II, 35.1982. Photograph © 2012, Museum of Fine Arts, Boston.

biographical compilation of deceptively ordinary *Vies minuscules* (*Minuscule Lives*) from 1984, or in the trilogy of artists' lives seen and told through the lens of witnesses living in their shadows (*Maîtres et serviteurs*, 1990), *Vie de Joseph Roulin* aims to rescue the narrative of this common man, this common man become inimitable icon in painting, from the margins. Roulin, a forgotten soul, a "being without memory,"[6] remains comparatively invisible. No matter how familiar the portraits of him (and of his family) may be today, the story they collectively tell has yet to be given its due.[7] Driven by an archaeological, almost demiurgic desire to exhume and envision the forgotten past, Michon's lushly told *tableau vivant*, his not quite still "Life" of Roulin, aims to do just that. As the author noted in one of an ever-growing corpus of interviews published over the last twenty years, "it is profoundly unfair that a man can live and die without ever being noticed. . . . This, among other things, is what I addressed in the *Lives*" (*RV* 23).[8]

Underpinning the text's resuscitation and consecration of Joseph Roulin's all but bygone story, however, lies another, equally estimable imperative, evident in the other narratives I examine in this study, to engage some of our most basic assumptions about the nature of visual art, about how works are consecrated as such, and about how we experience them optically, intellectually, and emotionally. More specifically, as it hints at Vincent van Gogh's troubled path to profitability, *Vie de Joseph Roulin* also relates the model's own efforts to grasp the foundations of art's ontology. Although he has been confronted on a very personal level with a figure who was to become one of the world's most recognizable artists, Roulin remains blind to the powers of the painter's genius and, crucially, to the worth of his work. By staging Roulin's struggle to negotiate the place the artist and his art occupy between the godly and the earthly, between high culture and base commerce, between the ritualistic and the everyday, Michon's exuberantly crafted imagetext not only makes modernity's own obsession with the perennial "enigma of the beaux arts" (*JR* 27) more visible, it critiques and seeks to demystify what we often take for granted about the institution itself.

## A Portrait in Words

Like *Triptyque* and *Un cabinet d'amateur*, *Vie de Joseph Roulin* is yet another testament to contemporary French fiction's penchant for telling tales of and about pictures. In the narrative Pierre Michon, like Claude Simon and Georges Perec before him, seeks to write the image, to emulate it and bring it to sight in words. The particular brand of fiction for which he has become famous, an ever-expanding corpus of texts characterized by their dazzling breviloquence—what Michon calls "le bref fulgurant," (*RV* 206)—are especially well suited to this task. Michon's intensely dense and compact bursts of prose testify to a desire to reveal and animate the aura of his subjects, to make them pulsate or "tremble in the short span of 60 or 120 pages" (*RV* 49), not unlike the energetic brushstrokes that distinguish van Gogh's eminent oil paintings, particularly the series of portraits from the 1880s and 1890s that aim to evoke the essence of the sitter not through mere resemblance but through striking bursts of vibrant color. In each concise tale Michon practices another form of restraint, one that eschews flourishing descriptions, reality effects, or chatty dialogue in favor of a fluid and self-contained montage of poetic images and potent ideas designed to resonate with readers long after the reading is done. For Michon this rigorous narrative economy is painterly in its aspirations. The form of short fiction that he so fastidiously practices has little to do from a compositional or structural perspective with the novel or with other deliberately protracted forms of storytelling that traditionally bask in their "duration." (Novels, quite simply, are too long. As Michon has said, they take too long to read, and allow too much hermeneutic leeway, to provide the reader with any lasting sense of totality [*RV* 25]). Rather, the author conceives of his compendious fictionalized biographies—often written in short spans of time—in terms that echo painting's own compositional unity. For painting, which Michon can't help but admire ("how can we not envy it?"), is a form that at once contains all its disparate elements, simultaneously displaying both "incipit and denouement" (*RV* 208).

More than any other work in his corpus, *Vie de Joseph Roulin* seeks to overcome the inherent inequity between painting and prose. It is through writing, in Michon's particularly resplendent style, that the text yearns to live up to painting's art of embodiment. Painting, as Michon has said, "is the grand art of incarnation. . . . Another world appears within, more real than the world" (*RV* 32). A fictional imagetext, a "textual picture" in every sense of the term,[9] *Vie de Joseph Roulin* pursues a similar effect in words by mobilizing language to "propel, in a noticeable way, the flesh of the world, its grain, its texture, its light."[10] The relative flatness of van Gogh's picture plane, especially in the Roulin family portraits, is given new depth of meaning in an exacting, at times unfamiliar, yet ultimately transcendent prose whose richness and complexity seek to make the images come alive, to materialize in a whirlwind of words become images. If in van Gogh's series of brilliant pictures Roulin consistently "appears exhausted . . . empty as a rhythm" (*JR* 8), the text recognizes how latent the possibility for transformation, through storytelling, really is: "He *could* be as lively as his shape" (*JR* 8, emphasis mine). The key, as the narrator remarks in one of the text's most important self-reflexive passages, lies in the incantatory nature of his prose:

> This hollow scansion, an inner rhythm of language, inflexible and deaf, that strangles what one is struggling to say, feeds it and fatigues it—I want it to bear his name; so that words and the rhythms grow old in Marseilles

> and remember Arles; so that words end up sprouting beards; they'll appear in Prussian blue; they'll be alcoholic and republican; they won't make sense of one drop of the paintings; but with some luck, or by kidnapping, perhaps words will once again become a painting; they'll be muzhik or boyar as the spirit moves me—and completely arbitrary, as usual—but will come visibly to light, manifest, and die. (*JR* 8)

Throughout *Vie de Joseph Roulin* references to color, light, and shading illuminate, and the rhythm of the narrative voice resounds to transform the inevitable stasis of the image into movement in words. The text on the page struggles to embody the man himself, to render him not merely visible but evidently so, "manifest." The narrator, conscious of his powers of "evocation," strives to summon the model to emerge before the reader-become-beholder as if he were conjuring an almost otherworldly "apparition": "Like a painter, it is an image, a human image, that I want to make appear" (*RV* 65). Not unlike van Gogh's own attempts to represent his painted subjects as if they were cloaked in a mystical aura—"I would like to make portraits which would look like apparitions to people a century later"[11]—Michon's similarly spectral aesthetic yearns to make life loom in the "mirror" of his prose (*RV* 32). The multilayered and decidedly lyrical tone that the author mobilizes in *Vie de Joseph Roulin*, a voice that melds lush, opulent language—what the author calls "Belle Langue"—with occasional recourse to a more rudimentary and vernacular idiom, renders the subjects in question, and their world, extraordinary, marvelous.[12] Throughout Michon aims to profit from the transformative power of language, as van Gogh did with paint, to coax the euphoric from the straightforward. "All of this enters into my strategy of apparition, from the written which drives itself toward the visible" (*RV* 61).

As with writers studied elsewhere in this book, Michon's interest in the relationship between word and image is evident in a number of works in his corpus, many of which probe the processes and stimuli responsible for artistic creation. Visual culture crops up in a number of ways. A mixture of subtle and more direct references to artists and artworks abound in the short narratives—themselves like portraits come alive in language—that comprise his groundbreaking first book, *Vies minuscules*.[13] Portions of *Corps du roi* (2002) are indebted to photographs of Samuel Beckett and William Faulkner, and his celebration of Arthur Rimbaud (in *Rimbaud le fils*, 1991) is engendered, in part at least, by Étienne Carjat's famous 1871 photograph of the young poet.[14] The idiosyncratic rise to prominence of such luminaries as Goya and Watteau is seen through the lens of lesser-known witnesses to their greatness in *Maîtres et serviteurs* (1990), while the third tale in that trilogy ("Trust this Sign") focuses on Lorentino, a minor disciple of Piero Della Francesca. *Le roi du bois*, published in 1996, offers another indirect look at a genius at work, this time baroque painter Claude Lorrain, in a tale narrated by his disaffected apprentice Gian Domenico Desiderii. Most recently, like *Vie de Joseph Roulin*, *Les onze* (2009) presents readers with an archaeological restoration of a painting brought to life—and back into historical consciousness—in prose. Set in Revolutionary France, *Les onze* chronicles the creation and legacy of François-Élie Corentin's spectacular image of the Grand Committee of Public Safety.[15] Commissioned by three of its eleven principal members in a gesture of ultimate ideological authority (but designed to be ambiguous enough to condemn the man depicted at its center, Robespierre, should public support for their efforts wane), the image recalls the political machinations and iconological ambitions of those who orchestrated the Terror. In its portrayal of the provincial painter who would become famous for this monumental work, *Les onze* is a book not merely about how masterpieces are born, but about how the history of art objects inflects the way we read and ultimately come to understand them.

While it is rooted in events essential to the founding of the modern French Republic, a period of national trauma that continues to haunt the collective imagination to this day, the story of the painting's genesis in *Les onze* is entirely fabricated. The painting, like the painter who ostensibly produced it, is a mere figment of the author's imagination. Though not as confounding as *Un cabinet d'amateur* before it, *Les onze* is a beguiling literary trompe l'oeil, a work of historical fiction based, in part, on fraudulent history. For Michon as for Perec, literature, and literary language more generally, is necessarily a form of lying. The best writers prevaricate like dentists pulling teeth ("This won't hurt a bit") who rely on the complicity of their patients (the readers) whose comfort and well-being depend on a somewhat reluctant suspension of disbelief. As in Perec's work, though, Michon's manipulation of the kind of literary trickery he wields so deftly in *Les onze* is precisely what leads to a certain element of truth for those readers capable of giving in to the ruse and consenting to its "beautiful fabrication": "my stories about painters are lies, but you have to believe them" (*RV* 74).

As is true in Plutarch's parallel *Lives* of illustrious Romans and Greeks (ca. 100 AD) and Giorgio Vasari's seminal *Lives of the Artists* (1550)—two predecessors who helped shape the genre that Michon adapts in his series of *Vies*, yet who were just as inclined to occasional moments of narrative fantasy—the vacillation between the real and imagined, between historically reliable facts and pure fiction, is equally at play in all of Michon's work (save, perhaps, the most outwardly "fictional" text of all, *La grande Beune* [1996]). This is especially true in his fictionalized biography of Roulin. Michon is not only one of contemporary France's most erudite writers; he researches his texts extensively.[16] *Vie de Joseph Roulin* is no exception to the rule. The narrative occasionally hints at the legwork involved in its own production. References to research consulted (*JR* 1) and correspondence read (*JR* 14–15) authenticate the story the narrator tells. These sources are integral to his project, even though the "all knowing books" (*JR* 5) dedicated to van Gogh contain only minimal information about Roulin's own life. (As the narrator muses, the postman would be surprised to see his name, let alone his portrait, mentioned in such scholarly tomes.) That said, *Vie de Joseph Roulin* is not truly biographical "in the sense of providing a chronological and documented account of [its subjects'] existence."[17] Given its author's fidelity to the guiding principles of fiction, the life it tells is in no way definitive, but merely "probable."[18] Quotidian events that must have occurred, but which are often neglected by official histories, are consistently tempered by the narrator's active imagination. Early on, to cite one of the most prominent examples, the narrator presents a scene that must have occurred, though the details cannot be accurately ascertained: namely, the first meeting between Roulin and van Gogh. The text suggests a certain degree of equivocation with regard to the facts. Perhaps, as the narrator notes, the two men bumped into one another in the Café de la Gare, which both van Gogh and Roulin were known to frequent. Or maybe they were introduced in the Place de l'Eglise by a common acquaintance, like the Zouave infantryman who was one of the first models to sit for the painter in Arles.[19] Why not imagine that one day van Gogh strolled over to the train station post depot to ship a package of canvases to his brother Theo in Paris by way of "*la petite vitesse*" (*JR* 18)? It certainly is conceivable that he met Roulin there, since the postman worked the counter from time to time. Perhaps it was on this occasion that the two took a liking to each other and spent the afternoon chatting over a drink at the café outside. Feasible, to be sure, likely even, but not necessarily true. While rare certainties are acknowledged—"We know, for example, that at the end of 1888, the Post Office transferred him from Arles to Marseilles" (*JR* 6)—hesitation about lesser-known facts abounds: "whether [it was] a promotion due to his zeal or a demotion due to his hangover, we don't know" (*JR* 6).[20] Throughout *Vie de Joseph Roulin* the narrator's consistent interventions evoke just how much he projects his own vision of the past. Note the frequent use of speculative clauses rife with ambiguity: "I assume he received several letters from Saint Rémy" (*JR* 8); "Perhaps an uncle pulled some strings and he joined the Post Office, and there he wasn't even a postman, as legend tells us and I amuse myself to imagine, not a mail carrier, but a desk clerk" (*JR* 13). The narrator's creative agency is explicitly deployed elsewhere as well: "Therefore, idyllically, I imagine him handling van Gogh's letters" (*JR* 9); "I would like to believe that once again he is surprised" before the sight of a painting (*JR* 26); "I hope with all my strength that the name of Mother Ginoux" does not figure on a petition to intern the artist (*JR* 29); "I want to see and hear" the first conversation between Roulin and a visitor to his home (*JR* 35). Not once does the narrator apologize for his obvious subjectivity. Rather, the text makes no attempt to hide who holds the strings: "they'll be muzhik or boyar *as the spirit moves me*" (*JR* 8, emphasis mine). If Michon therefore speaks of the text in terms of a corporal "apparition" and "incarnation," of writing that seeks to drive its subject to the edge of sight, *Vie de Joseph Roulin* consistently recalls how much it relies on the narrator's ingenuity. The text's implied readers are also called upon to wonder and dream up possible scenarios for the sake of fiction. It would not be inconceivable to think, for example, that Roulin died in the same hospital bed as Rimbaud—not because Rimbaud did, in fact, die in Marseilles, but because, in the end, "we"—narrator, author, and reader—"are romantics" (*JR* 50).[21]

For Dominique Viart, Michon's writings are "figural" in this regard.[22] Because much of what is known about Roulin's daily life—and about the intricacies of his relationship with van Gogh—cannot be verified, the "Life" that Michon proposes is necessarily conjectural. Given the text's focus on Roulin's consciousness, on his thoughts and ideals, on his own agency, a reliable witness or source text becomes unnecessary. Biographical specificity is, ultimately, negligible. Supposition, on the other hand, prevails. The narrative makes no overt pretense to verifiability so that it may more effectively enact Michon's interest in the legendary and epiphanic, in the "distortions of memory and the interventions of the ethereal" (*RV* 21).

Although it does not propose to live up to traditional hagiography's role, to "edify" its audience and prompt them to venerate the saintly ways of the subject in question, Michon's literary portrait of Roulin nevertheless inspires readers to regard the paintings afresh.[23] Van Gogh's images speak to the corrective power of art. The paintings, the narrator affirms, "should be seen by everyone because, strangely enough, as opaque as they seem, they make things clearer, more easily understood" (*JR* 40). Indeed, many critics believe viewers today have lost the capacity to truly see, to contemplate and read between the lines. As art critic Michael Kimmelman has remarked, over time the modern subject has lost the "urgency" to look. Vision has become harried by a saturation of the optical field: "So tourists now wander through museums, seeking to fulfill their lifetime's art history requirement in a day, wondering whether it may now be the quantity of material they pass by rather than the quality of concentration they bring to what few things they choose to focus upon that determines whether they have 'done' the Louvre. It's self-improvement on the fly."[24] Michon's short novel, on the other hand, taps into the "enigma of the visual" and luxuriates in an imaginary gallery of places and people become pictures: "Let's look at Arles where there's the little *Pont Langlois*, so tender and blue, an even bluer sky; *vaqueros*; zouaves; . . . fields of wheat or melons and an old, infallible sun" (JR 29). As it reminds us how important it is to look—"It's greatly effervescent, looking at painting" (RV 62)—*Vie de Joseph Roulin* suggests how transformative writing about art may be, as if to say, as Oscar Wilde once did, that a picture rendered in words "becomes more wonderful to us than it really is, and reveals to us a secret of which, in truth, it knows nothing."[25] Which is to say that narrative about painting often seeks to render the invisible visible and show readers even more than there is to see with the naked eye.

### *Accounting for Taste*

Like the other books in this study *Vie de Joseph Roulin* melds a genuine esteem for the power of pictures—the author, a self-professed iconolater, has spoken of his "reverence" for images (RV 61)—with a desire to expose the modern subject's complex relationship to the visible world. Critics have commented on Michon's particular use of history, on the role that painting plays within his corpus, on style, genre, on the influence of the avant-garde, and on how Michon's practice corresponds with a certain tendency in contemporary French letters to craft tales about the forgotten ("great books about inconsequential people," as Pierre Bergounioux writes). Little has been said, however, about the curious anachronism staged in *Vie de Joseph Roulin* that allows Michon to tackle what is clearly one of his most important preoccupations: namely, the relationship between art, our experience of it, and the role played by the institutions responsible for its sanctification, dissemination, and display.[26] As Michon's writing of the image stimulates a newfound appreciation of the Roulin portraits (and of painting more generally), it also explores how much one's ability to apprehend and enjoy a work of art is conditioned, and often obfuscated, by a series of extra-aesthetic concerns.

In *Distinction*, his seminal critique of theories of taste that understand the appreciation of beauty as a disinterested and universal phenomenon, Pierre Bourdieu suggests how certain social conditions account for differences in artistic appreciation among different viewers. In particular, Bourdieu sees education and upbringing, often difficult to disassociate from professional and economic status, as key factors in one's capacity to admire and fully grasp a work of art. "A work of art," he writes, "has meaning and interest only for someone who possesses the cultural competence, that is, the code, into which it is encoded."[27] As Michon's narrative makes consistently clear, Roulin, neither well educated nor particularly wealthy, lacks the proficiency required to find meaning in van Gogh's pictures and "read between the lines" (*JR* 9). His capacity to see (*voir*) is impeded by his lack of knowledge (*savoir*). A veritable blank slate when it comes to a culture that he never acquired, Roulin, as the narrator imperiously claims, "doesn't know anything about Art" (*JR* 7). He is surprised even to learn that painted canvases could be separated from their frames, rolled up and put into cylindrical containers for storage or shipment (*JR* 26); his insights into the nature of art are "of little help" (*JR* 7). Like most of the people whom van Gogh painted and befriended throughout his life, the postman remains utterly incapable of "making sense" (*JR* 8) of the work.[28] "Lost in a chaos of sounds and rhythms, colors, and lines, without rhyme or reason,"[29] like those dispossessed beholders who, for Bourdieu, lack the requisite codes, for Roulin the images will forever remain a "fabric of unreadable runes" (*JR* 27).

Throughout the narrative Roulin is persistently dumbfounded by van Gogh's work, and by the very idea of good taste. "How," the narrator asks, "could he teach us anything?" (*JR* 7). The postman has neither the foresight to recognize the legend in the making nor the words to effectively express how he feels. In order to compensate for this deficiency, the narrator takes the liberty of speaking in his place. Clearly a more adept linguist, and equipped with a more finely honed interpretive spirit than his modest subject, the narrator speaks from the privileged position of the present, well aware of how famous van Gogh would become in the century after his death. Conscious of his status as an enlightened scribe, from the first sentence to the last the narrator imagines what Roulin might have said about the artist and his work had he endeavored to speak at all.

This curious act of ventriloquism—Michon's own take on a kind of free indirect style mobilized so effectively by his forebear Flaubert—is well suited to Roulin because, as the narrator notes, it is often the most innocent and naïve of beholders who are most sensitive to majestic transformations: "no one is more sensitive to the book made man, they say, than those who don't read books" (*JR* 28). Given his overt lack of cultural capital, the postman is also the best channel through which to launch an ethical critique of the institution of art. As

Bourdieu claims, popular aesthetics—the taste of "ordinary" people—is always grounded in morality: "whether rejecting or praising, [the working class's] appreciation always has an ethical basis."[30] Popular taste ascertains whether a work of art is legitimate or not on the basis of the work's relationship with everyday things and experiences, and not on its relationship with or reference to other works of art: "The result is a systematic 'reduction' of the things of art to the things of life, a bracketing of form in favor of 'human' content, which is barbarism par excellence from the standpoint of the pure aesthetic."[31] In *Vie de Joseph Roulin* the postman embodies this ethos. In a pivotal early scene the narrator articulates for Roulin a potent idea that again raises the issue of aesthetics and thus alludes to the text's latent engagement not only with institutional critique—the theory that "explains why a work of art is a work of art"—but with ideas about what makes a work of art valuable or not.[32] As the narrator pictures it, Roulin, filled with a sense of pity for and devotion to van Gogh, must have wondered—though in not so many words—by what sort of cunning "ruse more perverse than the seizure of the notaries during the Republic of '93" can painting, a vocation like any other that one learns and transmits, produce "tangible things" destined to embellish the homes of the rich, or to hang in cathedrals and exalt the believers, or even to line the walls of the local prefecture "to call young men to a career, the army, the army, the Colonies," while, at the same time, it rejects the painter himself, who is condemned, as van Gogh was, to rot mad, hungry, and penniless at his death (*JR* 26–27). How, in other words, can the artist be so neglected and so alienated from the work that he so painstakingly produces, especially when this work is destined to become so valuable? In one of a series of ongoing reflections that attest to what the narrator believes to be Roulin's spirited yet innocent quest for meaning in the image, the text not only strives to explore the myth of artistic creation, but also to engage the equally complex mechanisms of art's true function. For "working-class people expect every image to perform a function."[33] Roulin's paucity of symbolic capital is responsible for what amounts to a form of aesthetic aphasia—"agape" as he is before the work of art (*JR* 7). His consistent confusion before the "enigma of the beaux arts" (*JR* 27) also represents a conclusive marker of his class. Though Michon's populist aesthetic seeks to relativize this position—as if to say that Roulin's blindness might ultimately lead to a more innocent, and thus instructive, form of insight—the text also stages what for sociologists like Bourdieu is one of art's principal operations: namely, to distinguish people from different social categories on the basis of whether or not they are capable of aesthetic appreciation. Which is to say that *Vie de Joseph Roulin* enacts how one's taste for pictures—and, perhaps more importantly, the lack of it—"classifies."[34]

### *The Art of the Deal*

Further on, the narrative reinforces this idea by differentiating Roulin's working-class naiveté from another character whose level of refinement, education, and expertise labels him as someone who, on the contrary, knows exceedingly well how to look. It is at this moment that the text's inquiry into how one who knows nothing of art might begin to make some sense of it takes a decidedly critical turn.

Not long after a fortuitous transfer that would allow Roulin to finish his postal career more comfortably in Marseilles, almost a decade after the death of van Gogh, a dapper young art dealer appears on the mailman's doorstep and introduces the world of business into the fold. Although Roulin first mistakes him for a painter, the visitor soon makes his motivations clear. "He's interested in Mister Vincent," Roulin tells his wife. "He saw our portraits in Paris" (*JR* 37). As the dealer confides, van Gogh has recently attracted the attention of urban tastemakers who are beginning to recognize his work as that of a great artist, as an oeuvre that will completely shake up the economics of the industry. Van Gogh's paintings—one of which hangs casually in Roulin's kitchen—are now worth their weight in gold.[35]

Though Roulin regards the visit as a veritable event, the dealer's stopover in Marseilles is merely one in a series of house calls in his grand tour of van Gogh's old haunts, a "sort of pilgrimage" (*JR* 37) to the south of France where the myth of the painter—and of modern painting—is in the making. The dealer's role in creating this myth is consequential. A clever sleuth, seeking out the new and noteworthy, the dealer goes to great lengths to acquire works that will one day "command exorbitant prices" (*JR* 40).

Although initially bewildered by the dealer's frank offer to purchase the painting van Gogh left him, the innocent retiree can't help thinking that those odd portraits of his family and their acquaintances in Arles, as opaque as they might have seemed, actually might "make things clearer and more easily understood" (*JR* 40). In a bizarre twist of fate, he surmises, those painterly trifles could have made Vincent rich in the end. For Roulin, this mysterious, almost magical post-mortem sanctification and valorization of van Gogh and his work remains an anomaly, albeit a happy one. For how, he wonders, can one possibly begin to legitimate the fusion of creation and commerce? "Who had decided that he was a great painter . . . and how had this transformation occurred?" (*JR* 40) In a moment that resonates with modernity's own struggle to articulate what makes art "art," to distinguish between an everyday ornament and a virtually priceless object, or to theorize the difference between mere things and expensive and critically viable cultural artifacts, *Vie de Joseph Roulin*'s engagement with the artworld through the mind of its naïve protagonist raises one of the very questions upon which the institution of art is built. As the narrator, speaking through Roulin, ponders, "Who can say what is beautiful and as a result, amongst men, is deemed worthless or worthwhile?" (*JR* 65). Who, after all, decides whether or not a work of art is valuable?

For Roulin, a proletarian at heart, the question is a knotty one. The very notion of art—of its evaluation, valuation, and subsequent fluctuation in value over time—does not sit well with his more communist sensibilities. Rather, the postman's staunch support of a progressive worldview—"when he heard [Roulin] sing the 'Marseillaise,' van Gogh said, he felt the whole spirit of the French Revolution reborn"[36]—calls for a more equitable kind of commerce than the one for which a free market system allows. As the narrator explains, Roulin idealizes a way of doing business without ill will, free from rampant speculation, complicated dealmaking, and shady sales. His idea of fair trade relies on transparency and privileges an ideal system where things have the same value as the money used to buy them. Commerce, he believes, should be "without the spitefulness that usually is the bread of their dealings . . . as if both words and teeth weren't meant to bite, the value of money were not the only thing people could see, as if other things were visible, were valued as highly" (*JR* 14). Like most people "lacking the specific competence" to appreciate painting, Roulin thus applies to works of art "the perceptual schemes of [his] own ethos."[37] This "republican prince," that "old, radical postman" (*JR* 48), belongs to a world in which a painting's value must logically correspond to what one sees in the image depicted within, like the cherished portraits of admirable men—socialists all—that hang on his kitchen walls.[38]

As Michon's narrative makes clear, however, for the dealer and the institutions that he represents, referentiality is hardly a factor in calculating what a work of art is worth. Nor is the detached appreciation of beauty one might experience before a painting, the "experiential aesthetics" that the narrator consistently invokes and that undergirds one of modernity's more influential theories of art.[39] Rather, *Vie de Joseph Roulin* sardonically posits that art is valuable when, quite simply, the market deems it so. Speaking on behalf of a man impassioned by politics but confounded by painting, the text answers Roulin's initial quandary in a decidedly cynical way by attributing responsibility for a work's worth to the "capitalists" ensconced upon high in their Manhattan office towers, "higher and holier than *Notre-Dame de la Garde*" (JR 44).

While readers may have the impression that that author uses this moment to lash out against the abusive practices of an increasingly deregulated global business environment in his own time—the mid-1980s—the reference to Wall Street is not entirely anachronistic. Michon's dealer, with his deft negotiating skills and focus on the bottom line, not only embodies an increasingly commercialized and international market for works of modern art at the *fin de siècle*,[40] he corresponds with the image of ruthless financiers and cultural businessmen that populate the pages of nineteenth-century fiction and criticism. During the latter half of the nineteenth century a number of writers who saw Wall Street principles as a conductor for many of the period's most able art brokers sought to denounce the conflation of art and capitalism.[41] Some critics also launched a generalized attack on the profession as a whole for its inherent lack of conscience. In a study of the art market that ultimately condemns the kind of behavior evinced by the dealer in Michon's tale—a tract that was published in 1888, the year Roulin came to know and befriend van Gogh—American journalist Sheridan Ford wrote that "Dealers everywhere understand how largely personal trust enters into their operations and yet, strange to say, in the business of buying and selling pictures the code of ethics or *morale* is less high than that which obtains in the grocery or boot and shoe trades."[42] Art traders, Ford maintained, have little time for aesthetics: "No time is wasted discussing merit, authenticity, or beauty."[43] Similarly, for Roulin, curious to know how pricing is set, the dealer has no reply other than to blame the market and find fault with "Americans who know what beauty is and by their dollars are able to prove it" (*JR* 44). Rather than indict himself and other members of his profession, the dealer consistently invokes the image of skyscrapers and the businessmen that occupy them in order to epitomize the unassailable power source driving an increasingly globalized marketplace. Not just a condemnation of the shrewd methods of the art trade, then, *Vie de Joseph Roulin* makes a surprisingly potent critique of the mercantilist system as a whole. As the narrator explains, condensing past and present, capitalism—in 1888 as well as in 1988—is an "unscrupulous" (*JR* 44) practice. The markets, including the market for works of art, have for over a century been capable of transforming something as mundane as a little yellow café in Arles—the dingy "artist's co-op" (*JR* 21)—into an image as well known as the iconic buildings that tower over New York City's famous skyline.

Despite his evident aversion to the abuses of the market system, in the end Roulin acquiesces and sells his portrait anyway. Although a fervent opponent of irresponsible and unfair trade, when he is confronted face to face with the human side of commerce—two men discussing the value of a work of art over a glass of pastis, say—it's "not that easy" to be critical (*JR* 48). Apologizing to the ghost of his radical hero Blanqui for having fallen prey to the almighty dollar, and with one last glance at the cherished but tattered red flag that hangs in his home, Roulin sells his portrait for a handsome profit and symbolically puts to rest his longstanding faith in Marx's revolutionary mole (*JR* 48).

Although van Gogh had once expressed his desire to produce portraits whose subjects, centuries later, might be seen by viewers as veritable "specters," Michon, in a statement tinged with regret, remarks that the paintings these days are about as visible as "the effigies of bank notes used to pay for them."[44] Echoing a view invoked in the epigraph, which is excerpted from Paul Claudel's fittingly entitled play *The Exchange* (1893–4), the author's assertion ultimately reminds readers that the market's arbitration of good taste, its seemingly subjective conflation of aesthetics and finance, often leads the public astray. Although *Vie de Joseph Roulin* somewhat begrudgingly acknowledges that everything ultimately has its price, as the epigraph wryly confirms, "Is everything worth exactly what it costs? Never" (*JR* 5).

### *Art = Capital*

Though Roulin gives in and sells his painting to the dealer, to "this young man who had learned to make good use of money" and "who would be better able to benefit from this painting of theirs" (*JR* 47), the narrative does not fault the postman for consenting to a force that proves beyond his control. Rather, *Vie de Joseph Roulin* disparages those parties involved in the larger machine that transforms objects into obsessions and art into capital. The narrative denigrates the businessmen who, like the "little capitalist" dealer (*JR* 48), are so crafty—"Sure [the dealer] was a bit of a crook, but they all are" (*JR* 47)—and exposes the cogs in a system that denies art its ritual status in favor of its value as an object of exchange. Indeed, the text seems to yearn for a more unadulterated, innocent means of ascribing value, one more in tune with Roulin's core Republican principles.[45] As it explores the changing status of the work of art at the dawn of the age of capitalistic consumption, *Vie de Joseph Roulin* laments the inevitable and inevitably modern transformation of art into commodity, preferring instead a situation in which art's value—a quality that is neither intrinsic nor readily visible—would somehow transcend the exigencies of commerce.

When examined in conjunction with its larger social and economic contexts, however, modern art must necessarily be considered in light of a complex network of exchange and distribution; this is true even of those artworks and movements that strive to disassociate themselves from such base concerns by stressing their own difference and independence from the affairs of the world. While modern art and money might initially seem "alien to one another," as they are for Joseph Roulin, the history of art has shown that, in fact, art and money have always been "endlessly intertwined."[46] If *Vie de Joseph Roulin* thus offers a meditation on the nature of value in art, aiming to demystify the very paradigms and institutions that decide what is beautiful and thus profitable, it also exposes the conceit that art is an object to be bought and sold like any other, as if to say that "the real material condition of modern art, masked by its pretense to universality, is that of a specialized luxury commodity. Engendered under capitalism, modern art became subject to the commodification from which nothing fully escapes."[47]

By making visible modern art's unavoidable complicity with

the market, *Vie de Joseph Roulin* engages a series of modern and contemporary works by artists that interrogate the nature of the artwork under capitalism. Despite earlier attempts, both in theory and in practice, to distinguish art's sovereignty with regard to the market—one thinks here of Clement Greenberg's militant championing of the autonomy of art, and especially of the avant-garde, in the face of kitsch—much artwork produced in the decades surrounding *Vie de Joseph Roulin*'s publication confronts rather directly the conflicted status of art as a commodity. While much of this work concerns itself inherently with what makes art "art," with aesthetics, beauty, and form; in a word, with the properties of art, it also compellingly considers the notion of "art as property,"[48] which is to say that these works, like *Vie de Joseph Roulin*, deliberate art's relationship to economics.

From Robert Smithson's 1500-foot-long *Spiral Jetty* (1970), permanently installed in an isolated corner of Utah's Great Salt Lake (though frequently under water today), and Bruce Nauman's numerous process pieces that he performed alone in the confines of his studio (*Dance or Exercise on the Perimeter of a Square (Square Dance)*, 1967–68), to Joseph Beuys's politically inspired, ritualistic "Actions" and Ana Mendieta's haunting bodily traces left in the earth (in the *Silueta* series, 1973–78), many of the most influential site-specific, land art, conceptual, and performance practices from the 1960s and 1970s work outside the traditional systems of display, ownership, and exchange. Though concrete records and traces (in the form of photographs, videos, props, artist's notes) of many of these often dematerialized and ephemeral works were inevitably absorbed by the market and museums—a commonplace situation for much cutting-edge work that constitutes what some might consider a "'betrayal' of its earlier aspirations"[49]—the artists, by initially eschewing traditional pathways of exhibition for these works, espouse an intrinsic anticommercialist sensibility. During the same period, other artists chose to work deliberately within the confines of museum and gallery spaces, but they did so in order to challenge in an explicitly subversive way the normative, ideological codes according to which these institutions operate. Well-known proponents of this sort of institutional critique include artists like American Michael Asher, Frenchman Daniel Buren, and German Hans Haacke. While Asher's interventions usually alter the museum's physical structures (removing partitions and adding walls; dividing gallery spaces; displacing artworks from one part of the museum to another), Buren's work frequently involves the installation of his trademark stripe fabrics, inside and outside the museum, in lieu of actual works of art. Many of Hans Haacke's set pieces from the 1970s and 1980s prove even more explicitly seditious. Haacke has made a career of exposing the business of art to those gallery and museum visitors who are not usually accustomed to thinking about art in conjunction with notions like high finance and corporate relations. In 1971 an installation that meticulously documented the Upper Manhattan real estate holdings of one of the city's most powerful slumlords was cancelled by the Guggenheim Museum's director on the grounds that it did not conform to the museum's mission of exhibiting self-contained "creative" works. As Arthur Danto points out, the genius of Haacke's gesture was that it provoked the museum to offer public resistance to a work about real estate, about business and incorporation, when, in fact, these notions are precisely what constitute the very atmosphere of many major museums.[50] For almost four decades now Haacke has continually sought to demystify art's autonomy from market concerns by publicly divulging the role banks, wealthy investors, and other business entities play in financing the purchase and managing the exhibition of art. At the same time his work reveals how certain corporations and other large firms (like Mobil or the British advertising giant Saatchi and Saatchi) profit symbolically and financially from their patronage. In an effort to supplant the romantic, idealized mythology that "emotionally sustains" those who work with art today, Haacke's practice aims to disclose how the artworld functions as an "industry" like any other.[51]

While much of the work I mention above seeks ways to bypass or even undermine traditional institutional constraints, particularly by implicating viewers in a self-reflexive process that encourages them to think critically about the ideologies that necessarily condition their viewing,[52] with time many artists began to accept capitalism's influence on art produced under a market economy. Like Marcel Duchamp and Andy Warhol before them, these artists more readily came to terms with the idea that, no matter how hard they may try, few alternatives exist: "the work of art in capitalist society cannot escape the status of a commodity."[53] To be sure, however, these works are no less ambiguous with regard to their position. If Mike Kelley's arts and crafts style installations—which include handmade afghan rugs and stuffed animal sculptures—invite viewers to reflect on the status of art as a commodity and as fetish, they also suggest how the notion of the gift and gift-giving might be mobilized to undermine that economy. Or, as Kelley concedes in an interview, maybe not: "If I give you this art-thing, it's going to escape the evils of capitalism. Well, of course that's ridiculous, because if you give this thing to Junior he owes you something. It might not be money, but he owes you something."[54] Louise Lawler's photographs of well-known works of art shown in various environments—in museums, galleries, and auction houses, but also on the walls in corporate offices and wealthy collectors' homes—are works of art in and of themselves. Yet they simultaneously expose art as an arbiter of taste—and thus as a marker of class—as well as a tool of corporate power. And while certain viewers of Andreas Gursky's more recent large-scale photographs of market environments—from images of high-end Prada boutiques and the Tokyo Stock exchange to the glorious cornucopia of products arrayed in a ninety-nine-cent store—might wonder at the aesthetic spectacle of global consumer culture, high and low, that these photographs project, others might find in it a latent critique of how widespread, uniform, and dehumanizing this very culture has become.

Like work by Kelley, Lawler, and Gursky, Barbara Kruger's series of photomontage imagetexts from the mid-1980s also offer a potent inquiry into the commodification of the cultural and the concomitant symbolization of the economic. In *Untitled (When I Hear the Word Culture, I Take Out My Checkbook)* (1985), a large 11.5 x 6 foot poster, the blunt slogan, overlaid on an appropriated image of a marionette that resembles the 1950s children's television icon Howdy Doody, borrows an earlier quotation by Jean-Luc Godard, which is used as the second epigraph to this chapter (image 6).[55] The piece deftly suggests how this sort of cultural appropriation transforms the low into high, as Howdy Doody magically gains access to the world of art galleries and museums. At the same time, it exposes art's inevitable, indeed natural, transformation into merchandise by the market. While Kruger seems to acknowledge that her own work is necessarily part of that market, one possible implication here is that the agents that control the buying and selling of works like this—the art dealers and collectors with their checkbooks at the ready—are dummies or puppets easily convinced that a work is worth something because someone (the artists or critics who really hold the strings) has deemed it so. Similarly, other

Image 6. Barbara Kruger, *Untitled (When I Hear the Word Culture, I Take Out My Checkbook)*, 1985. Photograph, 138 x 60 in. (350.5 x 152.5 cm). © Barbara Kruger. Norton Family Collection. Image courtesy of Mary Boone Gallery, New York.

verbal/visual signs like *Untitled (You Make History When You Do Business)* (1981), *Untitled (Buy Me, I'll Change Your Life)* (1984), *Untitled (I Shop, Therefore I Am)* (1987), and *Untitled (You've Got Money to Burn)* (1988) enact Kruger's critical position that cultural production is indistinguishable from the ideology of consumption that undergirds it.

Among those artists whose work illustrates precisely how "the logic of the arts and that of the economy [are] not incompatible but, in fact, consistent," Jeff Koons is perhaps the most spectacular.[56] Though hardly the first renowned artist to display everyday objects as a way to challenge the institutions that ascribe value to the work of art—as Dalia Judovitz writes, much contemporary art is indebted to Marcel Duchamp, whose famous readymade, *Fountain* (1917), subverts the notion of an artwork's inherent worth by virtually "commemorating the urinal which literally flushed the notion of artistic value down the drain"[57]—Koons's early work, in the *Pre-New, The New* (1979–80) and *Equilibrium* (1985) series, complicates the relationship between consumption and desire in an affirmative, optimistic, and complicit form of display (image 7). The immaculate vacuum cleaners and basketballs arranged in minimalist-inspired Plexiglass vitrines affirm and seemingly revel in the potential that base commodities might become works of art. Because these objects are encased in glass, they prevent the kind of handling of the materials that is necessary to utilitarian ownership. The objects remain forever "new" because they will never be used for their intended purpose. At the same time, as Koons has himself remarked, once a collector or institution purchases the piece, a new commodity is born, an artwork whose very sale is designed to increase the artist's own symbolic power.[58] Indeed, as someone who worked on Wall Street as a commodities broker before he began to make a living from his art, and who often deals directly

Image 7. Jeff Koons, *New Shelton Wet/Drys 10 Gallon, Double Decker*, 1981. Two Shelton wet/drys, acrylic, fluorescent lights, 82 x 28 x 28 in. (108.3 x 71.1 x 71.1 cm.). © Jeff Koons. Courtesy Jeff Koons Studio.

with the companies that produce the products displayed in his work (Hoover and Wilson, in the cases mentioned above), Koons is one of contemporary art's most forthcoming (and savvy) proponents of the role branding and business acumen play in the successful creation (and sale) of art.[59]

If Koons's work asks how an everyday object, isolated from its market context, becomes a work of art, and how this work of art can then be transformed into an object of exchange, *Vie de Joseph Roulin* seeks to understand a similar series of processes when a postman, members of his family, and traces of his everyday world materialize in icons to be bought and sold. A consideration of the particular cultural moment during which Michon wrote and published the narrative helps to affirm why this is so. The period in which artists like Koons, Kruger, Kelley, and Lawler came of age was a time of tremendous speculation in the art market. During the mid-1980s collectors, multinational corporations, and major financial institutions began to see fine art as a prime investment opportunity. The engines of capitalism had, in effect, "overtaken" contemporary art, "quantifying it and reducing it to the status of a commodity."[60] Other visual artists, such as Julian Schnabel and David Salle, produced popular work whose value was boosted by the status of their reputations, just as neoliberal governmental policies, fund raising, and marketing efforts "made it possible to conceive of relationships between the artist, the artwork, and the public in economic terms."[61] As a result, prices of Old Master paintings soared as much as the work of fashionable young painters. As art historian David Hopkins recalls, in "1987 and 1988, 121 paintings and drawings topped the million-dollar mark in American auctions compared with 14 in 1979 and 1980."[62] During the "consumer orgy" of the booming 1980s, and especially during the years when Michon wrote and published *Vie de Joseph Roulin*, art became inextricably linked with money.[63]

Some of the most spectacular auctions of that decade led to the sale of several key works by Vincent van Gogh. In March of 1987, the purchase of his *Still Life: Vase with Fifteen Sunflowers* (1888) by a Japanese insurance company for a record

$39 million—at the time the most ever paid for a work of fine art—became a global media sensation.[64] Eight months later, in November of 1987, another van Gogh still life from 1889, *Irises*, upped the ante even further, selling for the prodigious sum of $49 million. As Michon himself would write in 1988, clearly in response to these unprecedented transactions, van Gogh, who "incidentally" was also a painter, had, like many artists in those days, become a veritable "golden boy."[65] For Michon, the genius of van Gogh's work, no matter what we might think of its beauty, of its execution, or of the way it makes viewers feel, had been utterly surpassed by the staggering weight of its market value. *Vie de Joseph Roulin* attempts to work through this situation by revisiting the role the dealer and the market have played in the ultimate consecration of van Gogh as an artist, a phenomenon that Roulin recognizes but is hard-pressed to understand. A literary manifestation of what Olaf Velthuis calls "imaginary economics," Michon's narrative, like the works of art that I briefly survey above, constitutes a form of reflection, or even a "source of knowledge," about art's relation to broader economic issues.[66] It unearths the inconsistencies between the material and human conditions involved in the production of painting, how we make sense of it, and how it is publicly received, while simultaneously exposing and subverting the tendency to take the value of a work of art for granted.

### *The Price Is Right*

No matter how much the text invites readers to consider how artworks relate to the larger institutions that dictate what a work of art is worth, *Vie de Joseph Roulin*, like the other works in this study, is conscious of its own distinct textuality and brings visual culture to bear on the practice of writing. Michon's telling of a tale of pictures in prose not only affirms "the very powers and capacities"[67] of literary fiction, it self-reflexively confirms what makes literature unique. Michon's project, in *Vie de Joseph Roulin* and elsewhere, is driven in part by the desire to interrogate the very nature of writing. As Patrick Crowley has observed, Michon's work frequently engages in a series of reflections that have interested writers for decades, posing crucial questions such as "What is literature? What is the function of the author?"[68] While the author's fictionalized biography of Roulin can be read as a more generalized inquiry into the nuances of aesthetic evaluation and valuation, the narrative seeks to come to terms with how literature's value is calculated as well. As Michon has asked, "What makes a *text* a work of art?" (*RV* 15, emphasis mine.) While the focus on the sale of Roulin's painting in *Vie de Joseph Roulin* makes the conflation of art and commodity more visible, it also implicitly engages literature's position with regard to its own economy of dissemination and exchange.

In interviews that he has granted over the years, Michon seems acutely aware of the vagaries of the book market. Like many authors of his generation who seek to publish successful works of literature in a highly competitive field, the author is hardly immune to thinking about comparatively less "noble" factors such as book sales, the function of criticism, or the infiltration of what he calls "non-literature" on literary space. In a 1989 interview published in *La Quinzaine littéraire*, for example, Michon was asked to respond to a series of questions about the future of French fiction ("Where is French literature going?"). While the author acknowledges the influence of the avant-garde in his thinking about the role of high theory on modern French prose—noting the influence of Maurice Blanchot and the literary and critical trends associated with the *nouveau roman* and *Tel Quel*—his explanation for the subsequent reaction in French letters against an earlier emphasis on experimental formalism is not so much literary-historical as it is economic. "We talk a lot about this so-called 'return to narrative,' but I think that it is more a question of the book market than of literary art" (*RV* 14). Over time, Michon continues, the institutions responsible for the publication of French literature, including not only the publishing houses but the publicity machine that helps to sell books, have given in to a popular desire to read works that are more "facile" than many of those that were published during 1950s and 1960s, the heyday of a more theoretically oriented brand of avant-garde fiction. "The book market," Michon notes, "neither needs nor has the patience to disguise itself: it has for some time now replaced something it no longer bothers to call art with merchandise" (*RV* 16). For Michon, the literary world, occupied more and more by the unwavering presence of the mass media, increasingly influenced by consensus and motivated by trade, has been forced to conform and use "sales tactics" and other base machinations associated with a major commercial industry.

That said, no matter how much the world of business inflects the reception of literature, the market for books, as *Vie de Joseph Roulin* subtly implies, is quite different from the market for works of visual art. The essential characteristics that differentiate painting from prose ultimately determine how, where, and at what price we experience different kinds of art. For Gérard Genette, whose recent work constitutes a rigorous survey of those differences, the key lies in the notion of embodiment. Where painting is material, literature is immaterial. Nonmechanical visual art like painting and sculpture is physically unique, whereas literature manifests itself in different occurrences. Building on Nelson Goodman's distinction between the "allographic" and "autographic" arts, Genette proposes a schema that differentiates "works of physical immanence (material objects or perceptible events)" and "works of ideal immanence—that is, works consisting in a type common to several correct occurrences."[69] While these distinctions are important from an ontological standpoint, they also help to explain discrepancies in the way we consume art today. Literature does not quite rely on the same channels of distribution and exchange because works of literature—objects of "ideal immanence"—cannot be physically transformed. Books, like musical scores, are multiple manifestations of the same, unique work. Every time the singular numerical manifestation of a painting is physically transformed, on the other hand, the specific identity of that work changes. Because all works of physical immanence are defined by their "history of production,"[70] when the specific identity of a painting is altered—when one transforms it by physically manipulating it, or by reproducing it—its value changes concurrently. The relative value of a work of literature over time, on the other hand, is more stable than that of a painting whose identity depends, among other things, on the physical conditions of its support.

If, as we have seen, Michon's narrative suggests how the market for modern painting is responsible not only for a work's commodification but for the seemingly unending fluctuations in its monetary value, it also hints at how literature inherently avoids some of the same traps. While books, as material objects, are commodities to be bought and sold like any other, their price is not calculated in the same manner as other works of art. Though certain books, like select first or signed editions and original manuscripts, are occasionally purchased at astronomical prices—precisely because the market for these rarities necessarily must consider the "history of their production" and their provenance—they do not come close to attaining the sums reached by works of visual art.[71] Nor does the price of such literary works fluctuate in accordance with the ebb and flow of the increasingly globalized economy. During the "Great Recession" that many Western countries endured in 2008 and 2009, conditions for the sale and purchase of artworks vacillated in concert with plummeting, and then skyrocketing, values of the international stock markets as investors, initially weary about the speculative future of art, began to reenter the scene at the first signs of a potential recovery.[72] Accounting for inflation, the price of books, however, has remained comparatively stagnant over the years. This is to say that literature is not as dependent on the market for valuation, whereas painting is: "Impersonal and businesslike as prices seem, they are the numbers artists, collectors, and dealers live by."[73] In short, a work of literature's monetary value has not been and cannot be perverted by a market where, today, most books of similar lengths, destined for sale to trade, mass-market, or academic audiences respectively, sell for similar prices based not on any intrinsic aesthetic qualities, but on contingent factors like page length, print run, paper and ink quality, binding, and other production costs. Works of great literature in any language, sold as books or read in serial installments, on paper or in one of today's increasingly prevalent digital reader formats, are thus more accessible than original master paintings ever were or will be. Seen from such a "textually materialist" perspective—a way of reading that Michon's narrative implicitly encourages—*Vie de Joseph Roulin* positions literature as a decidedly democratic art form that corresponds more readily with Joseph Roulin's own revolutionary ideals.[74] As it yearns for a world in which the value of a work of art might be determined according to a set of purely aesthetic criteria, where it is not as easy to say that a painting or a text is worth more because it costs more, *Vie de Joseph Roulin* ultimately insinuates that the channels that enable the tactical yet necessary commerce of literature are much less fraught than the more mercurial markets for the buying and selling of its sister art.

# 4

# Remake

If you don't like the movies, bug off.

CHRISTIAN AUTHIER, *Deuxièmes séances*

Where Pierre Michon's *Vie de Joseph Roulin* invites viewers to see and reassess the work of Vincent van Gogh in their mind's eye, Tanguy Viel's groundbreaking second novel *Cinéma* takes readers to the movies by telling a film, in its entirety, in words.[1] The film in question, as the narrator divulges near the novel's conclusion, is famed director Joseph Mankiewicz's last motion picture, *Sleuth* (1972, released as *Le limier* in France). This brilliant thriller by one of the twentieth century's most acclaimed filmmakers recounts the machinations of Andrew Wyke (Laurence Olivier), a wealthy writer of detective fiction determined to entrap and humiliate the handsome young hairdresser who is sleeping with his wife. Not to be outdone, the coiffing lothario, Milo Tindle (Michael Caine), returns the favor in the end, luring Wyke into his own dangerous web of deceit and revenge. Revolving around an elaborate game of doubles, disguises, set-ups, and surprising twists, the film's plot is a complex one, necessitating a fair amount of attention on the part of the spectator. Indolent viewers beware: things onscreen are not always what they seem.[2]

Thankfully for readers of *Cinéma*, the novel appoints a knowledgeable guide to lead the way through the vicissitudes of Mankiewicz's labyrinthine tale. The anonymous narrator, a consummate devotee of the film, takes it upon himself to tell *Sleuth*, scene by scene, from the beginning through to "The End" (124). His obsessive-compulsive account of the picture exhibits a keen eye for detail and a flair for evocative storytelling. Yet his project is not altogether disassociated from certain hermeneutic concerns. The film is constantly "paused" in favor of a running interpretation and critical commentary: "But I'm getting ahead of myself. I speak, and the film stops moving forward" (40). In describing the film shot by shot, frequently interrupting its "projection" with an incessant series of self-conscious remarks and digressions ("that is what I'm thinking as I watch the film" [35]), the narrator can only hope that his passion for and understanding of *Sleuth* will be shared by a public that is appreciative enough of its playful elegance and puzzle-like complexity. "[I've] tried everything to make sure, to guarantee that, yes, nobody can resist this film" (51). Not merely a citation, a copy, or even a true "novelization" of the original scenario, Viel's exemplary imagetext wraps *Sleuth* in an explicitly self-conscious narrative frame.[3]

The narrator refers to his 124-page enunciation, diegesis and exegesis combined, as a "spoken reel" (*pellicule vocale* in French) (43). This particularly apt metaphor suggests how *Cinéma* stages the relationship between seeing (and listening to) a film and what one might have to say (and write) about it. As the narrator speaks of and with *Sleuth*—"so that the images and I speak together" (43)—rehearsing the story scene by scene, the film's images and dialogue are figuratively recorded onto the surface of the text in words.[4] The notion of the "spoken reel" exemplifies the novel's negotiation of the complex play of verbal and visual paradigms inherent to both media, and provides a useful point of departure from which to probe the greater significance of Viel's writing of Mankiewicz's film onto, and into, *Cinéma*. How does the novel write the film? What is at stake, for literary representation in particular, in doing so? What does *Cinéma* have to say about the relationship between literacy and visuality, and between reading and watching (and, of course, listening)? And finally, why does the status of that relationship matter in an age characterized by the unheralded propagation of popular visual forms?

## *Telling* Sleuth

After the opening credits have rolled *Sleuth* begins as follows: "A sports car, the red car belonging to Milo Tindle, rolls down the drive leading to the mansion, to the mansion that we see straight ahead, imposing. Tindle, that's his name, he's an Englishman, parks in the courtyard, on the gravel, with his red sports car and his fitted sportcoat, which was very fashionable in the seventies. He gets out of his red sports car (with his initials inscribed on the side, on the left door panel, etched into the paint, it's written: M. T., for Milo Tindle)" (9). Or at least that's how the narrator of *Cinéma* sees it. For in the novel *Sleuth* is not "projected" by an objective and inhuman machine, but rather by a first-person narrative voice that has its own way of telling. Asked to describe this same series of shots, another narrator might have neglected to mention the initials inscribed on Milo's car. Others might have found it unnecessary to reveal the character's nationality (readers learn further along that Tindle is inherited from the Italian, "Tindolini"). Still others would have forgotten to mention the historical flair of Milo's form-fitting jacket (a potent reality effect, evoking here the essence of disco-era European fashionability). Throughout the text, the narrator of *Cinéma* does not pronounce some universal version of what "one" sees on the screen, nor does he assert that this is his aim. Rather, the diegesis reflects his personal experience of the film, suggesting what he alone sees.

To compensate for the film's inherent complexity the narrator decides on a series of constraints to direct his particular way of telling. On the whole his narrative strictly follows the chronology of the film. Not doing so would diminish the "majesty of things as they appear on screen, majestic certainly with regard to their sequencing" (26). In *Sleuth* the timing of events is crucial. The narrator does, however, make an exception to this self-imposed rule, leaking one of the film's many surprises long before it actually occurs on the screen. In a scene that presents Wyke's staged assassination of Milo Tindle about three-quarters of the way through, the narrator discloses that while the first two bullets to leave his pistol's chamber were real—"to be more persuasive" (68)—the third was merely a blank: "Not that we never learn about it but, if I respected the chronology (it's deliberate that I don't respect it, because it would be less simple to do justice to the contours of the film), if I respected the chronology, then, we would only know about it twenty minutes later." (68–69) In this case the narrator sacrifices a crucial moment of shocking disclosure—viewers learn, "twenty minutes later," that the third bullet was a fake and that Milo is, in fact, still alive—so that he can stress the nuances of the film's structure. This change in narrative order attests to the narrator's desire to prevent his listeners from losing track of the plot.[5] It is also symptomatic of his need to convince his audience that the production of such a surprising twist is a truly ingenious feat. Throughout, *Cinéma* consistently exalts Mankiewicz's talent for filmmaking.

Despite the narrator's desire to "explain it all" (43), there are certain aspects of the film that he, surprisingly, does not

Image 8. Screen capture from *Sleuth*, 1972, directed by Joseph L. Mankiewicz. Palomar Pictures.

address. The seeming fidelity of his narration to the original—"everything is genuine, I'm not changing a single image" (67)—masks several inconspicuous absences. The most important of these is the film's title-sequence, which he simply overlooks.[6] On the screen, the opening credits are superimposed over a series of theatrical dioramas that enact some of the most legendary moments from Andrew Wyke's popular series of "Lord Merridew" detective novels (image 8). A variety of ornately decorated proscenium arches frame these static, intricately crafted scenes, and the painted curtains are unfurled to reveal the stage and the tiny figurines that inhabit its space as if in mid-act. At the end of the film the camera pulls back to reveal the stage upon which Wyke and Tindle are themselves figured, and the curtain that then falls affirms that these two men have been caught up in a drama not unlike one that we might read about in a popular mystery. Yet the film's explicit reference to the dramatic arts serves other functions as well. For one, it acknowledges the decidedly theatrical origins of the story. If in its almost faultless adherence to the classic unities of place, of action, and of time *Sleuth* seems as though it would be perfectly tailored for the theater, that is because it is: *Sleuth* was initially produced for the stage, opening in London in 1970 to rave reviews. A year later it was awarded Broadway's highest honor, the Tony for best play. The opening and closing sequences of the film therefore acknowledge the original generic status of the story and allow the film to credit the playwright—who also happens to be the film's screenwriter—Anthony Shaffer.[7] Although the narrator of *Cinéma* invokes "the great director, Joseph L. Mankiewicz" (107), he disregards *Sleuth*'s true authorship by making no mention of Shaffer, nor of the play, whatsoever. The novel effectively represses the theatrical origins of the film in order to concentrate on more specifically cinematic concerns—techniques that testify to Mankiewicz's own creative genius—like editing and shot composition. But the omission also signals the novel's affiliation with certain avant-garde critiques of notions of originality and authorial agency, a connection that will become more apparent further along in this chapter. In disregarding Shaffer's essential role in the genesis of the film—were it not for his words the screenplay would, quite simply, not exist—the novel effectively stages the "death of the author," thereby aligning itself with concerns about artistic agency that subtend work by a wealth of other artists whose practice, as we will see, is similarly appropriationist in nature.[8]

Despite this subtle yet no less important omission, the narrator's otherwise faithful rendering of the film puts a modern twist on the classic Horatian formulation of *ut pictura poesis*. Throughout, it reflects on the ability of language to make us see and on the authorial desire to invest words with the "presence" of those objects to which they refer. As the narrator of one of Vladimir Nabokov's novels remarks, "an author's fondest dream is to turn the reader into a spectator."[9] Through the notion of the "spoken reel," *Cinéma* enacts this very desire. The novel not only implicates readers in a process of reading, but of seeing and listening as well. This particular mode of writing aims to transmit onto the page precisely what is traditionally projected onto the screen. Moments when the narrative recounts the events of a film effectively stitch readers into its cinematic fabric. Despite the novel's many narrative interventions, *Cinéma* frequently manages to capture the intricacies of certain key scenes. The narrator's telling of the moment that precedes Andrew Wyke's "staged" murder of Milo Tindle, a masterful sequence during which the detective writer grants the adulterous hairdresser twenty seconds to escape the scene of the premeditated crime designed to frame him, is particularly successful in this regard. In this passage the text alternates between Andrew's sinister countdown and Milo's desperate attempt to escape:

> "eight," . . . the face blushing as the blood rises to his temples and climbs up to his brain, opening it, the door, the heavy wooden door . . . "nine," . . . and running to the car, running . . . "ten," . . . but they have to come off . . . "eleven," . . . these shoes, they have to come off to drive . . . "twelve," . . . one, then the other . . . "thirteen," . . . and they're stuck, these planks . . . "fourteen," . . . won't come off . . . "fifteen," . . . now turn the ignition, turn the ignition . . . "sixteen," . . . the ignition key . . . "seventeen," . . . but where are they, where are the keys . . . "eighteen," . . . and Andrew's voice, that we heard inside, getting closer, and which is outside now . . . "nineteen," . . . who is crushing the gravel with his loafers which settle next to the car . . . and . . . "twenty."

But he doesn't shoot, Andrew, only holds his hand high, wiggling the keys above Milo, condescendingly. (58–59)

The passage accurately mirrors, shot by shot, Mankiewicz's own montage of the scene (image 9). The narrator's citation of Wyke's sinister countdown in its original English lends an air of authenticity to the enunciation without hindering the comprehension of his Francophone narratees.[10] As is the case throughout the novel, the use of the present tense dissolves the gap between the text and the film—lacking any flashbacks or prolepses, *Sleuth* is told "in the present"—and thereby draws the reader closer to the action. Moreover, the passage invites readers to identify with a series of internal reflections that, while not explicitly voiced in the film, can nevertheless be attributed to the characters on screen. The text not only stages Milo's thought process as he tries vainly to escape what appears to be an almost certain demise, but also what the spectator, in an affective moment of identification with the protagonist, might be anticipating and hoping for as well ("the shoes must come off to drive!").[11]

The rhetorical device upon which such an effective evocation of the filmic relies is the classic trope of *ekphrasis*, the "verbal representation of a visible representation," most often a work of visual art.[12] In his critique of the *Salon de 1765*, Denis Diderot exemplifies the main objectives of this discursive figure. He notes, "I will describe the paintings for you. And my description will be such that, with a little imagination and enthusiasm we will realize them in space, placing the objects there just as we had seen them on the canvas."[13] Before embarking on his critique of the works on view in the *salon* that year, the author expresses a keen awareness of the challenges involved in transposing the various paintings on display into a discourse evocative enough to allow his readers

Image 9. Screen capture from *Sleuth*, 1972, directed by Joseph L. Mankiewicz. Palomar Pictures.

to "see" what there is to be seen. Yet if he recognizes the difficulties of rendering the image in words, he is also confident enough in his rhetorical capabilities, and in the subtleties of the figure of *ekphrasis* in particular, to foster the reader's visualization of the text in the mind's eye.

The kind of "screen writing" (or *écr(an)iture*) that the novel stages, a particular instance of *ekphrasis* in which the literary text aims to render a moving picture in language, functions according to a similarly idealistic paradigm. Initially, caught up in a moment of "ekphrastic hope,"[14] Viel's narrator is clearly as confident in language's capacity to rise above the essential impossibility of *ekphrasis* as Diderot was centuries earlier. His "spoken reel" seeks to create a discourse that might foster an experience if not exactly the same, then at least akin to watching and listening to a film. The narrator of *Cinéma* seemingly rewrites Diderot's ekphrastic paradigm as if to say, "I will describe *the film* to you. And my description will be such that, with a little imagination and enthusiasm, we will realize it in space, placing the *images and sounds* there just as we had *seen and heard* them *onscreen*."[15]

The conceit that readers might be able to hear and see the film is, of course, a mere illusion. As Tanguy Viel has himself pointed out, in the novel "a film becomes a book and, almost, vice versa."[16] This "almost" is essential, since it suggests Viel's uneasiness about telling a film in words. Not surprisingly, near the novel's conclusion, the narrator echoes his author's hesitation and reveals a profound suspicion of language's capacity to make readers actually see: "you have to understand, then, that what is said is not what is filmed, not at all, there's no comparison, no analogy is possible, as my friends say, and it's not a question of one being superior to the other, neither that nor anything else, but it's fundamental, it's like measuring the temperature with a barometer, like desperately wanting to make a table fly, it's as absurd as that" (109–10). In opposition to the utopian notion of a verbal description that can almost magically render the described object visible, *Cinéma*'s narrator acknowledges the impossibility of the ekphrastic ideal. The limits of his enunciation, and more generally the limitations of language to speak what he sees, become plainly apparent. Speaking and writing the image in an attempt to render it visible is a futile act that can only lead to dissatisfaction; using language to tell a film is like "measuring the temperature with a barometer." The very idea of it is as absurd as trying to "make a table fly."

The narrator's frustration stems from his awareness of the innate incompatibility between the verbal and visual fields. As Michel Foucault remarked, neither can be reduced, systematically, to the other's terms: "It is in vain that we say what we see; what we see never resides in what we say. And it is in vain that we attempt to show, by the use of images, metaphors, or similes, what we are saying; the space where they achieve their splendour is not that deployed by our eyes but that defined by the sequential elements of syntax."[17] Although language is an effective means of communication, words will always be an abstract and equivocal vehicle for expressing what one sees. Telling a picture is hardly the equivalent of showing it: "No amount of description . . . adds up to a depiction. A verbal representation cannot represent—that is, make present—its object in the same way a visual representation can. It may refer to an object, describe it, invoke it, but it can never bring its visual presence before us in the way pictures do."[18]

In other words, the textual that speaks the filmic is no substitute for the real thing. As the narrator of *Cinéma* finally concedes: "Surely speech won't change it, surely not. I have stopped thinking that my opinion could make a difference, and, I can say it now, frankly, I never believed it, never tried for a second to convince anyone, because, I must say: if Sleuth didn't succeed, then no one can, and I know it" (124). Coming to terms with the capacity of the "spoken reel" to influence its audience, the narrator admits to the eventual shortcomings of his own narrative project. Despite its numerous efforts to encourage readers to "see" (and to hear), to stitch its audience into the fabric of the film, to show readers through its telling, and to convince us of the film's stature, the novel concludes by maintaining that a film can never be replaced by what one might have to say about it. This is to say that the only way to experience the real thing is, quite simply, to see it for oneself.

## "*Reading*" Sleuth

In this way *Cinéma* complicates the mythical power of words to conjure up images available for the world to see. Unlike the other narratives studied in the previous chapters, texts which delight in their attempts to rival the image in words,

*Cinéma* offers a critique of *ekphrasis* and its drive to simultaneously empower and contain the image it describes. Yet if the novel explicitly suggests that "words can 'cite,' but never 'sight' their objects,"[19] it nevertheless encourages readers to seek meaning from the images they might see on screen. As it explores the modalities of writing the image, *Cinéma* represents a significant consideration of the ways spectators make sense of the images and sounds that comprise the cinematic experience. The novel not only explores what it means to recount a narrative like *Sleuth* in words, it traces the procedures inherent to "reading" motion pictures.

Like the narrators in Simon's *Triptyque*, Perec's *Un cabinet d'amateur*, and Michon's *Vie de Joseph Roulin*, the narrator of *Cinéma* examines the object of his gaze with a meticulous eye for detail, noticing not only the most glaring facts, but also elements that are only hinted at in the film, those "minuscule signs that crop up in the camera's field of vision" (56). He does so, in part, to capture the sensation of his first viewing, to reveal which of those minor details struck him from the very beginning. The narrator's attention to visual minutiae also points to his drive to understand how and why the narrative leads to the death of Milo Tindle at the hands of Andrew Wyke. The text acts as a record of a series of revelations that provide the "keys" (122) that unlock the film's many mysteries. The narrator's close scrutiny of the film mirrors a detective's scrupulous inspection of criminal evidence. Wyke's mansion, after all, is the scene of a crime.

The suppression of the film's continuity via the regular textual "pausing" and the subsequent isolation of certain shots enables the narrator to analyze the facts at his own pace. Contrary to the more passive, "dreamlike" experience usually associated with cinematic spectatorship, the narrator's videocassette recorder (62) allows him to view the film more actively by providing total control of the filmic "apparatus" whose access is usually denied to moviegoers in theaters.[20] The "freeze frame" (33) that results from the narrator's consistent pausing of the film is of utmost importance in that it grants him unlimited control over the motion picture's inherent temporality. This portioning of the film into a series of contiguous still images that the viewer is free to peruse at his or her own leisure echoes the practice of formalist film analysis inaugurated, in part, by Roland Barthes. In his essay "The Third Message," Barthes examines another set of subtle signs that appear in a series of film photograms from S. M. Eisenstein's *Ivan the Terrible* (1943), and posits three different levels of meaning manifest in these details: the denotative level; a second, more connotative-symbolic level, motivated by directorial decisions and therefore more easily recognizable, more obvious; and a third level, "obtuse meaning," a "meaning both persistent and fugitive, apparent and evasive" cloaked in those "accidental" signs that stubbornly defy categorization, those which surpass the limits of intellection.[21] In the examination and analysis of *Sleuth* that his narrative provides, the narrator fully engages Barthes's tridimensional paradigm. The denotative and obvious levels of meaning correspond to those images that the narrator chooses to tell or interpret. The third meaning, on the other hand, is more elusive. As Viel has said, "even if the narrator is, above all, a speculative type, he's looking to somehow render, in language, the third dimension that the screen proposes in trompe l'oeil: depth."[22]

An example of this search for a hidden depth to the image can be found near the beginning of the novel. Not long after the film's opening sequences, after Andrew and Milo have exchanged pleasantries, the novelist asks Milo, whom he knows to be sleeping with his wife, if he would like to marry her. "With your permission," is Tindle's irreverent response. Andrew, however, hardly skips a beat, and doesn't seem the slightest bit perturbed by Tindle's daringly blunt retort. Ever the stoic, Wyke makes it seem that Tindle's amorous escapades with his wife are of little concern to him. As he would like Milo to believe, this is not why he has been summoned to his Wiltshire home. Despite Andrew's nonchalant reaction, however, the narrator notices a hidden displeasure that is slightly discernible in the character's expression, a discreet tension that "might be missed the first time you see the film" (21). The narrator, sensing its importance, voluntarily emphasizes this crucial detail because it marks a moment of combativeness that recurs throughout the film, and those recurrences are important for the viewer's understanding (22).

Although for Barthes the obtuse meaning is irrelevant to the plot, for the narrator of *Cinéma* this detail is crucial.[23] According to his reading, the subtle tension reveals Andrew's true motives. In *Cinéma* these details, these images laden with meaning, correspond to the larger narrative whole and are an integral part of the story's development. For the narrator, even the most minor of details is essential to his quest for meaning.

The narrator's own visual sleuthing of the film goes hand in hand with a process of deliberation. In order to solve a crime or put together the pieces of an incomplete puzzle, the detective must be able to construct in his mind a coherent picture of the whole. The gaps in the knowledge provided by those details must be filled. The narrator of *Cinéma* does not simply read the clues, he projects the information that the film, as a result of editing, sometimes leaves out. In order to grasp all of its nuances, he occasionally proposes to replace what the film omits, frequently narrating in the novel what remains "disnarrated" in *Sleuth*.[24]

For example, immediately following the scene in which Andrew supposedly shoots and kills Milo, the screen fades to black. The following shot reveals Andrew, at home in his kitchen, calmly preparing his dinner, newspaper in hand. Here the narrator intervenes to explain the lacuna: "Just there, there was an ellipsis: just there two days in the film passed by in three minutes" (63). Following Andrew's vengeful simulation of Milo's murder with blank bullets, which takes place on a Friday afternoon, Milo has had time to recoup and plan his own revenge. He returns Sunday night, disguised as the so-called "Inspector Doppler," feigning an investigation into the death of "Milo Tindle." Andrew, clearly shocked, blind to Tindle's impeccable disguise, does not quite know what to make of the situation. At this point in the film, the tide has turned; one man's joke has become another's retribution.

The spectator never sees exactly how Tindle's own scheme materializes. Milo could have prepared his plot to frame Wyke over the weekend, but the film never makes this possibility explicit. In the novel, however, the narrator proposes to illustrate, precisely, how Tindle came back to the house while Andrew was away in order to "deposit clues, false clues, to be precise, since they accuse Andrew of Tindle's murder" (73). A few pages later, the narrator spells out his own theory as to how Milo managed to orchestrate his frame: "In truth, he came in through the same window on Friday, the window he came through in his clown costume, with his ladder and glass-cutter, to simulate the fake robbery. So, Saturday, of course, the pane was already cut and the window could be opened from the outside, that's how simple it was, and that's not even part of the dialogue, the camera just gives us a static shot of that window" (83). Reifying the ellipsis, this passage repositions events that the film only subtly suggests. Much occurs during this gap; in order to arrive at a conclusion as compelling as the one the narrator proposes, the spectator is required to practice a good deal of reflection. The film is so compelling for the narrator of *Cinéma* precisely because it demands a more analytical kind of spectatorship that necessitates sustained attention over multiple viewings. The film incites spectators to meditate on its details and crucial ambiguities, and to do some sleuthing of their own.

One of the most remarkable moments in which *Sleuth* deliberately deprives viewers of the facts occurs as the film begins: Mankiewicz, assuming a certain naiveté in the film's spectator, lays a trap during the opening credits by introducing a certain "Alec Cawthorne as Inspector Doppler." Alec Cawthorne, however, does not exist. The role of Inspector Doppler, as the narrator eventually admits, is played by Michael Caine, which is to say Milo Tindle incognito: "even in the credits there are fake names . . . I see how that can be annoying, especially to be tricked by a film's credits" (69–70). Whereas the film withholds this information, the text prematurely discloses Mankiewicz's clever paratextual ruse.

These instances in which the narrator explains certain aspects that might go unnoticed are so significant because they stage the mental processes of an ideal spectator. Formalist critic Boris Eikhenbaum proposed the concept of "inner speech" to help explain this phenomenon. According to Eikhenbaum's theory, in order to make sense of what occurs on the screen, the cinematic spectator fills the spaces created between two shots with language: "Perception and understanding of a motion picture is inextricably bound up with the development of inner speech which makes the connections between separate shots."[25] Eikhenbaum thereby conceives of this internalized verbal discourse as a double, or as a secondary lining of the film integral to its reception. That the narrator's "spoken reel" includes not simply his diegesis of the film but his comments and thoughts as well testifies to the idea that meaning in film is produced in conjunction with the perceptual *and* linguistic processes of each spectator. Those moments in which the narrator reveals "what I think about when I watch the film" (35) effectively articulate what Eikhenbaum intends by inner speech. *Cinéma*'s rewriting of Mankiewicz's film from the perspective of an informed and active spectator thus stages the cognitive processes activated when spectators aim to make sense of the movies.

## *Watching* Sleuth

If *Cinéma* acknowledges its own limitations as a text and suggests how it is that spectators make sense of films in words, it also introduces a subtle critique of the dangerously seductive powers of popular cinema and its place in society today. In consuming *Sleuth* to such a degree, the narrator has himself—and not altogether unknowingly—been consumed. Thanks to a well-worn copy of the film and his trusty VCR, the narrator is such an informed and active viewer precisely because he has seen the film "tens, even hundreds of times" (49). He meticulously records the impressions, emotions, and thoughts provoked by his almost daily viewings in a notebook bought expressly for that purpose (50). The distracted narrative style that characterizes his narration attests to what can be described as the narrator's psychic sickness. While they certainly give life to Viel's prose, the text's impossibly long, epanorthotic sentences—filled with pauses, changes of rhythm, and the narrator's self-conscious, hesitating corrections—are frenzied and manic.[26] He even admits to suffering from a "fragile mental state" (62). The film is, in the narrator's own words, "everything for me" (63). Acquaintances are judged according to their responses to *Sleuth* (104). On one occasion, a simple remark by a friend ("I knew it!") at a crucial turning point in the movie provokes a powerful shock in the narrator, flabbergasted that even he was incapable of coming to the same conclusion (33). *Sleuth* plays such an important role in the narrator's life that the two become dangerously conflated: "because in reality, in the film" (103). Elsewhere, in an ultimate metaleptic gesture, the "real" is again virtually fused with the "reel" as the characters take on a life of their own and break away from the confines of the screen: "They are always there for me, they live next to me, and seeing them everywhere, recognizing them in the street, they resemble everyone else too" (79). The narrator's zealous attraction not to the cinema in general but to one fetishized film in particular—a *Sleuth*-ophilia, as it were—clearly borders on the pathological. In fact, careful readers of this chapter may have remarked an earlier citation (see p. 143) in which the narrator refers to *Sleuth* as "Sleuth," a typographical variant that suggests how the film quite literally takes on a life of its own. In the end the narrator's existence is wholly dependent on this one picture. As he admits, "I have no life outside the film" (96).

Although the extremes to which the novel goes in developing the narrator's obsession border on the parodic—certain readers might even be prompted to question the narrator's eccentric behavior and ask, "Mais, qu'est-ce que c'est que ce cinéma?" ("What's with all the drama?")—it does, nevertheless, offer a subtly nuanced critique. The novel presents *Sleuth* as an all-encompassing and dehumanizing distraction, a powerful spectacle that penetrates the narrator to his core. If *Cinéma* encourages readers to see the film, it warns that those with cinephilic inclinations should do so in moderation.

In the end the novel's negotiation of the inherent similarities and differences between writing and the movies implicitly ponders the fate of literature today. Like the other novels examined elsewhere in this book, although *Cinéma* is clearly responsive to the ubiquity of popular visual culture, it nevertheless testifies to the available power and potential of the written word. In confronting the film in its own way, absorbing it within the fabric of fiction and engaging it to such dynamic ends, the novel recuperates and reactivates *Sleuth* from its inevitable disappearance into the dustbin of cinematic history (a predictable fate, in spite of its four Academy Award nominations). In other words, Viel's novel self-consciously challenges the assumption that film will undoubtedly make literature obsolete. Instead, *Cinéma* taps into the vast pool of celluloid resources in order to show that a less defeatist option is just as likely: namely, that in an age when mass visual culture threatens to disintegrate the culture of the book, film might be destined not to suppress literature, but rather to enrich it.

### *Reverberations of the Readymade*

Given the particularly umbilical relationship between text and film, it is not surprising that Viel almost decided on an alternative, more suggestive title: "To be honest, I almost called it "Remake," but it sounded too coercive or too close to conceptual art. Though it's true that the book explores issues like originality, erasure, the recycling of an object within a new network of meaning, I am also rather happy that it is not merely a theoretical play on the definition of art or a variation on the ready-made."[27] Despite his desire to eschew any overt art-historical references, Viel's comments nevertheless testify to the crucial debt *Cinéma* owes to the legacy of the historical avant-garde and the resuscitation of many of its most potent critical strategies in postwar art. More specifically, in its exhaustive appropriation of *Sleuth*, *Cinéma* merges with a long tradition of artistic provocation that rejects the conventionally modernist pretensions to originality and artistic agency. If much of *Cinéma*'s literary significance is derived from its innovative reframing of Mankiewicz's film, from the specific and stylistically distinct way in which it tells the film, and from the way it engages more existential questions linked to identity, madness, and doubles, I want to suggest in what follows that its larger significance can be attributed to the way it reflects the cultural context within which it was produced.

The practice of appropriation is, if not the most important, then undoubtedly one of the most influential developments in the visual arts during the last half-century.[28] The act of explicitly reproducing, copying, reframing, wrapping, and citing purloined images that was popularized in much art of the 1960s continued to appeal to artists in the United States and in Europe throughout the 1980s and 1990s. Visual artists who work in the mode of appropriation effectively raid the realm of visual culture—lowbrow, highbrow, or middlebrow—and repackage preexisting signs in innovative and conceptually sophisticated contexts. Freed from a particular history that deemed what kinds of objects were worthy of its attention, art from the 1960s and beyond exploited even the most mundane artifacts of everyday mass culture. Richard Prince, for example, one of the major figures from the 1980s who continues to play an active role in the contemporary art scene, has worked with a decidedly "popular" archive of images. Prince's celebrated "reprotographs"[29] of everyday, commercial iconography and pictures most usually associated with the world of mass consumption conform to the logic of bricolage that structures the appropriationist gesture. The images that he chooses to remake take on new meanings once they are visually distorted, removed from their original context, and exhibited in an entirely unanticipated environment. Prince lifts publicity images from magazines or billboards and re-

Image 10. Richard Prince, *Untitled (Cowboy)*, 1989. Ektacolor photograph, 89 x 123¼ x 3 inches (226.1 x 313.1 x 7.6 cm). © Richard Prince. Courtesy Richard Prince Studio.

produces them, strips them of any accompanying text, and exhibits them on the walls of a gallery or a museum. The artist's pilfering of popularized corporate iconography functions on several levels.

Take, for example, his shrewd borrowing, in *Untitled (Cowboy)* (1989), of one of the most enduring symbols of the American masculine ideal: the Marlboro Man (image 10). In its adoption and recasting of a relatively cheap, mass-produced advertisement as a work fit for exposure in a temple of high art, Prince's cowboy image is consistent with the kind of institutional critique made famous by the historical avant-garde in the early part of the twentieth century. Moreover, given the initially "spectacular" quality of the image—the Marlboro Man was initially designed by a corporate powerhouse to cover the country's ubiquitous billboards and seduce consumers nationwide—Prince's caption-free *détournement* renders the image quaintly innocuous. The silent spokesman for the cigarette giant is still just as virile and proud, yet the artist's rephotograph relieves him of his duties as one of the world's hardest-working marketing pawns. Since the image is a mechanically reproduced copy, it also acts as a direct affront to the classic ideal that a true work of art must be created with a subjective hand. As Prince notes: "Essentially, my own desires have very little to do with what comes out of myself, because what I put out (at least in part) has already been out."[30] *Untitled (Cowboy)* evinces a decidedly critical stance toward the cult of originality. It turns the conventional belief that a work of art is defined as such because of its inherent stylistic uniqueness into a mere cliché (and this quite literally).

Whereas Prince mechanically reproduces photographs, Mike Bidlo replicates modern masterpieces by hand. Many of Bidlo's paintings and sculptures include full-scale copies of works by Cézanne (ironically entitled *Not Cézanne*), Matisse (*Not Matisse*), Picasso (*Not Picasso*), and Warhol (*Not Warhol*) that are virtually indistinguishable from the originals. However, unlike a conventional forgery whose level of "success" is based on how well it suppresses its status as a copy—the collective aim of Kürz and Raffke in Perec's *Un cabinet d'amateur*—every one of Bidlo's fakes publicly celebrates and promotes its artifice.

At the same time, however, there is something to be said about the artistry of Bidlo's gesture. Much like Jorge Luis Borges's tale of Pierre Menard's verbatim facsimile of *Don Quixote*, a copy that nevertheless exhibits a discernible contrast in style from the original, Bidlo's work also re-presents the same "text" while simultaneously letting his own character shine through.[31] As Bidlo notes, "I think everyone brings their own signature and personality into their work, even if they're making replicas."[32] Still, the strength of Bidlo's art lies not so much in his ability to craft flawless forgeries. Forgers have been doing that for years. Rather, Bidlo's achievement as an artist is more a result of the conceptual foundation upon which his work is constructed, most specifically in its harnessing the power of the false to challenge the notions of the autonomy and inherently subjective nature of the art object.[33] His copies represent a denial of the very idea of originality and reveal what can occur when the copy deigns to challenge the level of innovation inherent in its model. In Bidlo's work the fake, as it were, is more.[34]

Artists who choose to appropriate other works do not always limit their choices to still images. The film library has proven itself to be another excellent trove to raid. To that end, a group of artists working with film and video as a support have recently revisited classic films and incorporated them in their art with surprising results. Unlike typical cinematic remakes, feature films that simply tend to "update and modernize earlier texts in terms of their generic possibility,"[35] these works, much like Viel's novel, transform the original films and open them up to a new world of meaning. Frenchman Pierre Huyghe, for example, works frequently with preexisting pictures. His 1995 installation piece, fittingly entitled *Remake*, is a reenactment of Alfred Hitchcock's *Rear Window* (1954). Huyghe's version, however, looks nothing like what one would expect from a studio production. The artist employed a group of nonprofessional actors, given their lines only hours before filming began in their own homes, to play the roles immortalized on screen by James Stewart and Grace Kelly. Under Huyghe's direction, the makeshift cast recreated the original film, with remarkable fidelity, in its entirety. In the standard two-channel gallery installation,

Hitchcock's original film is played beside the remake, so that Huyghe's version of the master film seems like an uncanny, yet decidedly Hitchcockian home movie.[36]

Another multichannel installation that engages a similar problematic is *The Third Memory* (2000), a reenactment of an infamous *fait divers* that was itself adapted, remade as it were, in Sidney Lumet's celebrated feature *Dog Day Afternoon* (1975) (image 11).[37] Like *Remake*, the installation positions the artist's sparse filmic restaging of the facts side by side with a projection of Lumet's comparatively big-budget interpretation. Much like the experience of reading Viel's novel, *Remake* and *The Third Memory* confront the viewer simultaneously with a film, a restaging of the film, and with their own memories of the film, or, in the case of *The Third Memory*, with their experience of a spectacularly mediatized event. Consequently, to see *Sleuth* after having read *Cinéma* is a different experience altogether, much as viewing *Rear Window* or *Dog Day Afternoon* would differ for a spectator already familiar with Huyghe's installations and vice versa. *Cinéma*, *Remake*, and *The Third Memory*—like work by Bidlo (after Pollock), Prince (after the Marlboro advertisements), Manet (after Titian), Sam Taylor-Wood (after Wallis), and any artist or writer whose work explicitly and openly cites other texts—are simply more forthcoming with their latent intertextuality than most, making readers and viewers readily aware that theirs is a composite of sorts. "All writing is gloss and intergloss," Antoine Compagnon writes, following Montaigne.[38] Or, to use a more contemporary idiom, every work of art, whether the creator is conscious of it or not, has undoubtedly been assembled to varying degrees in an inherent process of "cut and paste."

Although Prince, Bidlo, and Huyghe all appropriate recognizable images, thereby tapping into the collective memory

Image 11. Pierre Huyghe, installation view: *The Third Memory*, 2000. Double projection, beta digital, video on monitor, Duration 9 minutes, 46 seconds. Courtesy of the artist and Marian Goodman Gallery, New York and Paris. © 2010 Artists Rights Society (ARS), New York/ADAGP, Paris.

and presenting spectators with innovative interpretations of familiar cultural objects, they do so to rather diverse critical ends. Whereas Prince's rephotographs explore our identification with mass-media images, Bidlo's forgeries are effective critiques of the notion of the "masterpiece" and all that that term implies. Huyghe's work, in comparison, explores the way viewers process and interpret images and the ways reality and fiction subsequently become intertwined in memory. At the same time, despite these diverse critical underpinnings, every act of appropriation, no matter what the subject matter or media, shares an inherently antihumanist critique of the relationship between art and originality. From Warhol to Huyghe, James Rosenquist to Jenny Holzer, and Robert Rauschenberg to Louise Lawler, each of these artists undermines the modern tradition that defines the work of art as a unique, synthetic creation.

In 1982 Sherrie Levine, one of the most conceptually sophisticated of the contemporary appropriation artists, published an artist's statement—a virtual appropriationist manifesto—that underlines this dominant concern:

> The world is filled to suffocating. Man has placed his token on every stone. Every word, every image, is leased and mortgaged. We know that a picture is but a space in which a variety of images, none of them original, blend and clash. A picture is a tissue of quotations drawn from the innumerable centers of culture. Similar to those eternal copyists Bouvard and Pécuchet, we indicate the profound ridiculousness that is precisely the truth of painting. We can only imitate a gesture that is always anterior, never original. Succeeding the painter, the plagiarist no longer bears within him passions, humors, feelings, impressions, but rather this immense encyclopedia from which he draws. The viewer is the tablet on which all the quotations that make up the painting are inscribed without any of them being lost. A painting's meaning lies not in its origin, but in its destination. The birth of the viewer must be at the cost of the painter.[39]

In a rather fatalistic portrait of the state of culture in the 1980s, Levine conceives of the world as a giant palimpsest in which every sign that is produced reveals itself to be a composite of other signs. Every work of art, every text, refers to a series of anterior works whose influence is always automatically inscribed from within. Each work of art, in other words, is already an intertext destined to represent reality to the second degree. Since the creation of objectively new images has been deemed impossible, the artist has no choice but to turn toward the massive public archive of cultural artifacts and begin sifting through its contents.

In a deftly self-reflexive move, Levine's statement performs the very act of textual appropriation that it champions. Her conception of a world characterized by an inescapable circulation of images consciously cites, rewrites, and reactivates, almost verbatim, Roland Barthes's own theorization of a culture in which every text is to be considered a "tissue of citations."[40] In his 1968 account of the "death of the author" Barthes rejects the very possibility of a singular, subjective agent responsible for the creation of a work of art. The "author," that mythical figure previously venerated as the sole source for meaning in a text, is exposed as a purely artificial construct that must be "distanced" from the scene of meaning. In his place Barthes's essay positions the modern reader, burdened with his own cultural baggage yet free to explore the textual spaces left behind and opened up to an infinite network of meaning. For Barthes the true significance of a work of art lies not in its origin but in its destination.

Levine's conceptually oriented practice performs Barthes's downgrading of the origin of the work of art in favor of its reception. Most striking in this regard are her photographic appropriations of prominent pictures by such pioneers as Walker Evans and Edward Weston, repackaged images that "speak of the diminished possibilities for originality in an image-saturated culture."[41] While at first look these images might appear to celebrate the genius of these modern masters, upon closer inspection they actually subvert the legitimacy of the "originals." In implying that all representation is "a tissue of quotations" Levine's appropriations aim to dismantle the "master" status of Evans's and Weston's pictures, offering in the process a potent critique of the modernist myth of creative agency.[42]

In a later essay Barthes locates one of the primary sources of this critique in the paradigmatic example of Marcel Duchamp's readymade, noting that Duchamp's practice transforms the chosen object into a text.[43] Like the writer whose own text makes meaning from a chain of words, each selected from a paradigmatic pool of signs, Duchamp's readymade takes objects out of their contexts—not simply things that seem manufactured but that are veritably mass-produced—and repositions them in a new system of signification. None of the work that I have mentioned until now would have been possible were it not for Duchamp's conceptual breakthrough decades earlier.[44] The readymade, which Duchamp devised in 1914, several years before he would definitively decide to abandon painting, was decisive in paving the way for the emergence of a postmodern logic of appropriationist "postproduction" in which cultural artifacts are not merely recycled, but reinvented and reconsumed.[45]

The term "readymade" refers as much to the physical object as to the initial gesture in which the artist chooses an article—a urinal, say—and then names it and displays it. In doing so the artist symbolically declares that "this [comb, shovel, bicycle wheel, hat rack, etc.] is a work of art." The entire process is subversive to say the least, since it undermines the conventional foundations upon which the very notion of art is based. As Duchamp explains, the creation of the readymade involves a process radically antithetical to the artistry and subjective expression most traditionally associated with painting. It is, in effect, an act of "non-art."[46]

Image 12. Marcel Duchamp, *L.H.O.O.Q. Mona Lisa*, 1919. Retouched readymade. Musee National d'Art Moderne, Centre Georges Pompidou, Paris, France. Photo Credit: CNAC/MNAM/Dist. Réunion des Musées Nationaux/Art Resource, New York. © 2010 Artists Rights Society (ARS), New York/ADAGP, Paris/Succession Marcel Duchamp.

Among the various kinds of readymades that Duchamp produced throughout his career, those referred to customarily as "assisted readymades" are most closely linked with the kind of appropriation of images championed by Warhol and later by artists such as Levine, Bidlo, Huyghe, and, as I argue, Tanguy Viel. Unlike the "standard" readymade, in which the object is chosen and exhibited more or less as it was found, the assisted readymade is an appropriated image or object that has been "rectified" with visible alterations. Among the best-known of these images is the oft-cited *L.H.O.O.Q Mona Lisa*, which first appeared in 1919 (image 12). In this notorious work, Duchamp defiled a reproduction of the *Mona Lisa*, strategically outfitting the figure with a patch of unflattering facial hair. An artistically seditious piece that challenges the very pillars of modernist aesthetics, this iconoclastic symbol of the avant-garde is no less derisive (note the scandalous homophone in the image's title: *elle a chaud au cul* ["she needs a good screw"]).[47] Like almost all of Duchamp's work, this image relies on a witty play with naming and language, and exposes the work to a variety of interpretations that go well beyond the initial challenge to the institutional function of art.[48]

Given Tanguy Viel's desire to avoid any overt references to the culture of the readymade ushered in by Duchamp and further championed by the work of those contemporary artists that I mention here, a reference to the original Mona Lisa that appears as an epigraph in Viel's *Cinéma* seems curious: "A girl of eight, when asked why she thought the Mona Lisa seemed to be smiling, answered: 'Coming home one night from work, Mister Lisa asked his wife: "Did you have a nice day my dear?" And Mona Lisa answered, smiling: "Leonardo da Vinci came to make my portrait. Fancy that!"'" (7).

Attributed to behavioral scientist Paul Watzlawick, this citation is indeed a fitting way to begin a novel about watching and reading a film, since it thematizes the act of visual interpretation. Both Duchamp, in *L.H.O.O.Q*, and the child of Watzlawick's quip resemble the narrator of *Cinéma* in that they all recontextualize an image within a new system of meaning. Duchamp's own "reading" of da Vinci in *L.H.O.O.Q.* does not share in the child's innocence, yet both manage to open the original to a series of new interpretations—no easy task considering that da Vinci's portrait is among the most overinterpreted and, paradoxically, the most mysterious works in the history of art.

Like Duchamp's rectified picture, the child's anecdote positions da Vinci's masterpiece as the site of a joke. There is much humor, after all, to be found in the Mona Lisa's moustache, and *L.H.O.O.Q.* has rightly been deemed the "plastic equivalent" of a pun.[49] Tanguy Viel is clearly aware of the importance of the power and prevalence of wit in Duchamp's work, and he engages it playfully in another published text from 2003, "La dernière conférence de Marcel Duchamp" ("Marcel Duchamp's Last Conference"). In this short piece, Viel imagines the artist at his last public appearance, restless and fidgety as he responds to claims about the connection between humor and the readymade. Before a group of earnest scholars who hope to hear the artist "explain himself," a humble Duchamp remarks that, contrary to what certain critics of his *Fountain* might believe, the choice to expose a urinal at the now infamous Armory show in 1917 was not intended to be funny: "One thing is certain. I was always very serious when it came to art. Humor, for me, humor in art, that was not a great motivator, it was not, let's say, the driving force behind my research. . . . And humor, you know, I say this for me, but really, humor in art, I'll tell you what I think, humor in art, it never existed, no, no artist ever really dreamed about it."[50] As critics of Duchamp would object, the role of humor in the work is too complex to be downplayed in such a way. Humor, manifest in the innumerable puns and play on words especially, is integral to the Duchampian project since it fosters an experience that relies less on visual perception than it does on cognition.[51] Viel's imagined pastiche of Duchamp's lecture is therefore a rectified readymade in its own right: his narrative revolves around a figure that "looks" and "sounds" like Duchamp, but whose ideas do not quite correspond with the original.

Many of the puns upon which Duchamp's work relies, *L.H.O.O.Q.* and *Fountain* included, capture the constant movement and tension between humor and critical seriousness that is paramount to the artist's oeuvre.[52] Consider, for example, the 1917 readymade *Trébuchet* (Trap). This clever piece—a coat rack, hooks and all, nailed to the floor—functions as both a verbal and a visual pun. The title is itself a polysemic "trap" since *trébuchet* is a homophone for the term *trébucher*, meaning "to stumble over." Not only do viewers of the work run the risk of literally tripping over the object on the floor, the title also poses its own linguistic trappings.[53] Given Viel's own interest in Duchamp, it is not surprising that *Cinéma* performs a similar kind of polysemic play.[54] Along with its more obvious connotations, the title also invites readers to interrogate the absurdity and artificiality of the narrator's obsessive gesture (one might say that the narrator *fait son cinéma*, which is to say that he is being overly dramatic).

The dependence on the viewer's intellectual faculties, the combination of both vision and reasoning, is crucial to understanding the readymade as a physical manifestation of ideas, or as a work of "conceptual" art *avant la lettre*. In order to grasp the full significance of the readymade, it does not simply suffice to engage the work optically. Rather, the critically aware viewer must consider a host of other factors, most particularly the role of language: in the readymade's title, in any writing that is graphically present in the work, or in the syntagmatic sequence of words associated with the object in question. In order to make sense of a piece as subtly complex as *Fountain*, for example, the viewer must consider both the aesthetic qualities of the urinal—its almost feminine curves and milky smooth porcelain surface do not entirely deprive viewers of at least some visual pleasure—as well as the word "Fountain" itself, the words "R. Mutt" inscribed on the bottom left of the piece, and the images that the inverted *pissoir* inevitably invokes (*eau de toilette*?). In other words, there is more to the readymade than what initially meets the eye. Each piece is part of a collective effort to fulfill the institutional critique championed by the historical avant-garde, a critique that questions "the very principle of art in bourgeois society according to which the individual is considered the creator of the work of art."[55] But the specificity of each object chosen to enact the institutional critique proffers a world of meanings and associations that prove that the Duchampian readymade is more than a merely self-reflexive enterprise. The selection of the object in *Cinéma*'s own take on the rectified readymade is equally important. How can we explain *Cinéma*'s rewriting of *Sleuth*, in particular? Why this film? Moreover, why choose a film in the first place?

Mankiewicz's motion picture seems like an obvious choice for the subject of a cinematic obsession since, with its complex plot and virtuoso performances, it warrants more than one viewing. It is also fitting that it should engage the thematic of the double—Milo Tindle returns near the end of the film incognito, disguised as the inquisitive sleuth "Inspector Doppler"—since the novel can be considered a literary doppelgänger of sorts. Moreover, the struggle for control that the film stages between a writer and a hairdresser—pitting a man who works with words against another who is concerned primarily with image—serves as an allegory for the larger tension between the realms of the verbal and the visual that the novel addresses so directly near its conclusion.

The fact that the narrator watches the film via the medium's most readily consumable format, the videotape, is also significant. Viewing conditions, as he notes, are far from perfect (62), whereas to see the film in the theater is to experience *Sleuth* "in its entirety" (62). Anne Friedberg provides a useful explanation for this curious inconsistency in Benjaminian terms. She notes that what a film loses as a result of the passage from the cinema to the living room is its essential essence as a work of art. "The market of commodified video-movies available to the home viewer has meant that the 'aura' of the original moment of cinema exhibition disappears."[56] The very invocation of the term "aura" in today's complicated cultural landscape of digital reproduction and virtual reality is a slippery move, to say the least. However, the narrator's "spoken reel," the record of which is the novel itself, can nonetheless be read as an attempt to reverse the decline of the filmic aura in an age of televisual reproduction since it provides a space which cultivates the reemergence of the essence of the film, as seen on videotape, via the mediation of language.

The appropriation of Mankiewicz's film in *Cinéma* assumes much of the same critique that Duchamp and his postmodern progeny have in mind, repudiating modernist claims to subjective ingenuity. However, as with the readymade or its more contemporary manifestations, Viel's novel also responds to defeatist notions about the impossibility of true innovation in a culture in which every work inevitably refers back to the past. Following the logic of bricolage, *Cinéma* manages to craft something new from something old. Echoing Levine's acquiescent defense of appropriation—"We can only imitate a gesture that is always anterior, never original"—Viel ponders the relevance of artistic originality in a postmodern age when he writes, "Has the time come for new ideas? Because maybe that's it, writing today: not categorizing literature according to a new creed, but there too, picking up the pieces and rebuilding from the ruins."[57] In a world that is saturated with verbal and visual texts, the creation of the new must necessarily involve the recycling of the past: "The repetition of things, repetition, that is what will save us."[58] For Viel, as for Levine, all representation is already ready-made. The only worthwhile gesture that can be made to save the arts from stagnation is to overtly cite other signs. After all, as Barthes has suggested, the world is made up of signs, and signs are meant to be repeated.[59]

Although it was produced in a world composed of simulated and serial images, at the height of a period during which, as some believe, "stylistic innovation is no longer possible," Viel's novel deploys a logic of appropriation to prove just how productive reconstructing from the ruins can be.[60] *Cinéma*, like *L.H.O.O.Q.* before it, looks to the past in an effort to forge the new. Fortunately for today's consumers of culture, the repetition of signs and frequent pillaging of the imaginary museum common to much artistic production is ultimately so rewarding precisely because the reclamation of the past opens each text to a new world of meaning. The reactivation of Mankiewicz's almost forty-year-old film within Viel's fiction suggests how a re-presentation of the past prevents it from being completely conclusive and teleological. Viel's appropriation rescues *Sleuth* from potential disappearance. Like Michon's *Vie de Joseph Roulin*, it hints at the power of words to vivify and resuscitate a work of art that, for all intents and purposes, had been forgotten.[61] In the end, *Cinéma*'s literary repackaging of Mankiewicz's motion picture acts as a vehicle for reviving the past and replacing it back into the flow and circulation of history. Derived from the Greek word *kinêma*, "cinema," after all, is synonymous with movement.

# Conclusion

Among contemporary French fiction's most compelling imagetexts, Jean-Philippe Toussaint's fifth novel, *La télévision* (1996), engages the proliferating flux of images in society today by telling a tale of and about the most consequential visual medium to have emerged during the second half of the twentieth century.[1] The protagonist, a lackadaisical forty-year-old French art historian on leave in Berlin, decides to take a self-imposed sabbatical from watching television so that he can better concentrate on his research. No matter how hard he tries, however, he can't seem to get a break. Television or some simulacral derivative thereof crops up within his field of vision virtually everywhere he goes, its reach seemingly infinite. Screens of all shapes and sizes prove pervasive, visible in places both expected (on display in an electronics store or lodged behind a security desk at a local museum) and fortuitous ("Across the way stood a block of apartment buildings, so close that you could see the televisions in the various living rooms" [123]). Television's most fervent spectators, incapable of appreciating just how dire their situation has become, gaze in a zombie-like trance when the tube is on, and gossip about the latest programming whenever it's turned off. If television ostensibly acts like a window onto the world, real windows, illuminated from the inside at night, take on the quasi-televisual feel of "glowing screens" (24). Even the local papers, the narrator notes, have been colonized by television's relentless charge, their pages covered in program listings that leave less and less room for the news (36). No wonder Toussaint chose to set his story in a city whose "giant looming TV transmitter" (133), positioned atop the landmark Fernsehturm tower, dominates the German capital's skyline at over twelve hundred feet high.

Like a number of recent "cathode fictions" from France that tell tales of and about television, *La télévision* continually disparages the detrimental influence of the medium by deploying discourses critical of its alienating and tranquilizing effects.[2] The narrator, as Warren Motte writes, has evidently "read his Guy Debord," but his predominantly cynical disposition resonates with a long list of equally captious commentaries by other notable thinkers such as Pierre Bourdieu, Serge Daney, Theodor Adorno, and Jean Baudrillard, just to name a few.[3] Television sets, according to Toussaint's narrator, are like "sacred" objects, worshipped religiously by the unassuming masses (84). The images they project "arouse no passion, produce no explosion, but rather, encouraging our somnolence and flattering our phlegmatism, content themselves with anesthetizing us" (67). The potential effects are positively discouraging. Television, the narrator notes, replaces conversation, deprives us of at least three of our five senses, occupies more and more space in the daily newspapers, and keeps everyone stuck inside when the weather is nice. Watching TV—"the same undifferentiated images, without margins or titles, without explanation, raw, incomprehensible, noisy and bright, ugly, sad, aggressive and jovial, syncopated, all equivalent" (10)—drags the narrator down, "swept up in that vain inertia, that insatiable spiral, searching for even more vileness, still more sadness" (10). The novel is not unlike the "youthful work" of Nam June Paik and Wolf Vostell (159), two pioneering video artists whose experimental sculptures and installations from the 1950s through the 1980s frequently deployed television sets and manipulated their images to question, make visible, and ultimately resist the medium's tendency to make listless and passive subjects of us all. Similarly, Toussaint's novel tells this particular story about televisual pictures to condemn their impact and point out their principal flaws: "nothing ever happens on television, and the most insignificant incident of our personal lives always touches us more meaningfully than any joyous or catastrophic event we might witness on television" (66).

Though the novel consistently excoriates the medium's ills, it can't help but elicit a latent fascination with television and its place in the visible world. For all his griping, the narrator's position is decidedly more tongue-in-cheek than many of the most staunchly iconoclastic discourses that he channels. *La télévision*'s anxiety about the image and its adverse effects is tempered by its protagonist's comically insouciant attitude.[4] Not only does his renunciation of television include a number of quirky loopholes—the rules do not apply, for example, should he find himself watching while out and about in Berlin, or while feeding the plants in his neighbor's apartment—as he gives in to the reach of televisual culture, awestruck as much as he is horrified by the ubiquity of society's numerous screens, he decides to buy a second set in the end. Resistance is futile. Complicity, on the other hand, is much less taxing. As unavoidable as television might seem to him—even the subject of his book project on sixteenth-century artist Titian, whose surname is Vicellio, seems haunted by the pull of TV—the narrator recognizes that it is also, at best, an annoying distraction. After all, other activities provide an easy means of escape. From listening to music and thinking (about life, but about working too) to walking through the local parks and swimming in neighborhood pools (perhaps the most productive way he spends his time), the narrator manages to avoid falling completely under television's spell. Perhaps most importantly, he finds ample time to read (and not merely the TV guide [17]). At one point he luxuriates in a "succulent" leather-bound edition of Alfred de Musset's collected works, a text whose extensive critical apparatus of notes and appendices are "delightful to gnaw at reflectively" (50). Later he compares the utterly transitory nature of the televisual effect to literature's power to enchant. Television's blatant superficiality can hardly match the book's capacity to tap into the depths of the reader's imagination (95). Clearly, as the novel suggests in these brief paeans to literary culture, "This will *not* kill That." The image's rise has not, in fact, brought about literature's demise. Rather, as Toussaint playfully shows, narratives still have the power to enlighten and enthrall those willing to resist, if even for a moment, contemporary visual culture's increasingly expansive grasp.[5]

No matter how anxious toward images it might initially appear, *La télévision* affirms in another crucial way how pictures often serve as excellent fodder for fiction. Though the narrator is plagued by procrastination, incapable of writing more than two words of his scholarly monograph, his inability to work, paradoxically, engenders the novel itself. The story he has to tell is ultimately told. No matter how iconoclastic his position may seem, looking at pictures, the novel suggests, is ultimately a powerful engine for literary creation. Narratives like Toussaint's that tell pictures to such a degree work through their uneasiness about the image's influence. In doing so, they reveal the extent to which visual culture has and continues to be a veritable boon for the craft of fiction.

Years earlier, in a 1975 catalogue essay on Gérard Fromanger's hybrid "photogenic" paintings, Michel Foucault recognized this idea with an almost oracular clarity. Rather than examine explicitly how literature has been transformed by its engagement with pictures, however, Foucault focuses on the frenzied circulation of images in the plastic arts, a phenomenon whose roots he traces back to the nineteenth century. Ever since the advent of the industrial age artists and technicians, painters, photographers, and entrepreneurs have explored novel ways of encouraging the vicissitudinous migration of images from one medium to the next. Between cameras and easels, from canvases and plates to papers and newspapers, "with all the new powers acquired there came a new freedom of transposition, displacement, and transformation, of resemblance and dissimulation, of reproduction, duplication and trickery of effect."[6] Thanks to the resourcefulness of artists steeped in what, at the time, were newfangled processes of graphic fabrication and alteration—enhancing photographs with watercolors or pastels, experimenting with the superimposition and manipulation of negatives, photographing paintings, drawings, or sculpture, or developing photographic images directly onto sensitized fabric—pictures of many kinds began to flow freely from one material embodiment to another, slowly liberating themselves from the confines of any one medium such that "no medium, no language, no stable syntax could contain them."[7] That trend only continued to intensify over the course of the twentieth century, as the various visual arts merged progressively onto the larger thoroughfare of transitory images, a crowded highway for the flow of pictures.[8]

One gets the sense in reading Foucault's essay that he is genuinely enthusiastic about the renewed capacity for *all* forms of representation, and not just the visual arts, to experiment with one another. As he celebrates the unhampered flux of visible signs in contemporary culture his inspired call to arms—"let *everyone* join the game of images, and start to play"[9]—gleefully encourages this type of interartistic, transdisciplinary exploration and, as I would suggest, welcomes storytellers to enter the fray.

As we have seen, a number of France's most innovative writers have seemingly taken Foucault's invitation to heart. From Simon's intricately crafted picture puzzle and Perec's equally dizzying trompe l'oeil tale, to Michon's commemorative *tableau vivant* and Viel's verbal appropriation of Mankiewicz's moving picture, the stories these writers tell play "scientifically and pleasurably, in, with, and against the powers of the image."[10] They experiment in various ways with pictures, picturing, and ways of seeing, and envision the complex relationship between the verbal and the visual, and between literature and visual culture, today. They invent new works to look at in our mind's eye, and revive forgotten ones readers might have seen before. They engage with the work of visual artists, critics, and with theories of visual art, proposing their own distinctly literary contribution to art's most influential legacies. And no matter how much the hegemony of the visual continues to grow, narratives that tell stories about pictures inherently acknowledge literature's lasting appeal. A picture may be worth a thousand words, but as the narrator of *La télévision* maintains with a reader's (and a writer's) pride, books are so worthwhile because they "always offer a thousand times more than they are" (95).

Finally and no less importantly, the narratives studied here encourage readers to reconsider the deeper significance of what has become a boundless yet deceptively innocuous propagation of the visual in contemporary society. For isn't the very notion of the "civilization of the image" that I mention in the introduction to this study synonymous with "the process of making images civilized, of reducing them to clichés"?[11] And what is a cliché if not a hackneyed, overused, and overconsumed image, one that remains underestimated? Imagetexts cope with a world in which the circulation of signs is left virtually unchecked by refusing to take the image and its prominence for granted.

This is not to say, of course, that all images have been reduced to mere commonplace. In fact, some pictures are better than others at asserting themselves. Some images more effectively show just how prevailing a force they really are. As Victor Burgin has noted, the stakes for the most prominent and imposing images are certainly high: "No iconoclasm has befallen images; their shattering has left them stronger than when they were whole. Images are now as much a material force in and between societies as are economic and political forces. Contemporary visual culture—the combined product of 'the media' and a variety of other spheres of image production—can no longer be seen as simply 'reflecting' or 'communicating' the world in which we live: it contributes to the making of this world."[12] One has only to think of the heated polemic sparked by the release of recent films such as Mel Gibson's *The Passion of the Christ* (2004) and Michael Moore's *Fahrenheit 9/11* (2004), or of the infamous and highly polemical "Sensation" exhibition of paintings, sculptures, and installations by a group of young British artists at the Brooklyn Museum a decade ago.[13] The same is true of those pictures that perhaps best illustrate the widespread, "worldmaking" potential of visual representations: from the infamous (and infamously controversial) drawings of the prophet Mohammed published by the Danish press in 2005 and the scandalous photographs of prisoner abuse at Iraq's Abu Ghraib prison to the harrowing eyewitness snapshots and videos of the World Trade Center towers under terrorist attack, the last of which are undoubtedly the most traumatic pictures in recent memory. There is no denying that images like these are the antithesis of mere cliché. Their production and dissemination constitute a monumental "event" in its own right.[14]

Still, these pictures seem to be the exception to the rule. For although most images may be noticeable, many are often never quite "seen," since to "see" a picture truly, as I understand it here, is to take the time to acknowledge and internalize its deeper significance. Like Roland Barthes, who writes of scouring a pile of family snapshots in search of one that could capture the essence of his deceased mother, we often recognize subjects in images but it is rare that we find the dissimulated yet "essential" narratives that lie below the surface.[15] Or, as Marianne Hirsch confirms, echoing Barthes, "we see but are unable to look and unable to transform the field of vision into insight and meaning—unable to articulate, in clear terms, the relation between images and words."[16] A better understanding of the conjunction of the verbal and the visual—in works of literature, to be sure, but in other media as well—is thus so important today precisely because the post-9/11 world demands that we learn to read the images we see with more attention and care, and that we become more sensitive to the stories we tell about them.

# Notes

## *Introduction*

1. Stafford, *Good Looking*, 86–87.
2. For an excellent analysis of the relationship between visual spectacle and political clout in seventeenth-century France see Apostolidès, *Le roi machine*. On the spectacular nature of popular visual culture in nineteenth-century France see, among others, Vanessa Schwartz, *Spectacular Realities*; Samuels, *Spectacular Past*; and Crary, *Techniques of the Observer*.
3. de Certeau, *Practice of Everyday Life*, xxi.
4. Barthes, *Camera Lucida*, 119.
5. Hans Belting discusses our contemporary "imagomania" in *L'histoire de l'art: Est-elle finie?*, 68–69. Marjorie Perloff develops the idea of the "videation" of culture in her study *Radical Artifice*, 74. Harold Bloom evokes the "tyranny of the visual" in a culture marked by the decline of the literary in an interview from *The Charlie Rose Show*, WGHB-TV, July 11, 2000 (quoted in Black, *Reality Effect*, 3). Also see Régis Debray on the shift from the *graphosphère* ("period ushered in by the advent of printing") to the *videosphère* ("the hegemony of image-sound"), both of which were preceded by the *logosphère* ("incited by the invention of writing, but in which speech remains the primary means of communication") in Debray, *Introduction à la médiologie*, 42–51. Translation mine.
6. Sontag, "Interview with Gérard Lefort."

7. Barthes, "La civilisation de l'image," in Barthes, *Œuvres complètes I*, 1410–11.
8. See Weber, "Fewer Noses Stuck in Books." This article reports the findings of a 2002 survey conducted by the National Endowment for the Arts entitled "Reading at Risk: A Survey of Literary Reading in America." More recently, a 2008 study by the French market research group TNS-Sofres showed that while the number of regular readers remained stable in France from 1981 to 2008, those readers are reading fewer and fewer books. TNS-Sofres, "Les Français et la lecture."
9. Scarpetta, *L'impureté*, 66. Translation mine.
10. Salvayre, *Contre*, 17. Translation mine.
11. James Elkins has done the most work to expand our understanding of what we mean when we talk about pictures in the graphic sense. See, for example, Elkins, *Domain of Images*.
12. For a fine analysis of this "family tree" of images, see Mitchell, *Iconology*, 9–10.
13. I refer here to curator Douglas Crimp's understanding of the term, which he chose as a title for a 1977 gallery show of work by artists who explore sources from a variety of different media. The word "picture" conveys "not only the work's most salient characteristic—recognizable images—but also and importantly the ambiguities it sustains. As is typical of what has come to be called postmodernism, this new work is not confined to any particular medium. . . . *Picture*, used colloquially, is also nonspecific: a picture book might be a book of drawings or photographs, and in common speech a painting, drawing, or print is often called, simply, a picture." Crimp, "Pictures," 75.
14. See Mongin and Pizoird's interview with de Baecque, "Ce qu'on fait dire aux images." Translation mine.
15. For one of the best-known examples of the new visual semiology of the 1950s see Barthes, *Mythologies*. On the philosophical turn toward visual culture and aesthetics see, among others, Merleau-Ponty, *L'œil et l'esprit*; Marin, *Détruire la peinture*; Rancière, *Le destin des images*; and Nancy, *Au fond*

*des images*. Some of the most popular reflections on photography include Bourdieu, *Un art moyen*; Barthes, *La chambre claire*; and Dubois, *L'acte photographique*. The bibliography of French film criticism and theory is too expansive to address here. See instead Abel's impressive two-volume history *French Film Theory and Criticism*.

16. Daniel Bergez gives readers a good idea of just how many important French writers, following in Diderot's footsteps, regularly wrote art criticism. His nonexhaustive list includes: "Stendhal, Musset, Gautier, Champfleury, les Goncourt, Baudelaire, Zola, Huysmans, Mirbeau, Laforgue, Suarès, Proust, Valéry, Barrès, Apollinaire, Artaud, Breton, Aragon, Malraux, Bataille, Paulhan, Genet, Leiris, Beckett, Ponge, Bonnefoy, Dupin, Pleynet, Noël, Juliet, . . ." (ellipsis mine: the list goes on). Bergez, *Littérature et peinture*, 196.
17. See, to cite one of the most recent and most lavishly illustrated volumes on the subject, *Écrire la peinture*, ed. Dethurens.
18. One might also think of the image of *Christ Walking on Water*, an image that quite tellingly resembles the protagonist of Maupassant's *Bel-Ami* (1885), or Claude Lantier's impressionistic canvases (meant to bring to mind the work of Cézanne) in Zola's *L'œuvre* (1886).
19. For more on the influence of photography on nineteenth-century French literature, see Thélot, *Les inventions littéraires*; Grojnowski, *Photographie et langage*; and Ortel, *La littérature*.
20. Hamon, *Imageries*, 7. Translation mine. Baudelaire mentions French culture's increasingly expanding archive of images in his *Salon de 1959*. Quoted in Hamon, *Imageries*, 8. Translation mine.
21. See, most notably, Blaise Cendrars's *Les Confessions de Dan Yack* (1927) and *Le plan de l'aiguille* (1927), Paul Morand's *France-la-Doulce* (1934), and Raymond Queneau's *Loin de Rueil* (1944), each of which explores, in very different ways, the nature of moviemaking and the ways that film represents the world.

22. One might add to this (very abridged) list other works of fiction that engage extensively with pictures or take the image as theme: for example, Patrick Deville's *Longue vue* (1988), François Bon's *Calvaire de chiens* (1990), Marie Redonnet's *Candy Story* (1992), Patrick Modiano's *Chien de printemps* (1997), and Pierre Assouline's *Le portrait* (2007).
23. Mitchell, *Picture Theory*, 109. Similarly, Peter Wagner theorizes the "iconotext" as "an artifact in which the verbal and the visual signs mingle to produce rhetoric that depends on the co-presence of words and images." See Wagner, "Ekphrasis, Iconotexts, and Intermediality," 16. On less substantial uses of pictures in fiction, see Torgovnick, *Visual Arts*. For Torgovnick, purely decorative use of the visual arts occupies the lowest place on the "continuum of degree." It "sends us to another discipline, but not for long. It asks us to think about the visual arts, but not too hard" (17).
24. Vouilloux, *La peinture dans le texte*, 17. Vouilloux opposes the "homoplasmic" text—in which the "verbal substance" of the text refers to another form (like a visual representation)—to the "heteroplasmic," in which the image is visible alongside the words on the printed page.
25. Although there are a number of varied approaches to the notion of *ekphrasis*, and while recent attempts have been made to expand its reach to include descriptions of other visual forms (and not simply works of art), I rely here on James Heffernan's most succinct formulation. Heffernan's conceptualization of *ekphrasis* distinguishes it from two other modes with which it is often confused: namely pictorialism, where language creates effects similar to those created by pictures, and iconicity, when words and letters on a page are arranged to resemble what they signify (as in a "calligrammatic" poem for example). See Heffernan, *Museum of Words*, 3. For a more expanded definition of the term see Krieger, *Ekphrasis: Illusion*.
26. Mitchell, *Picture Theory*, 11–13.
27. For a concise synthesis of this return to aesthetics in French thought of the 1990s, see Samuels, "Aesthetic Theories."

Also see the special issue of the *Magazine littéraire* devoted to "Philosophie et art: La fin de l'esthétique?" no. 414 (November 2002), which includes articles by such notable thinkers as Jacques Rancière, Alain Badiou, and Jean-Marie Schaeffer.

28. Mitchell, *Picture Theory*, 16.
29. As Stephen Cheeke argues, writing the image, whether in poetry or prose, is as much a critical and revelatory act as it is a creative one. See his *Writing for Art*, 185–86.
30. See Bal, *Reading Rembrandt*, 4–5.
31. A word about terminology: While the bulk of the images that I engage in the chapters to follow can be classified as visual art (photographs, paintings, films), as I understand it the visual arts belong to the larger field of visual culture, a field that, as Nicholas Mirzoeff posits, includes a variety of forms destined to be looked at, from oil painting and sculpture to "new media" like television and the Internet. I argue throughout *Pictures into Words* that the way writers treat the visual arts in the texts that I study hints at larger questions about the role that pictures—in the more general sense that is encompassed by a more expansive term like "visual culture"—play in our society today. See Mirzoeff, *Visual Culture*, 3.
32. Patt, "Introduction," in *Searching for Sebald*, ed. Patt, 85n218.
33. Mitchell, *Picture Theory*, 210.
34. I borrow the notion of "flatness" from Thomas Friedman's bestselling book on globalization, *The World Is Flat*.
35. Stafford, *Good Looking*, 11.
36. "More than ever we distrust the unaided eye, which has been dizzied by regimens of pain relievers, antidepressants, reducing pills, low-calorie fasts, to say nothing of intoxicants and hallucinogens. As glasses (and sunglasses) have become fashion accessories, make-up 'corrective,' and dressing (for success) illusionary, the Cold War, the Vietnam War, the Afghan War, the 'War on Drugs,' the wars in the streets of Los Angeles and Sarajevo have seemed to demand an optic of surveillance through shatterproof lenses. The assisted eye

of the late twentieth century has been an eye on the defensive, protecting from nuclear missiles, subversives, guerillas, or from rapists, snipers, ultraviolence, ultraviolet. We watch our backs with rearview mirrors, our storefronts with parabolic mirrors, our prisoners through one-way mirrors." Hillel Schwartz, *Culture of the Copy*, 207.

37. Virilio, *Vision Machine*, 75.
38. Jay, *Downcast Eyes*, 14.
39. In her aptly titled *Good Looking*, cited above, Barbara Stafford offers a compelling alternative to the kind of antivisual thinking that Jay's book examines. Aiming to counter discourses that elicit the treacherous nature of images and condemn modern vision's inability to "see" through them, she argues instead for a renewed faith in "good images" and "good looking." Against a spate of recent iconoclastic claims that "images do only destructive work within our institutions," Stafford suggests that "images should be freed from the idealist identification with trompe l'oeil, the contemptuous judgment that they always pretend to fool the viewer into thinking that unreal things are real." See, especially, her "Introduction: Visual Pragmatism for a Virtual World," *Good Looking*, 2–17. Stafford's critique of Jay lies in what she feels is the "cursory and derivative" treatment, in *Downcast Eyes*, of earlier manifestations of antivisual thinking, especially in the eighteenth century. Stafford discusses this "prehistory" of Jay's modern and postmodern "antiocularcentrism" more extensively in her *Artful Science*. Finally, although Jay does suggest that the "antiocularcentric" phenomenon is most prevalent in contemporary France, he does, to his credit, maintain that "other examples of a similar attitude will no doubt occur to readers familiar with different national traditions." Jay, *Downcast Eyes*, 14n72.
40. Torgovnick, *Visual Arts*, 214.
41. Meltzer, *Salome*, 1.
42. The specific struggle for aesthetic primacy between painting and poetry, Jean Hagstrum explains, was rooted in a sociological distinction: until the time of Leonardo, Raphael, and

Michelangelo, painting and sculpture were considered purely mechanical arts, while poetry, although not much better off, had at least "come into the curriculum [of the 'liberal arts'] through the door of rhetoric and logic and had never suffered from the stigma that its practitioner dirtied his hands in physical labor." In time, however, poetry would be relegated to the position of a schoolboy destined to learn from the more accomplished master. Hagstrum, *Sister Arts*, 67. For a more extensive history of the origins of the *paragone*, see Fallay d'Este's introduction in *Le paragone*, 10–48.

43. Poster, *Cultural History*, 39.
44. Debray, *Introduction à la médiologie*, 51. Translation mine.
45. Adair, "Umberto E.," 40.
46. Vidal, "French Letters," 70.
47. Cited in McShine, *Andy Warhol*, 463.
48. Paul Virilio explains this phenomenon by pointing to a "defect" in literature, noting that "its images don't constitute figures. And the decline of writing comes principally from the fact that graphic, photographic and videographic images have replaced mental images." Virilio, "Interview with Jérôme Sans," 118.
49. Franzen, "Reader in Exile," 165. The assassin to whom Franzen is referring is the furry (and purple) dinosaur host of a popular children's television program.
50. Indeed, as art historian Marc Jiminez has recently proposed, the culture of the image has ultimately proven more democratic than dictatorial: "The civilization of the image has not killed the civilization of the text. Images, including contemporary art works, as fascinating, seductive, or atrocious as they may be, leave traces that, still, turn to language to develop and help constitute the relationship between the original and its copy, reality and fiction, truth and illusion . . . so that we can stop being fooled by their power and, especially, by the power of those who create them and impose them upon us." Jiminez, *Regards sur l'image*, 8. Translation mine.
51. See, for example, Stephens, *Rise of the Image*.

## 1. Puzzling Pictures

1. See Genette, *Figures III*, 185.
2. Saïd, *World, Text, Critic*, 101.
3. Nicolas Poussin, *Blind Orion in Search of the Rising Sun*, 1658. Oil on canvas. 46 7/8 x 72 in. (119.1 x 182.9 cm). The Metropolitan Museum of Art, New York.
4. Duverlie and Simon, "Interview," 52.
5. Simon, "Preface," *Orion aveugle*, unpaginated. *Orion aveugle* was published in a series called "Les sentiers de la création" ("Pathways to Creation") that included works mixing text and image by a number of well-known artists and writers like Miró, Butor, Le Clézio, and Dubuffet, among others. Translation mine.
6. Britton, *Simon: Writing the Visible*, 4.
7. Simon, *Triptyque*. Citations refer to the English translation, *Triptych*. Simon's multifaceted engagement with the visual arts has been addressed by a number of critics. Many of these include extensive analyses of the role of visual culture in *Triptyque*, in particular. See, for example, Sykes, *Les romans de Claude Simon*; Loubère, *Novels of Claude Simon*; Evans, *Simon and Transgressions*; Duffy, *Reading between the Lines*; and Ferrato-Combe, *Écrire en peintre*.
8. Simon is very forthcoming with respect to the generative role that Francis Bacon, Jean Dubuffet, and Paul Delvaux play in the text. See, for example, Goux and Poirson, "Un homme traversé par le travail," 40.
9. A fourth, secondary narrative sequence—in which a circus clown and his partners perform under a Big Top filled with spectators—is also woven into the fabric of the novel. For Michael Evans, this sequence suggests the virtual impossibility of locating any firm point of stability or fixity in the text. Evans, *Simon and Transgressions*, 198–200.
10. I borrow this concept from Jean-Louis Hippolyte's study of ambiguity in contemporary French literature, *Fuzzy Fiction*. Hippolyte locates the birth of modern, fuzzy fiction with the publication of Claude Ollier's deliberately vague and uncertain *Fuzzy Sets* in 1975, just two years after the release of *Triptyque*.

11. Foster, "Postmodernism: A Preface," xii.
12. For an excellent survey of this powerful epistemic and aesthetic shift, see Best and Kellner, *Postmodern Turn*. Additionally, Ihab Hassan usefully enumerates some of the major figures on the cultural stage (including writers, visual artists, choreographers, philosophers, cultural critics, political philosophers, musicians, and architects) who helped usher in these changes. In Hassan, *Postmodern Turn: Essays*, 85.
13. Not only did Simon train formally as a painter, studying under André Lhote in his twenties, throughout his career he entertained personal contacts with such luminaries as Raoul Dufy, Pierre Soulages, and perhaps most importantly, Jean Dubuffet. Beginning with a letter that the painter addressed to the author after the publication of *Orion aveugle* in 1970, the two entered into a period of fruitful correspondence that lasted fourteen years. See Simon and Dubuffet, *Correspondance*.
14. See, for example, the reproductions of manuscript pages from *La bataille de Pharsale* in Dällenbach, *Claude Simon*, 26 and 68.
15. Whereas the first, *Album d'un amateur*, mixes short, descriptive texts with both color and black and white photographs taken over the years in locations around the world—including Russia, India, Japan, Mexico and the United States—the second, *Photographies: 1937–1970*, save for a brief preface, lets the pictures speak for themselves.
16. Simon was not completely satisfied with the way this project turned out. Letters to the production staff and director suggest that his directives to ensure the film's fidelity to the text were not followed as closely as he would have liked. See Calle-Gruber, ed., *Les triptyques*, 57–88 especially.
17. Dällenbach, *Claude Simon*, 203n39. Translation mine.
18. Dällenbach, *Claude Simon*, 48. Translation mine.
19. For an analysis of Simon's decidedly complex relationship to photography, see Glacet, *Claude Simon chronophotographe*.
20. While this is most characteristic of the novels Simon produced during the early 1970s, a major aspect of the author's

literary project involves elevating the status of the descriptive from its auxiliary role as subservient to the development of action. See his discussion of Tynianov's hypothesis that literary fiction might be considered a pretext for the accumulation of descriptions in *Discours de Stockholm*, 16.

21. Simon, *Discours de Stockholm*, 27. Translation mine.
22. See Lessing, *Laocoön*.
23. Frank, *Idea of Spatial Form*.
24. The expression is attributed to Jacques Lacan. See Simon's discussion in "La fiction mot à mot," 73.
25. Simon, "La fiction mot à mot." Translation mine.
26. Neumann, *Échos et correspondances*, 11.
27. From the interview from 1979 with Jean-Maurice de Montrémy in *La croix. L'événement*, October 18, 1985. Cited in Ferrato-Combe, *Écrire en peintre*, 33. Translation mine.
28. For D. N. Rodowick, the "figural defines a semiotic regime where the ontological distinction between linguistic and plastic representations breaks down." Rodowick's discussion of the "figural," though centered on ways electronic and new media resist the classic opposition between the verbal and the visual, seems especially relevant to *Tryptique*. Rodowick, *Reading the Figural*, 2.
29. Baxandall, *Patterns of Intention*, 3.
30. Simon is clearly aware of the distinction, as his comment on a particular passage from Stendhal makes clear. As Simon tells it, while writing *Vie de Henry Brulard*, Stendhal could not remember whether he was actually a participant in a particular event described in the text or whether he had simply confused reality with the same event as it appeared in an engraving with which he was familiar. For Simon, what Stendhal fails to have realized is that "he was not describing the engraving, but the image that he had constructed of it." Simon, *Discours de Stockholm*, 26. Translation mine.
31. As Gérard Genette suggests, even in the most seemingly objective of texts, a speaker's voice always remains implicitly present in the background. See Genette, *Figures II*, 65.
32. Pugh, "Interview with Claude Simon," 8.

33. "I write my books as one would make a painting. Every painting is at first a composition." Simon and Piatier, "Entretien." Translation mine.
34. Duffy, *Reading Between the Lines*, 115.
35. Duffy, *Reading Between the Lines*, 128. Simon has remarked, in particular, that Bacon's *Lying Figure* (1969) was significant in this regard. See Duverlie and Simon, "Interview," 53.
36. Mougin, *L'effet d'image*.
37. Louvel, *L'œil du texte*, especially chapter 4, "La description 'picturale': pour une poétique de l'iconotexte."
38. Cited in Lotringer, *Claude Simon: Analyse, théorie*, 427. Translation mine.
39. Simon, *Discours de Stockholm*, 22.
40. Gandelman, *Le regard dans le texte*, 17.
41. The reference is to Jean Dubuffet, who likened *Triptyque* to a "Persian rug": "This is a book that one cannot read, if to read is to begin on the first page and end on the last. Here, one does not finish. . . . One can read it just as well from the end to the beginning." Dubuffet, "A propos de *Triptyque*, 1149. Translation mine.
42. Writing in *Le Monde*, Jacqueline Piatier comments on becoming lost in the text: "Where are we then? Meticulously, every reference to an ostensibly real world is destroyed the moment you begin to notice it." In Calle-Gruber, *Les triptyques de Claude Simon*, 60. Translation mine.
43. Whereas Stuart Sykes wonders whether the drowning actually occurs—"a young girl, abandoned by her babysitter who left to join her lover in a neighboring bar, drowns (?) in the river" (Sykes, *Les romans de Claude Simon*, 169)—Andrea Goulet points out that, despite its status as a disnarrated scene, traces of the little girl's drowning are implicit on the level of the text. She goes on to read this omission as a "narrative blind spot" that occurs as a result of the text's deliberate blurring of the mimetic and "anti-mimetic" functions. See Goulet, "Blind Spots and Afterimages." For his part, Ralph Sarkonak refers to the little girl's death by drowning—subtly suggested, he argues, by a network of implicit echoes

scattered throughout the text—as a crucial "unsaid" (or *non-dit*). Sarkonak, "Comment noyer le poisson."

44. See, for example, Sherzer, *Representation*, 25–31, and Neumann, *Échos et correspondances*, 30–31. Others have sought to reconstruct precise schemata that locate each picture and the sequences that they place *en abyme*. See, for example, Evans, *Simon and Transgressions*, 191–207, as well as Lotringer, "Cryptique." Still, other critics hesitate with regard to what, exactly, occurs. J. A. E. Loubère, for example, peppers her description of the urban sequence with a series of ambiguous verbs and modifiers that keep readers wondering: "The man of the pair appears to be the bridegroom. . . . The woman of the night couple seems to be the barmaid. . . . Her companion, perhaps the man who appears in some of the stills." See Loubère, *Novels of Claude Simon*, 203.
45. Michael Evans, *Simon and Transgressions*, 207. For Evans, the consistent shifting between the three narrative strands suggests another implicit structuring metaphor: namely, the Moebius strip.
46. See Jean Baudrillard's 1976 essay, "The Hyper-realism of Simulation," 1019. In the 1980s, Baudrillard's take on the "hyperreal" would become less pessimistic as he "stopped worrying" and began instead to "giddily embrace" the notion of a world populated by images without referents. Martin Jay, *Downcast Eyes*, 433.
47. Alistair Duncan calls *Triptyque* and *Leçon des choses* "the most formalist of the reputedly formalist novels." In Duncan, *Simon: Adventures in Words*, 119.
48. Lynn Higgins points out that with the period of formalist experimentation in the 1970s, Simon "left historical topics for a short while." Higgins, *New Novel, New Wave, New Politics*, 215.
49. Loubère, *Novels of Claude Simon*, 227.
50. Britton, *Writing the Visible*, 16. That said, the "pastoral" setting in *Triptyque* might constitute a memory from the author's past: Simon has mentioned that his vision of the landscape was inspired by childhood vacations to the commune of Les Planches-près-Arbois in eastern France. See Calle-

Gruber, *Les triptyques*, 42. Scenes for the German film adaptation of *Triptyque* that correspond with the pastoral sequence were filmed in Les Planches.

51. Jameson, *Postmodernism*, 141.
52. Guy Neumann notes that most criticism from the 1970s and 1980s approached *Triptyque* on a purely textual level. See Neumann, *Échos et correspondances*, 13. Ralph Sarkonak sees this as a logical trend, especially given the context: "At the time, the concept of depth was much maligned. . . . The text was a machine whose very functionality was ripe for study." In "Comment noyer le poisson," 38–39. Translation mine.
53. Clement Greenberg, "Modernist Painting," in Greenberg, *Collected Essays and Criticism*, 4:85–86.
54. Greenberg, "The New Sculpture," in Greenberg, *Collected Essays and Criticism*, 2:317.
55. Greenberg, "Sculpture in Our Time," *Collected Essays and Criticism*, 4:60.
56. One of the most striking accounts of this effect of painting on the beholder's body is Diderot's celebrated critique of Joseph Vernet's landscapes at the *Salon de 1767*. In this, one of the earliest works of modern art criticism, the author explores the surfaces of the paintings from the inside, as he is mystically transported into the frame, sharing the space with the figures depicted within. Denis Diderot, *Œuvres complètes*, vol. 16.
57. The aftershocks of Greenberg's influence were felt well into the 1960s, most notably in the work of critics schooled in a similar kind of formalism. See, for example, Fried, "Art and Objecthood."
58. Wallis, "What's Wrong with this Picture?," xiii.
59. Krauss, "Sculpture in the Expanded Field," 41.
60. Krauss, "Rauschenberg and the Materialized Image," 40.
61. Both a detail from *Charlene* (1954) and a photograph of a piece entitled *Canyon* (1959) are reproduced in *Orion aveugle*. A detail from *Charlene* serves, notably, as a backdrop for the inside title page.

62. Simon, "La fiction mot à mot," 87.

63. While Claud Duverlie argues that Rauschenberg's painting organizes the forms and structures of *Les corps conducteurs*, Jean Duffy's careful comparison of image and text confirms that the painting is also responsible for generating many of the narrative's words and themes. See Duverlie and Simon, "Pictures for Writing," and Duffy, *Reading*.

64. Simon, "Parenthèse." The text is an excerpt from an unpublished Simon work entitled *Complément d'information*.

65. From an interview with Lucien Dällenbach in Dällenbach, *Claude Simon*, 180–81. Translation mine.

66. Gopnik and Varnedoe, *High and Low*, 94.

67. Duffy, "Artistic Biographies," 175.

68. It is no wonder, then, that the German producers of the short cinematographic adaptation of *Triptyque* chose to call their film *Die Sackgasse*, or *L'impasse* in French.

69. In Dällenbach, *Claude Simon*, 180. Translation mine.

70. Krauss, "Rauschenberg and the Materialized Image," 43.

71. In Lotringer, *Claude Simon: Analyse, théorie*, 420. Translation mine.

72. See Ferrato-Combe, *Écrire en peintre*, Duffy, *Reading Between the Lines*, and Duverlie and Simon, "Pictures for Writing."

73. Rauschenberg is cited in Joseph, "A Duplication Containing Duplications," 133.

74. See Krauss, *Voyage on the North Sea*.

75. Krauss, "Sculpture in the Expanded Field," 38.

76. Loubère, *Novels of Claude Simon*, 220.

77. Joseph Conrad, *Nigger of the Narcissus*, 141.

## 2. *Faking It (Phony Pictures)*

1. Perec, *Un cabinet d'amateur*. Citations from the text refer to the English translation: Perec, *A Gallery Portrait*, in *Three by Perec*.

2. Throughout this chapter, for lack of a better word, I refer to Perec's text as a novel (albeit a short one). There is, however, no specific paratextual marker that designates it as such.

3. As he noted in a 1980 radio interview, Perec set out to encrypt elements from each chapter of *La vie mode d'emploi* within each of the paintings described in *Un cabinet d'amateur*. For more on *La vie mode d'emploi* as intratextual source material for *Un Cabinet d'amateur* see van Montfrans, *Perec: La contrainte du réel*, chapter 7 especially. See also Rosienski-Pellerin, *PERECgrinations ludiques*.
4. In an essay from 1967 on "Writing and Mass Media," Perec considers the generally harmful effects of new, primarily visual forms like television, comics, film, and advertising for the status of "classic" art. "Écriture et mass-media," *Preuves* 202 (December 1967), in *Perec: Entretiens et conférences*, 1:95. Translation for this and all subsequent citations from this collection are mine.
5. Manet van Montfrans has shown that Perec most probably modeled his own *Kunstkammer* painting on *Le cabinet d'amateur de Corneille van der Geest lors de la Visite des Archiducs* (1628) by the Dutch artist Guillaume van Haecht. Perec owned a Ravensburger puzzle (3000 pieces) that depicted this very painting. Van Montfrans, *Perec: La contrainte du réel*, 294. Van Montfrans has also shown how the exact number of paintings represented in Raffke's collection is not, in fact, one hundred (by his count, there are ninety-five or ninety-seven in total, depending on whether or not one considers the two German still-life paintings mentioned in the first part of the narrative, but perhaps not reproduced in Kürz's canvas). See van Montfrans, 331.
6. As the narrator clarifies, this kind of infinite regression only gives the impression that it continues indefinitely. The most scrupulous of viewers are able to make out eight successive generations of the painting within the painting, the last copy appearing as a minuscule smudge (21).
7. While the narrative's English translation privileges the term "story," as Gérard Genette notes, the term *Histoire de*, as it is employed in a title or subtitle, is inherently ambiguous since it designates "at once the object of an enunciation as well as the enunciation itself." Genette, *Seuils*, 84. Translation mine.

8. Quoted in *Perec: Entretiens et conférences*, 1:247.
9. Massumi, "Realer than Real."
10. Matthieu Lindon, in a catalogue copy for *Un Cabinet d'amateur*'s second printing. Quoted in Rosienski-Pellerin, *PERECgrinations ludiques*, 78. Translation mine.
11. Georges Perec, "Species of Spaces," 39.
12. "With respect to the work which can serve as a ground for it, [the parergonal frame] merges into the wall, and then, gradually, into the general text. With respect to the background which the general text is, it merges into the work which stands out against the general background." Derrida, *Truth in Painting*, 61.
13. Perec, "Ceci n'est pas un mur." All translations are mine.
14. Perec, "Ceci n'est pas un mur," unpaginated.
15. Perec, "Ceci n'est pas un mur," unpaginated.
16. Perec, "Ceci n'est pas un mur," unpaginated.
17. Camille, "Simulacrum," 35.
18. Massumi, "Realer than Real."
19. Milman, *Le trompe-l'œil*, 7.
20. Marin, "Representation and Simulacrum," 315.
21. "In *Un cabinet d'amateur*, one could not represent the painting. Though one could certainly describe it." Perec, "Entretien Georges Perec/Bernard Pous," in *Perec: Entretiens et conferences*, 2:194.
22. I refer here to what is perhaps the earliest recorded example of the power of the simulacrum to seduce its beholder. In this anecdote, which Pliny the Elder recounts in his *Natural History*, Parrhasios challenges Zeuxis, one of Ancient Greece's most successful artists, to a painterly battle of imitation. Zeuxis responds with an image of grapes so lifelike that a group of hungry birds hovering in its vicinity approaches the canvas for a bite. Parrhasios, on the other hand, presents a painting of a curtain so realistic that Zeuxis asks him to move it aside and reveal the painting that lies underneath. In Pliny the Elder, *L'histoire naturelle*, 352–53.
23. Perec's earliest, unpublished novel, *Le condottiere*, is the story of a forger (Gaspard Winckler) who attempts to cre-

ate a false painting in the style of Antonello da Messina. When his attempt ends in failure, Winckler decides to murder the person who initially commissioned the painting. References and allusions to the portrait will reappear in later texts including *Un homme qui dort* (1967), *W ou le souvenir d'enfance* (1975), and *La vie mode d'emploi* (1978). For a survey of other instances of the fake in Perec's corpus see Bénabou, "Faux et usage de faux."

24. Perec and Burgelin, "Le nouveau roman et le refus du réel," in *L. G.* Translation mine.
25. From the editorial of the journal's first issue, published in May, 1972. Reprinted in Perec, *Perec: Entretiens et conférences*, 1:133.
26. Perec, *Perec: Entretiens et conférences*, 1:37.
27. Perec, *Perec: Entretiens et conférences*, 1:56.
28. See, for example, his comments in "Notes sur ce que je cherche."
29. Kofman, *Camera Obscura* 4.
30. Perec, "Pour une littérature réaliste," in *L. G.*, 63.
31. Durham, *Phantom Communities*, 20. As Deleuze writes, "It is not in the great forest and woodpaths that philosophy is elaborated, but rather in the towns and in the streets—even in the most artificial in them." Deleuze, "Plato and the Simulacrum," 265.
32. Perec, "Pour une littérature réaliste," 65.
33. Plato, *Republic*, 330.
34. Plato, *Republic*, 331.
35. "Through his doublings and multiplications, the mimetic artist introduces 'improprieties' (a 'poison') into a social system ordered according to the rule that everything and everyone should be in its/his/her 'proper' place. . . . In brief, mimesis is excommunicated not because it is a threat to truth, but because it is a threat to order." Prendergast, *Order of Mimesis*, 9.
36. Deleuze, "Plato and the Simulacrum," 262.
37. Deleuze, "Plato and the Simulacrum," 263.
38. Camille, "Simulacrum," 31–44.

39. "Each time one wants to rigidly adhere to a system, there is something that gets stuck. In order to function freely within that system, then, one has to voluntarily introduce a minor error. Klee's idea is well known: 'Genius is an error in the system.'" Cited from an interview with Jean-Jacques Brochier in *Perec: Entretiens et conférences*, 1:240–41.
40. The novel, structured according to a knight's tour through every square on a 10x10 chessboard, only comprises ninety-nine chapters when, logically, it should comprise one hundred.
41. Camille, "Simulacrum," 40.
42. Perec, "Ceci n'est pas un mur," unpaginated.
43. I borrow the expression *détrompe-l'œil* from the artist Daniel Spoerri. Usually associated with the French *nouveau réalisme* of the 1960s, Spoerri's work subverts the illusionist quality of painting by presenting, rather than representing, the real. In certain pieces the artist affixes real objects (leaves, toy dolls, water faucets) to the canvas so that they interact with the pictorial composition, all the while providing a third dimension that the spectator could quite easily reach out and touch.
44. As Perec remarked, speaking of *La vie mode d'emploi* in 1978, "I am inspired by what we call hyperrealism." Perec, *Perec: Entretiens et conférences*, 1:219. In a later interview from 1981 he notes, "If there is an image that truly speaks to me, it would be hyperrealist painting, where the accumulation of details renders the object completely dreamlike. It's an unreal sort of reality." In *Perec: Entretiens et conférences*, 2:189.
45. Along with Deleuze, whose contributions to the debate were discussed earlier, see, for example, Jean Baudrillard's 1976 essay "The Hyper-realism of Simulation," 1018–20; Foucault, *This Is Not a Pipe*; and, later, Marin, "Representation and Simulacrum," 315.
46. The primary motivation driving Hebborn's crusade is subversive, to say the least. His work proudly aims to assault "those vulgar, avaricious creatures with good backgrounds, smart accents, fine educations and infinite pretensions, who control

the art trade from the top and for whom a work of art is as good or bad as the amount it fetches." Cited in Landesman, "A Crisis of Fakes." Throughout his life Hebborn was self-conscious about his working-class background and relative lack of education, and took pride in the success with which he was able to fool those with years of academic training. Ultimately, Hebborn went so far as to publish a how-to guide to forgery—*The Art Forger's Handbook* (London: Cassell, 1997)—in which he aimed to prove that anyone with a little patience and a bit of technical skill could craft a modest fake. The guide's publication, however, was not popular with everyone; shortly after the book's Italian release Hebborn was found murdered in a park near his home in Rome. The perpetrators of this crime were never found.

47. Van Meegeren's paintings are true simulacra in the sense that they do not copy authentic works by great masters. Rather, the works for which he was tried are paintings that could pass for Vermeer originals. They are, in other words, copies without explicit models.

48. As David Bellos points out, during the year Perec spent at the Lycée Henri-IV—where he was assigned an oral presentation on André Gide's 1925 novel *The Counterfeiters*—the Paris Museum of Fakes exhibited a selection of van Meegeren forgeries. Cited in Bénabou, "Faux et usage de faux," 27. For a more complete account of van Meegeren's career see Lopez, *Man Who Made Vermeers*.

49. Irving, *Fake!*.

50. Burgelin, *Les parties de dominos*, 199. See also Mazzorato, "*Citizen Kane*," and van Montfrans, *Perec: La contrainte du réel*, 194–95. Coincidentally, like *Un cabinet d'amateur* for Perec, *F for Fake* was the last work Welles completed before his own death.

51. The lives of both forgers were destined to end dramatically. Kürz, as we learn, suddenly disappeared in a Long Island Rail Road accident that killed twenty-three people on August 12, 1914. De Hory is rumored to have committed suicide in 1976.

52. Tiphaine Samoyault cleverly notes that the name "Raffke" might allude directly to *F for Fake* in that the letters can be rearranged to spell "faker," with an extra "f" left over for good measure. Samoyault, "Le collectionneur," 96.
53. In this way, the film occupies a space opposite an earlier, incomplete film, *It's All True* (1941), which blends fictional scenes with documentary footage from a trip to Brazil.
54. Deleuze, *Cinema* 2, 147–55. For Deleuze, Welles's film is illustrative of the new kind of cinema, developed around the 1960s, which dismantles the classic relationship between the virtual and the real.
55. Koos, "Abysmal Play," 79–80. These narrative "cracks" have much in common with the visual "cracks" which appear in several of the trompe l'oeil facades that Cuchi White photographed and published in *L'œil ébloui*. In figure 8 in that book in a London façade painted by Ken White, one of the simulated windows has shattered, revealing the layer of brick that lies underneath and exposing the painting as a trompe l'oeil. Upon closer inspection, however, we realize that the brick is itself painted; the artist has simulated a second layer of simulation underneath. Perec's hyperrealist poetics function in much the same way.
56. The name "Kleidröst," as certain critics have remarked, alludes, in French, to a certain robe-grille, or "Robbe-Grillet." See, for example, Rosienski-Pellerin, *PERECgrinations ludiques*, 116.
57. Perec, "Ceci n'est pas un mur," unpaginated (emphasis mine).
58. Perec, "Ceci n'est pas un mur," unpaginated.
59. Perec, "Ceci n'est pas un mur," unpaginated.
60. Welles is citing Rudyard Kipling. See "The Conundrum of the Workshops," Kipling, *Complete Verse*, 272.
61. Buchloch, "Andy Warhol Line," 66.
62. Danto, *Transfiguration of the Commonplace*, 56.
63. Danto, *Beyond the Brillo Box*, 53.
64. See, for example, Herwitz, *Making Theory, Constructing Art*, especially chapter 1, "Setting the Stage: Arthur Danto's Reading of the Avant-Garde," 25–32. Herwitz neatly poses the

question that Danto avoids: "If Warhol's primary reason in making these boxes was to stimulate the thought that they are (really) identical to ordinary ones, differing only by their presence in the gallery and a theory to back them up, why did he make them oversize, why do they look both painted and mass produced, what is the reason for their comedy?" That said, however, there are two points to be made in defense of Danto's claims. For one, it seems that critics of his particular reading of Warhol rely on the idea—or the misconception, depending on one's point of view—that vision is objective. As I mention above, the differences between a real Brillo box and a Warhol simulacrum may be visible, but only to those who choose to look for them. Danto, like the more easily fooled readers of Perec's novel, was himself duped by the illusion, at least for a moment or two. And it is precisely at this moment, when those distinctions between the art object and the "real thing" it represents are indiscernible, that what Danto would refer to as the deeper philosophical implications of Warhol's work begin to crystallize. Whether or not viewers pick up on the differences later on does not, therefore, render Danto's argument null and void. Secondly, although Danto does ultimately elide the inevitable differences between the industrial boxes and Warhol's copy without much discussion, he does, all the same, acknowledge their existence. He admits, albeit sheepishly, that certain viewers might see through the trompe l'oeil illusion and notice that, although it may look like it, Warhol's *Brillo Box* is not a "real" Brillo box after all. Yet, as he writes, "the differences surely cannot constitute the difference between art and reality" (*Beyond the Brillo Box*, 7).

65. Danto, *Beyond the Brillo Box*, 7.
66. Deleuze, "Plato and the Simulacrum," 262.
67. Danto, *After the End of Art*, 125.
68. Perec, "Ceci n'est pas un mur," unpaginated.
69. Duchamp's 1921 readymade entitled *Why Not Sneeze Rose Sélavy* consisted of a birdcage containing, among other things, marble cubes shaped to look like sugar. The Boltanski

reference is to a work from 1969 entitled *Recherche et présentation de tout ce qui reste de mon enfance*. Boltanski's art, particularly his interest in the relationship between memory, photography, and the Holocaust, resonates with Perec's own artistic project, and the two frequently refer to each other's work. See, for example, Pô, "Perec et Boltanski."

70. Danto, *Beyond the Brillo Box*, 5.
71. See Clark, *Farewell to an Idea*, 2–13.
72. Danto, *After the End of Art*, 125.
73. Danto, *Beyond the Brillo Box*, 9.
74. Whereas Danto locates the beginning of the end in Warhol, Nowak's own theorization of art in the posthistorical era emerges earlier with a painting that was exhibited in 1913. Perhaps not inconsequentially, this was the year in which Marcel Duchamp's cubist-inspired work *Nude Descending a Staircase* scandalized viewers when it was displayed at the Armory show in New York.
75. Perec, *Perec: Entretiens et conférences*, 2:330. Translation mine.

### 3. *Tableau vivant*

1. Michon, *Vie de Joseph Roulin*. References and all citations refer to Wyatt Alexander Mason's translation, *The Life of Joseph Roulin*, published along with the three narratives that comprise Michon's *Maîtres et serviteurs*, in *Masters and Servants*, 3–51. References in the text to citations from *The Life of Joseph Roulin* are made parenthetically (JR).
2. In the first (and largest) portrait he made of Roulin in the summer of 1888 (see image 5) van Gogh depicts Roulin seated at a table against a light blue wall. With time subsequent portraits would become more complex, the backgrounds more intricate and stylized.
3. I use the term "novella" here for lack of a better term. Along with "short novel" (*roman court*), Michon occasionally refers to his texts as *récits*, which I translate as "narrative" and privilege throughout this chapter. See Michon, *Le roi vient*, 23–24. This and all subsequent translations from this text are mine. References in the text to citations from *Le roi vient* are

made parenthetically (RV). For a survey of attempts to classify and categorize the generic specificity of Michon's work, see Crowley, *Michon: Afterlife of Names*, 155–59.

4. On the significance of Saints' Lives as a model for the kind of fictionalized biography that Michon practices throughout his corpus, see Jefferson, "Pierre Michon's Lives of the Saints," in *Biography*, 333–51.
5. The significance of the image of Roulin for art history, on the other hand, has not been lost on scholars and curators of van Gogh's work. Curator Kirk Varnedoe's 2001 exhibition at the New York Museum of Modern Art, Van Gogh's Postman: The Portraits of Joseph Roulin, was the first exhibit to focus exclusively on the impact of Roulin on van Gogh's life and art. See Varnedoe, "Joseph Roulin."
6. Demanze, "Les illustres et le minuscules," 244. Translation mine.
7. Some of the museums worldwide that house portraits of Roulin and other members of his family include the New York Museum of Modern Art, The Metropolitan Museum, the Winterthur Kunstmuseum in Switzerland, the Boston Museum of Fine Arts, the Detroit Institute of the Arts, the São Paulo Museum of Art in Brazil, the Barnes Foundation outside Philadelphia, and the Van Gogh Museum in Amsterdam.
8. Sylviane Coyault-Dublanchet rightly points out that Michon's work is comprised as much of "minuscule deaths." The passing of each character that is charted, or at the very least mentioned in each story is what makes the hagiographic aspect of his texts possible. See Coyault-Dublanchet, *La province en heritage*, 194.
9. Mitchell, *Picture Theory*, 109.
10. Pouilloux, "Une prose de voyant," 866.
11. Van Gogh, in a letter to his sister Willemien, June 5, 1980. The citation appears on the back cover of the Verdier edition of *Vie de Joseph Roulin*, in a short text that elucidates the larger stakes of Michon's project.
12. For example, the narrator describes Roulin as *fort en gueule*

*et bon bougre* (10, in the French edition) ["a big talker, voluble and occasionally profane" (6)], while van Gogh is often referred to as the *rouquin* (30, in the French) ["redhead" (22)]. For more on the vacillation between a more classic and familiar tone, see Michon, *Le roi vient*, 122–23 and 207.

13. For a compelling analysis of Michon's practice of visual citation, see Coyault, "Les *Illuminations* de Pierre Michon."
14. None of these images are reproduced on the pages of these books. That said, Michon has collaborated with artists on two works that meld photographs and text: *Les passants immobiles* and *L'Irlande*.
15. Michon began work on *Les onze* in 1993, precisely two hundred years after the Reign of Terror. "Perhaps," as one journalist has written, "he had had enough of the [bicentennial] commemorations of 1789." Jacobs, "Je vais vous demander d'acheter un livre."
16. As Dominique Viart writes, "Michon's writing is very well informed, it is nurtured by a huge library that this bookworm never ceases to explore." Viart, "What Makes People Write?" 19.
17. Jefferson, *Biography*, 335.
18. Pouilloux, "Une prose de voyant," 869.
19. A Zouave is a soldier trained to serve in Africa, though they later fought in Indochina. While the first battalions of Zouaves were comprised of mostly Algerian Berbers, French settlers in the Maghreb were eventually recruited. Van Gogh painted two portraits of this particular soldier, Lieutenant Paul-Eugène Milliet, whose regiment was garrisoned in Arles after returning from deployment in Tonkin during the Sino-French war.
20. According to van Gogh's letters, however, Roulin was keen on the transfer since it offered a higher salary and better working conditions. See, for example, Letter 738 (To Theo, January 19, 1889) in http://vangoghletters.org/vg/.
21. While Wyatt Mason's translation of the term *romanesque* as "romantic" suggests the narrator's recourse to an active imagination, the original French term hints at how con-

scious the narrator is of the fabricated nature of his tale, of its resolute fictionality. For Michon, the term *romanesque* (in French) resonates with "invention." See Michon, *Le roi vient*, 61.

22. Viart, "Pierre Michon, un art de la figure."
23. Robertson, *Medieval Saints' Lives*, 17. Michon's project is not designed to encourage readers to model themselves on the "saintly" lives of his historical subjects. Rather, as Ann Jefferson argues, for Michon the writer's duty is, ultimately, to "glorify literature." See Jefferson, *Biography*, 336.
24. Michael Kimmelman, "At Louvre."
25. Wilde, "The Critic as Artist," 367.
26. See, for example, the essays collected in Farron and Kürtös, *Pierre Michon entre pinacothèque et bibliothèque*, and Castiglione, ed., *Michon: L'écriture absolue*. Pierre Bergounioux writes about Michon's "minuscule" lives in *L'invention du présent*, 83.
27. Bourdieu, *Distinction*, 2.
28. In a short memoir published in 1957, in which she describes her experience posing for van Gogh, Adeline Ravoux notes that "at this time, very few people understood the painting of van Gogh." See Ravoux, "Souvenirs sur le séjour."
29. Bourdieu, *Distinction*, 2.
30. Bourdieu, *Distinction*, 5.
31. Bourdieu, *Distinction*, 44.
32. I borrow the definition of the institutional theory of art from philosopher George Dickie. See Dickie, *Evaluating Art*, ix.
33. Bourdieu, *Distinction*, 5.
34. Bourdieu, *Distinction*, 6.
35. The text suggests that the painting in question is a portrait of Roulin (40 and 45). Reference to the "fat dahlias" that are visible on the canvas point to the version now owned by the Museum of Modern Art in New York. Either way, it is unlikely that Roulin owned a portrait of himself. We know from van Gogh's correspondence that he in fact sent Roulin two canvases in January 1890, during his internment in the asylum at Saint-Remy-de-Provence: one depicting a white

farmhouse in an olive field, and another representing a wheat field with a mountain vista in the background. Both are currently owned by private collectors. See letter 836 to Theo van Gogh in http://vangoghletters.org/vg/.

36. Varnedoe, "Joseph Roulin," 11.
37. Bourdieu, *Distinction*, 44.
38. As the narrator notes, these include images of Blanqui, Gambetta, Rossel, and Rigault (Michon, *Joseph Roulin* (9)). Louis Auguste Blanqui (1805–81) was a notable French socialist. Léon Gambetta (1838–82) was a prominent Republican statesman. Louis-Nathaniel Rossel (1844–71) and Raoul Rigault (1846–71) were heroes of the Paris Commune in 1871.
39. As George Dickie explains Monroe Beardsley's evaluational theory, "a work of art is valuable because it is the cause of a valuable aesthetic experience of which the work of art is the objective part." Dickie, *Art and Value*, 75.
40. See Jensen, *Marketing Modernism*.
41. Briefel, *Deceivers*, 118–19.
42. Ford, *Art: A Commodity*, 13.
43. Ford, *Art: A Commodity*, 14.
44. The citation appears on the back cover of the Verdier edition of Michon's text. Translation mine.
45. Michon has said that his books about painters and their models constitute a way to lay bare ("mettre à plat") the notion of value. See *Le roi vient*, 135.
46. Jensen, *Marketing Modernism*, 10. As Jenson goes on to say, "That we have continued to insist on this division, even while ever escalating the domain of money in the world of art, has been an essential feature of modernism" (11).
47. Crimp, "Redefining Site Specificity," in *On the Museum's Ruins*, 155.
48. Campbell and Durden, *Variable Capital*, 115.
49. Kwon, *One Place After Another*, 4.
50. Over the years, as Danto argues, museums had "been subtly transformed into a showroom for classy investments."

Arthur Danto, "Hans Haacke and the Industry of Art," 132–33. Danto's essay was first published in 1987.

51. Haacke, "Museums, Managers of Consciousness."
52. Kwon, *One Place After Another*, 24.
53. Foster, "(Dis)Agreeable Objects," 13.
54. Miller, "Interview with Mike Kelley," unpaginated.
55. When the American film producer (played by Jack Palance) in Jean-Luc Godard's film *Le mépris* (*Contempt*, 1963) utters these words, he appropriates a more sinister saying from German *Luftwaffe* commander Hermann Goering, who once declared: "When I hear the word 'culture,' I reach for my revolver."
56. Velthuis, *Imaginary Economics*, 14.
57. Judovitz, "Art and Economics," 195.
58. Koons is clearly aware of the inherent ambiguity in his work: "The message was not to be seduced. Not to give up your economic power base. At the same time, anybody who bought one of these pieces would be giving in to this seduction. So it was also enhancing my power." In Bonami, ed., *Jeff Koons*, 43.
59. See Thompson, *$12 Million Stuffed Shark*, 80.
60. From the catalogue of the Whitney Biennial in 1989. Quoted in Velthuis, *Imaginary Economics*, 86.
61. Velthuis, *Imaginary Economics*, 26.
62. Hopkins, *After Modern Art*, 206.
63. See Campbell and Durden, *Variable Capital*, 115.
64. Incidentally, media coverage of this sale lasted longer than anticipated. A debate about the authenticity of the painting brewed for a number of years. For more on the story surrounding the disputed painting, see van Tilborgh and Hendriks, "The Tokyo *Sunflowers*."
65. From the back cover of the Verdier edition of *Vie de Joseph Roulin*.
66. Velthuis, *Imaginary Economics*, 12.
67. Torgovnick, *Visual Arts*, 214.
68. Crowley, *Michon: Afterlife of Names*, 13.
69. Genette, *Work of Art*, 16. Genette is not entirely schematic in

this book, and acknowledges a subset of intermediate practices, like concrete poetry or performance art, that straddle these two regimes.

70. Genette, *Work of Art*, 22.

71. While Prince Henry the Lion's twelfth-century Book of the Holy Gospels fetched $20.7 million when it was sold at Sotheby's in 1983, Bill Gates paid $30.4 million in 1994 for Leonardo da Vinci's *Codex Leicester* manuscript. These record-shattering books sales, however, pale in comparison to prices attained for many of the world's most famous paintings which, even when not adjusted for inflation, regularly sell for more than $50 million.

72. See, for example, Melikian, "Art Market."

73. Velthuis, *Talking Prices*, 4.

74. See Brown, "Introduction: Textual Materialism."

## 4. *Remake*

1. Viel, *Cinéma*. All translations are mine.

2. As critic Alain Garsault put it, "the spectator is prone to ask what, exactly, did he just see?" Garsault, "Le petit clown rouge," 22. Translation mine.

3. On literary novelizations of films, see Baetens, "La novellisation, un genre contaminé?" As Baetens notes, *Cinéma* does not correspond completely to the definition of that genre. However, it exemplifies, in part at least, what Gavriel Moses has termed the "film novel." For Moses, novels such as F. Scott Fitzgerald's *The Last Tycoon* (1925), Vladimir Nabokov's *Laughter in the Dark* (1960), and Manuel Puig's *Kiss of the Spider Woman* (1979) explore the various interactions between film, life, and literature. Like *Cinéma*, these novels might focus on the apparatus of film, on its production or its reception, or engage, implicitly or explicitly, various theories of film. See Moses, *Nickel Was for the Movies*.

4. The narrative makes no attempt to transcribe or even mention the film's musical score.

5. This desire to make things somewhat easier for his francophone narratees also explains the simultaneous translation of

his *pellicule vocale* into French: «Everything is in English in the film when you see it in its original version, but here I'm making as if it were the French version, so that it's easier to follow what's happening, so that you get a better sense for what you risk missing otherwise» (28).

6. Although the narrator will later discuss the opening credits (69), he focuses solely on the text, never mentioning the accompanying images.
7. The original play is published along with stills from the film in Shaffer, *Sleuth*.
8. See Roland Barthes, "La mort de l'auteur," in *Œuvres complètes*, 2:491–95.
9. Nabokov, *Despair*, 16.
10. The narrator assumes that his audience understands rudimentary English, how to count from one to twenty at the very least. This is not the first time he reproduces the English text in order to more effectively capture the nuances of the film.
11. "But *what* does the spectator identify with during the projection of a film? Because he has to identify with something. . . . The spectator, evidently, identifies with the fictional *character*." See Metz, "Le signifiant imaginaire," in *Le signifiant imaginaire*, 66–69. Translation mine.
12. Heffernan, *Museum of Words*, 3.
13. Diderot, *Salon de 1765*. Hamon, *La description littéraire*, 131. Translation mine.
14. Mitchell, *Picture Theory*, 152. Given the fact that both film and prose fiction develop over time in a linear way, I would suggest that film lends itself more readily to verbal description than those "still" forms like painting or photography. Of course, reading a literary text is free from temporal constraints; readers progress through a text at their own pace. Film, on the other hand, cannot be seen any faster or any slower than it is projected without affecting the viewer's perception. That the narrator of *Cinéma* watches *Sleuth* repeatedly with the help of a VCR only eases the process of transposition from image to text in his "spoken reel." The paused image that the VCR allows, like the film still, "flouts logical

time." Barthes, "The Third Meaning," in *Responsibility of Forms*, 62.

15. Some critics have claimed that Diderot's way of seeing in the *salons* is, precisely, proto-cinematic. For Brigitte Peucker, for example, the philosopher's descriptions of the images on display "evoke the myth of total cinema." Peucker, *Incorporating Images*, 109.
16. Viel and Aubron, "Éléments," 150. This and all subsequent translations are mine.
17. Foucault, *Order of Things*, 9.
18. Mitchell, *Picture Theory*, 152.
19. Mitchell, *Picture Theory*, 152.
20. Baudry, "Le dispositif," 64.
21. Barthes, *Responsibility of Forms*, 44.
22. Viel and Aubron, "Éléments."
23. "The obtuse meaning is discontinuous, *indifferent* to the story and to the obvious meaning." Barthes, *Responsibility of Forms*, 55.
24. This term, discussed by Gerald Prince in an essay on the larger phenomenon of the "disnarrated," refers to the narrative content that would fill the gap created by an ellipsis. In other words, the nonnarrated is that part of a narrative which must have happened but which the story omits. See Prince, "The Disnarrated."
25. Eikhenbaum, "Problems of Film Stylistics." Eikhenbaum's essay was originally published in 1927. The date is significant since it reveals that Eikhenbaum devised his theory during the period directly preceding the advent of cinematic sound. The rise of the "talkies," however, does not necessarily discount the notion of inner speech, since all films imply an underlying discourse despite the presence of dialogue. Cited in Willemen, *Looks and Frictions*, 41.
26. This is typical of all of Viel's novels. See my article "Viel's Manic Fictions."
27. Viel and Aubron, "Éléments."
28. "In my own view, the major artistic contribution of the decade [the 1970s] was the emergence of the appropriated image." Danto, *After the End of Art*, 15.

29. Muir, "Signs of a Beginning," 56.

30. Foster, *Recodings*, 66.

31. The obvious objection to my comparison of Bidlo to Borges is that while Menard's copy is an allographic gesture, like all writing, Bidlo's *Not X* copies are autographic. Whereas an accurate copy of a text, or of a musical score for that matter, will always be an "equally genuine instance" of that text, a replica of a painting, even the most exact copy, will always remain a forgery, never to be considered a "new instance" of the work. Written texts and musical scores, in other words, are "unfakable." The irony of Borges's story, however, is that, for the narrator, Menard's achievement is precisely a result of his *Quixote*'s stylistic difference from the original; in other words, Menard succeeds in creating an autographic copy of a written text, which, as Nelson Goodman would argue, is impossible. See his chapter on "Art and Authenticity" in *Languages of Art*, 99–123.

32. Bidlo and Rosenblum, "Mike Bidlo," 193.

33. Bidlo made a name for himself not simply with his painterly appropriations, but also as a result of his uniquely appropriationist performance pieces in which he stages reenactments of artists "at work." His 1982 performance *Jack the Dripper at Peg's Place*, for example, was derived from the infamous story in which Jackson Pollock urinated in Peggy Guggenheim's fireplace. He also remade Yves Klein's shocking performance piece *Anthropometry of the Blue Period* from 1960—in which the artist dragged nude women, smeared with paint, across a canvas laid on the floor—and recreated gatherings at Warhol's Factory. These performances enlarge the critical scope of Bidlo's project in their interrogation not simply of a work's authenticity, but also of the subjective agency and originality of the artistic process itself.

34. Along with Borges and Bidlo, a third "conceptual forger" made waves in the art world of the 1970s. Hank Herron's perfect copies of Frank Stella's geometric abstractions led one critic to proclaim that Herron's ingenious simulations were "Stellas *plus*, Stellas and *more*." Cheryl Bernstein, the critic

in question, went on to champion Herron's contribution to late-modern art as even more important than that of Stella himself, noting that "any comparison of Herron and Stella would have to concede that the former's power and potentiality, his superior pictorial structure, his more exclusive visual mode, and lastly, his more fully depicted literal shape, based as they are on the reproduction of the latter's work, vastly intensifies the conflict between them." The genius of this critique, of course, is that Herron and Bernstein are themselves fakes, created by the [real] art historian Carol Duncan in 1970 as a parody of the kind of art criticism that was being published in the most theoretically savvy reviews. Despite the hoax, Duncan's/Bernstein's ambitious essay, clearly influenced by the influx of continental theory in American intellectual circles at the time, was praised by the art establishment and accepted as an insightful and altogether valid article, even though the paintings that she discusses do not exist. Although her critique does make a legitimate, albeit slightly precocious argument, today Duncan's gesture is appreciated for its conceptual potency, effectively staging the very act of appropriation and simulation that it takes as its subject. See "The Fake as More, by Cheryl Bernstein," as well as Duncan's comments on the "Bernstein affair" in part 4 of Carol Duncan, *Aesthetics of Power*. The success of Duncan's hoax was so great that the true identity of the article's author was not revealed until 1986. For a revised version of that essay, which blew Duncan's critical cover, see Thomas Crow, "The Return of Hank Herron: Simulated Abstraction and the Service Economy of Art," in Crow, *Modern Art* 69–84.

35. Stern, "*Emma* in Los Angeles," 226.
36. Curiously, there seems to be a small cottage industry of video artists whose work appropriates classic Hitchcock films. Stan Douglas's *Subject to a Film: Marnie* (1989) recreates the crucial robbery scene from the Hitchcock film of the same name and reprograms it in a loop, so that the heroine is forever trapped at the scene of the crime. Douglas Gordon's *24 Hour Psycho* (1993) is a technologically adapted version of Hitch-

cock's celebrated thriller in which the artist has slowed down the action to just two frames per second, stretching the duration of the film to last an entire day. Finally, for *Scottie's Bedroom* (1994) David Reed, a painter who works occasionally in video, has digitally inserted one of his own paintings into a scene depicting the hero's bedroom in *Vertigo*. This scene, looped onto video, is projected on a television in the installation which also features a bed and the original Reed painting, configured to resemble, in a clever *mise en abyme* of the film, Scottie's bedroom. Although each artist experiments with the original film to different effects, they all rely on the public's collective memory of these Hollywood classics. For his part, Tanguy Viel has also turned his attentions to Hitchcock's legacy in the pantheon of world cinema in his most recent short text *Hitchcock, par exemple*.

37. On August 22, 1972, motivated by the high cost of his lover's impending sex change operation, John Wojtowicz attempted to rob a Brooklyn branch of the Chase Manhattan Bank. During the heist he held a group of the bank's customers hostage for fourteen hours, which proved to be ample time to transform the event into a massive media spectacle. The perpetrator served time in jail, and was released in 1979. Wojtowicz himself figures in Huyghe's recreation of the events of that day in 1972, produced in a sound studio outside of Paris, scantly decorated to resemble the scene of the hold-up. Interestingly, at one point during the reconstruction, Wojtowicz describes an exchange of gunfire that had taken place during the heist as having occurred "in the real movie." Like the narrator of Viel's novel, Huyghe's "narrator" has been similarly infected by the conflation of life and art.
38. Compagnon, *La seconde main*, 9. Translation mine.
39. Levine, "Statement," 48. Reprinted in Harrison and Wood, *Art in Theory*, 1039.
40. Barthes, "La mort de l'auteur," *Œuvres complètes II*, 491–95.
41. Owens, "Sherrie Levine at A&M Artworks," 115.
42. In that almost all her work recontextualizes work by male

artists, Levine's appropriations also offer a feminist critique of the male-dominated scene. As she remarks, "A lot of what my work has been about since the beginning has been realizing the difficulties of situating myself in the art world as a woman, because the art world is so much an arena for the celebration of male desire." Levine, "Interview with Jeanne Siegel." For a compelling reading of Levine's appropriations as "woman's work," see Singerman, "Seeing Sherrie Levine."

43. Barthes, "Réquichot et son corps," *Œuvres complètes II*, 1633.

44. Many of the most renowned appropriationists have appropriated works by Duchamp. In the 1960s, both Richard Pettibone and Elaine Sturtevant were among the first to have produced such replications (Sturtevant prefers to call her works "repeated" Duchamps rather than appropriations). More recently, Sherrie Levine remade Duchamp's *Fountain* (1917) in a series of polished bronze urinals. Mike Bidlo, has also placed Duchamp's groundbreaking gesture *en abyme* with a series of fountain drawings and a painted a replica of the *Nude Descending a Staircase* (1912). Finally, in another, but certainly not the last contribution to this seemingly infinite play with the past, Michael Mandiberg caused a stir with his series of third degree appropriations, posted on the Internet, of Levine's 1981 rephotographs of Walker Evans's 1936 originals (*http://www.aftersherrielevine.com*). Mandiberg's take on what he feels is an esoteric conceptual practice is ironically entitled *After Sherrie Levine*. However, Mandiberg's critical affront against appropriationist practices might have been even more trenchant had he chosen to appropriate Levine's own appropriations of Duchamp.

45. See Bourriaud, *Postproduction*.

46. Duchamp and Roberts, "I Propose to Strain the Laws of Physics," 62.

47. Salvador Dali referred to it as a work of "ultra-intellectual aggression." Naumann, *Duchamp: Art of Making Art*, 80.

48. David Joselit argues that the strategic topographical place-

ment of the title in Duchamp's reproduction (i.e., in her lap) is the key to understanding the artist's identification of language with the feminine body. Dalia Judovitz, on the other hand, reads the title as an expression of the logic of exchange between the spectator and the work: *L.H.O.O.Q.* can be read as "LOOK." Both critics, however, agree that the reference to the feminine in the title ("L," or *elle*) is undermined by the "hairy" masculinization of the image. See Joselit, *Infinite Regress*, 91–92, and Judovitz, *Unpacking Duchamp*, 141–42.

49. Paz, *Duchamp: Appearance Stripped Bare*, 21.
50. Viel, "La dernière conférence," http://www.remue.net/cont/viel.html. Translation mine.
51. For a thorough account of Duchamp's word play, see George H. Bauer's performative essay: Bauer, "Duchamp's Ubiquitous Puns."
52. See Judovitz, *Unpacking Duchamp*, 117–18.
53. Even the term "readymade" itself is based on the principle of polysemic signification. As Judovitz explains, "The label 'readymade' designates a work, which is 'already' made by mass production, but whose readiness to be 'made' into art is delayed by its technological history and whose terms are unassimilable to an artistic terminology." Judovitz, *Unpacking Duchamp*, 76.
54. The specter of Duchamp has continued to haunt much of Viel's work after *Cinéma*. In *Maladie*, a short text about a manic hypochondriac who happens to be suffering from an unidentifiable, symptomless disease, the narrator lists those objects that he has been forced to leave behind after a series of moves imposed upon him by his condition. Along with a chess set, his editions of Bossuet, some china, a laptop computer, and a dog, the narrator also laments, quite tellingly, the loss of a "cherished photo of Marcel Duchamp." Viel, *Maladie*, 34. More recently, the author penned a catalogue entry for an exhibition in France dedicated to Duchamp's influence on contemporary art in which he writes, "If I dared, dear Marcel, I would say that the ready-made is to our century

what Lascaux was to prehistoric man." See Viel, "Cher Marcel Duchamp." Translations mine.

55. Bürger, *Theory of the Avant-Garde*, 52.
56. Friedberg, *Window Shopping*, 139.
57. Viel, "Idées en pente." Translation mine.
58. Viel, "La dernière conférence."
59. Barthes, "Droit dans les yeux," in *Œuvres complètes III*, 737.
60. Jameson, "Postmodernism and Consumer Society," 115.
61. Viel's novel would not be the last iteration of *Sleuth*. In 2007 Kenneth Branagh released his own feature-length version of Shaffer's play starring Michael Caine in Olivier's former role and Jude Law in Caine's former role, with a newly adapted screenplay written by Harold Pinter.

### *Conclusion*

1. Toussaint, *La télévision*. Citations refer to the English translation, *Television*.
2. See Blatt, "Revolution Will Be Televised."
3. Motte, "Toussaint's TV Guide," 180.
4. This is characteristic of many of Toussaint's narrators. See Hippolyte, *Fuzzy Fiction*, 25–31.
5. Given the virulence of most antitelevisual (and antivisual) critiques, it is not surprising that a number of other contemporary novels about television propose the written word, and narrative, as a salutary alternative to the nefarious power of the cathode ray tube. For example, in Raymond Jean's *Transports*, the story of a man caught red-handed cheating with his mistress on live television during an internationally broadcast soccer match, the protagonist, wearied by the "mediatized rape" that he has endured, finds solace in the pages of Alain Robbe-Grillet's *La Jalousie* (1957). And in Michel Tournier's *La goutte d'or*, a novel that condemns the cult of the image in modern France from the perspective of an innocent Berber immigrant recently arrived in the metropolis, words (in the form of poetic lyrics or calligraphy) have the capacity to heal, to serve as "an antidote to the subjugation by the image"

(256, translation mine). See Jean, *Transports*, and Tournier, *La goutte d'or*.

6. Foucault, "Photogenic Painting," 83.
7. Foucault, "Photogenic Painting," 84.
8. Foucault regards Fromanger's own technique—which consists of projecting photographic images onto a canvas and painting over the shadows, adding touches of brilliant color throughout—as an inevitable extension of art's historic dipping into the larger pool of visual representations.
9. Foucault, "Photogenic Painting," 103 (emphasis mine).
10. Foucault, "Photogenic Painting," 89.
11. Flaxman, "Introduction," in *Brain Is the Screen*, 9. As Deleuze himself writes, "Civilization of the image? In fact, it is a civilization of the cliché where all the powers have an interest in hiding images from us, not necessarily in hiding the same thing from us, but in hiding something in the image." Deleuze, *Cinema 2*, 21.
12. Burgin, *In/Different Spaces*, 21.
13. On the controversy surrounding this exhibition see Berman, "Museums in the Age of Giuliani."
14. Solomon-Godeau, "Remote Control." For W. J. T. Mitchell, statements like these about the power of images today are often exaggerated: "Images of guns don't kill; guns do. . . . The fantasy that images and visuality are the decisive political forces of our time is, in fact, one of those collective hallucinations that should be a problem for investigation in visual culture, not one of its critical axioms." Mitchell, "Interdisciplinarity and Visual Culture," 542. Of course, Mitchell's retort was written over a decade before the death of Theo van Gogh, murdered in cold blood on the streets of Amsterdam in 2004 in retaliation for the depiction of Muslim women in his 2004 film *Submission*.
15. Barthes, *Camera Lucida*, 65–66.
16. Hirsch, "Collateral Damage," 1212.

# Bibliography


Abel, Richard. *French Film Theory and Criticism: A History/Anthology*. 2 vols. Princeton: Princeton University Press, 1993.

Adair, Gilbert. *The Postmodernist Always Rings Twice*. London: Fourth Estate, 1992.

Apostolidès, Jean-Marie. *Le roi machine: Spectacle et politique au temps de Louis XIV*. Paris: Minuit, 1981.

Authier, Christian. *Deuxièmes séances*. Paris: Stock, 2009.

Baecque, Antoine de, with Olivier Mongin and Alexandra Pizoird. "Ce qu'on fait dire aux images: L'historien, le cinéphile et les querelles du visuel. Entretien avec Antoine de Baecque." *Esprit* (March-April 2003): 19–34.

Baetens, Jan. "La novellisation: un genre contaminé?" *Poétique* 138 (April 2004): 235–51.

Bal, Mieke. *Reading Rembrandt: Beyond the Word and Image Opposition*. Cambridge: Cambridge University Press, 1991.

Barthes, Roland. *Camera Lucida: Reflections on Photography*. Translated by Richard Howard. New York: Farrar, Straus and Giroux, 1981.

———. *La chambre claire: Note sur la photographie*. Paris: Minuit, 1965.

———. *Mythologies*. Paris: Seuil, 1957.

———. *The Responsibility of Forms: Critical Essays on Music, Art, and Representation*. Translated by Richard Howard. Oxford: Basil Blackwell, 1986.

———. *Roland Barthes: Œuvres complètes*. 3 vols. Edited by Eric Marty. Paris: Seuil, 1993, 1994, 1995.

Baudelaire, Charles. *Œuvres completes*. Paris: Robert Laffont, 1980.

Baudrillard, Jean. "The Hyper-realism of Simulation." Translated by Charles Levin. In *Art in Theory, 1900–2000: An Anthology of Changing Ideas*, edited by Charles Harrison and Paul Wood, 1018–20. Oxford: Blackwell, 2003.

Baudry, Jean-Louis. "Le dispositif: Approches métapsychologiques de l'impression de réalité." *Communications* 23 (1975): 56–72.

Bauer, George H. "Duchamp's Ubiquitous Puns." In *Marcel Duchamp: Artist of the Century*, edited by Rudolf Kuenzli and Francis M. Naumann, 127–46. Cambridge MA: MIT Press, 1991.

Baxandall, Michael. *Patterns of Intention: On the Historical Explanation of Pictures*. New Haven: Yale University Press, 1985.

Belting, Hans. *L'histoire de l'art: Est-elle finie?* Translated by J.-F. Poirier and Y. Michaud. Nîmes: Jacqueline Chambon, 1989.

Bénabou, Marcel. "Faux et usage de faux chez Georges Perec." *Le cabinet d'amateur: Revue d'études perecquiennes* 3 (Spring 1994): 25–36.

Bergez, Daniel. *Littérature et peinture*. Paris: Armand Colin, 2004.

Bergounioux, Pierre. *L'invention du présent*. Saint Clément de Rivière: Fata Morgana, 2006.

Berman, Marshall. "Museums in the Age of Giuliani." *Art in America* 87, no. 12 (December 1999): 37–43.

Best, Steven, and Douglas Kellner. *The Postmodern Turn*. New York: Guilford Press, 1997.

Bidlo, Mike and Robert Rosenblum. "Mike Bidlo talks to Robert Rosenblum." *Artforum* 41, no. 8 (April 2003): 192–95.

Black, Joel. *The Reality Effect: Film Culture and the Graphic Imperative*. New York: Routledge, 2002.

Blatt, Ari J. "The Revolution Will Be Televised, or Didier Daeninckx's Cathode Fictions." *Yale French Studies* 114 (December 2008): 144–55.

———. "Tanguy Viel's Manic Fictions." *Contemporary French and Francophone Studies* 14, no. 4 (2010): 373–80.

Bonami, Francesco, ed. *Jeff Koons*. Chicago: Museum of Contemporary Art, 2008.

Bourdieu, Pierre. *Distinction: A Social Critique of the Judgement of Taste*. Translated by Richard Nice. Cambridge MA: Harvard University Press, 1984.

———. *Un art moyen: Essai sur les usages sociaux de la photographie*. Paris: Minuit, 1965.

Bourriaud, Nicolas. *Postproduction: La culture comme scénario, comment l'art reprogramme le monde contemporain*. Paris: Les presses du réel, 2003.

Briefel, Aviva. *The Deceivers: Art Forgery in the Nineteenth Century*. Ithaca: Cornell University Press, 2006.

Britton, Celia. *Claude Simon: Writing the Visible*. Cambridge: Cambridge University Press, 1987.

Brown, Bill. "Introduction: Textual Materialism." *PMLA* 125, no. 1 (January 2010): 24–28.

Buchloch, Benjamin. "The Andy Warhol Line." In *The Work of Andy Warhol: Dia Art Foundation Discussions in Contemporary Culture 3*, edited by Gary Garrels, 52–69. Seattle: Bay Press, 1989.

Burgelin, Claude. *Les parties de dominos chez Monsieur Lefèvre: Perec avec Freud—Perec contre Freud*. Strasbourg: Circé, 1996.

Bürger, Peter. *Theory of the Avant-Garde*. Translated by Michael Shaw. Minneapolis: University of Minnesota Press, 1984.

Burgin, Victor. *In/Different Spaces: Place and Memory in Visual Culture*. Berkeley: University of California Press, 1995.

Calle-Gruber, Mireille, ed. *Les triptyques de Claude Simon: Ou l'art du montage*. Paris: Sorbonne Nouvelle, 2008.

Camille, Michael. "Simulacrum." In *Critical Terms for Art History*, edited by Robert S. Nelson and Richard Shiff, 35–48. Chicago: University of Chicago Press, 2003.

Campbell, David and Mark Durden, eds. *Variable Capital*. Liverpool: Liverpool University Press and the Bluecoat, 2007.

Castiglione, Agnès, ed. *Pierre Michon: L'écriture absolue*. Saint-Étienne: Universitaires de Saint-Étienne, 2002.
Certeau, Michel de. *The Practice of Everyday Life*. Berkeley: University of California Press, 1988.
Cheeke, Stephen. *Writing for Art: The Aesthetics of Ekphrasis*. Manchester: Manchester University Press, 2008.
Clark, T. J. *Farewell to an Idea: Episodes from a History of Modernism*. New Haven: Yale University Press, 1999.
Compagnon, Antoine. *La seconde main: Ou le travail de la citation*. Paris: Seuil, 1979.
Conrad, Joseph. *The Nigger of the Narcissus*. New York: Doubleday, 1914.
Coyault, Sylviane. "Les *Illuminations* de Pierre Michon." In *Pierre Michon entre pinacothèque et bibliothèque*, edited by Ivan Farron and Karl Kürtös, 35–55. Bern: Peter Lang, 2003.
Coyault-Dublanchet, Sylviane. *La province en héritage: Pierre Michon, Pierre Bergounioux, Richard Millet*. Geneva: Droz, 2002.
Crary, Jonathan. *Techniques of the Observer: On Vision and Modernity in the Nineteenth Century*. Cambridge MA: MIT Press, 1992.
Crimp, Douglas. *On the Museum's Ruins*. Cambridge MA: MIT Press, 1993.
———. "Pictures." *October* 8 (Spring 1979): 75–88.
Crow, Thomas. *Modern Art in the Common Culture*. New Haven: Yale University Press, 1996.
Crowley, Patrick. *Pierre Michon: The Afterlife of Names*. Bern: Peter Lang, 2007.
Dällenbach, Lucien. *Claude Simon*. Paris: Seuil, 1988.
Danto, Arthur. *After the End of Art: Contemporary Art and the Pale of History*. Princeton: Princeton University Press, 1998.
———. *Beyond the Brillo Box: The Visual Arts in Post-Historical Perspective*. Berkeley: University of California Press, 1998.
———. "Hans Haacke and the Industry of Art." In *The Wake of Art: Criticism, Philosophy, and the Ends of Taste*, edited by Gregg Horowitz and Tom Huhn, 129–38. Amsterdam: G + B Arts International, 1998.

———. *The Transfiguration of the Commonplace: A Philosophy of Art*. Cambridge MA: Harvard University Press, 1981.

Debray, Régis. *Introduction à la médiologie*. Paris: Presses Universitaires de France, 2000.

Deleuze, Gilles. *Cinema 2: The Time-Image*. Translated by Hugh Tomlinson and Robert Galeta. Minneapolis: University of Minnesota Press, 1989.

———. "Plato and the Simulacrum." In *The Logic of Sense*, edited by Constantin Boundas, translated by Mark Lester with Charles Stivale, 291–303. New York: Columbia University Press, 1990.

Demanze, Laurent. "Les illustres et les minuscules: Pierre Michon lecteur de Plutarque." In *Fictions biographiques XIXe–XXie siècles*, 129–38. Toulouse: Presses Universitaires du Mirail, 2007.

Derrida, Jacques. *The Truth in Painting*. Translated by Geoff Bennington and Ian McLeod. Chicago: University of Chicago Press, 1987.

Dethurens, Pascal, ed. *Écrire la peinture: De Diderot à Quignard*. Paris: Citadelle et Mazenod, 2009.

Dickie, George. *Art and Value*. Oxford: Blackwell, 2001.

———. *Evaluating Art*. Philadelphia: Temple University Press, 1988.

Diderot, Denis. *Œuvres complètes*. Edited by Jean Varloot. Paris: Hermann, 1990.

———. *Salon de 1765*. Paris: Hermann, 1985.

Dubois, Philippe. *L'acte photographique*. Bruxelles: Éditions Labor, 1983.

Dubuffet, Jean. "A propos de *Triptyque* (Une lettre de Jean Dubuffet)." *Critique* 37, no. 414 (1981): 1149–50.

Duchamp, Marcel, and Francis Roberts. "I Propose to Strain the Laws of Physics." *Art News* 67, no. 8 (December 1968): 62.

Duffy, Jean. "Artistic Biographies and Aesthetic Coherence in Claude Simon's *Jardin des plantes*." *Forum for Modern Language Studies* 35, no. 2 (1999): 175–92.

———. *Reading Between the Lines: Claude Simon and the Visual Arts*. Liverpool: Liverpool University Press, 1998.

Duncan, Alistair. *Claude Simon: Adventures in Words*. Manchester: Manchester University Press, 2003.

Duncan, Carol. *The Aesthetics of Power: Essays in Critical Art History*. Cambridge: Cambridge University Press, 1993.

Durham, Scott. *Phantom Communities: The Simulacrum and the Limits of Postmodernism*. Stanford: Stanford University Press, 1998.

Duve, Thierry de. *Résonances du readymade: Duchamp entre avant-garde et tradition*. Nîmes: Éditions Jacqueline Chambon, 1989.

Duverlie, Claud, and Claude Simon. "Claude Simon: The Crossing of the Image." Translated by J. Rodgers. *Diacritics* 7, no. 4 (Winter 1977): 47–58.

———. "Pictures for Writing: Premises for a Graphictology." Translated by Elizabeth Bails. In *Orion Blinded: Essays on Claude Simon*, edited by Randi Birn and Karen Gould, 200–218. Lancaster PA: Bucknell University Press, 1981.

Eikhenbaum, Boris. "Problems of Film Stylistics." *Screen* 15, no. 4 (Winter 1974–75): 7–34.

Elkins, James. *The Domain of Images*. Ithaca NY: Cornell University Press, 1999.

Evans, Michael. *Claude Simon and the Transgressions of Modern Art*. London: Macmillan, 1988.

Fallay d'Este, Lauriane. *Le paragone: Le parallèle des arts*. Paris: Klincksieck, 1992.

Farron, Ivan, and Karl Kürtös, eds. *Pierre Michon entre pinacothèque et bibliothèque*. Bern: Peter Lang, 2003.

Ferrato-Combe, Brigitte. *Écrire en peintre: Claude Simon et la peinture*. Grenoble: ELLUG, 1998.

Flaxman, Gregory. *The Brain Is the Screen: Deleuze and the Philosophy of Cinema*. Minneapolis: University of Minnesota Press, 2000.

Ford, Sheridan. *Art: A Commodity*. New York: Rogers and Sherwood, 1888.

Foster, Hal. "(Dis)Agreeable Objects." In *Damaged Goods: Desire and the Economy of the Object*, edited by Brian Wallis, 13–18. New York: The New Museum of Contemporary Art, 1986.

———. "Postmodernism: A Preface." In *The Anti-Aesthetic: Essays on Postmodern Culture*, edited by Hal Foster, ix–xvi. Seattle: Bay Press, 1983.

———. *Recodings: Art, Spectacle, Cultural Politics.* Seattle: Bay Press, 1985.

Foucault, Michel. *The Order of Things: An Archaeology of the Human Sciences.* New York: Vintage, 1994.

———. "Photogenic Painting." In Gilles Deleuze and Michel Foucault, *Gérard Fromanger: La peinture photogénique*, edited by Sarah Wilson, translated by Dafydd Roberts, 81–104. London: Black Dog, 1999.

———. *This Is Not a Pipe.* Translated by James Harkness. Berkeley: University of California Press, 1982.

Frank, Joseph. *The Idea of Spatial Form.* New Brunswick NJ: Rutgers University Press, 1991.

Franzen, Jonathan. "The Reader in Exile." In *How to Be Alone*, 164–78. New York: Picador, 2002.

Fried, Michael. "Art and Objecthood." In *Art and Objecthood: Essays and Reviews*, 148–172. Chicago: University of Chicago Press, 1998.

Friedberg, Anne. *Window Shopping: Cinema and the Postmodern.* Berkeley: University of California Press, 1994.

Friedman, Thomas. *The World Is Flat: A Brief History of the Twenty-First Century.* New York: Farrar, Straus and Giroux, 2005.

Gandelman, Claude. *Le regard dans le texte: Image et écriture du Quattrocento au XXe siècle.* Paris: Méridiens-Klincksieck, 1986.

Garsault, Alain. "Le petit clown rouge." *Positif* 154 (1973): 16–23.

Genette, Gérard. *Figures II.* Paris: Seuil, 1969.

———. *Figures III.* Paris: Seuil, 1972.

———. *Seuils.* Paris: Seuil, 1987.

———. *The Work of Art: Immanence and Transcendence.* Translated by G. M. Goshgarian. Ithaca NY: Cornell University Press, 1997.

Glacet, Aymeric. *Claude Simon chronophotographe: Ou les*

*onomatopées du temps*. Lille: Universitaires du Septentrion, 2007.

Gogh, Vincent van. *Vincent van Gogh: The Letters*. Edited by Leo Jansen et al. 6 vols. London: Thames and Hudson, 2009. Also online at http://vangoghletters.org/vg/.

Goodman, Nelson. *Languages of Art: An Approach to a Theory of Symbols*. Indianapolis: Hackett, 1976.

Gopnik, Adam and Kirk Varnedoe. *High and Low: Modern Art and Popular Culture*. New York: Museum of Modern Art, 1990.

Goulet, Andrea. "Blind Spots and Afterimages: The Narrative Optics of Claude Simon's *Triptyque*." *Romanic Review* 91, no. 3 (May 2000): 289–311.

Goux, J. P. and André Poirson. "Un homme traversé par le travail: Entretien avec Claude Simon." *La Nouvelle critique* 105 (June-July 1977): 32–44.

Greenberg, Clement. *Clement Greenberg: The Collected Essays and Criticism*. Edited by John O'Brian. Chicago: University of Chicago Press, 1993.

Grojnowski, Daniel. *Photographie et langage*. Paris: José Corti, 2002.

Haacke, Hans. *Unfinished Business*. Edited by Brian Wallis. New York and Cambridge MA: New Museum of Contemporary Art and MIT Press, 1986.

Hagstrum, Jean H. *The Sister Arts: The Tradition of Literary Pictorialism and English Poetry from Dryden to Gray*. Chicago: University of Chicago Press, 1958.

Hamon, Philippe. *La description littéraire: Anthologie des textes théoriques et critiques*. Paris: Macula, 1991.

———. *Imageries: Littérature et image au XIXe siècle*. Paris: José Corti, 2001.

Hassan, Ihab. *The Postmodern Turn: Essays in Postmodern Theory and Culture*. Columbus: Ohio State University Press, 1987.

Heffernan, James. *Museum of Words: The Poetics of Ekphrasis from Homer to Ashbery*. Chicago: University of Chicago Press, 1993.

Herwitz, Daniel. *Making Theory, Constructing Art: On the Authority of the Avant-Garde*. Chicago: University of Chicago Press, 1993.

Higgins, Lynn. *New Novel, New Wave, New Politics: Fiction and the Representation of History in Postwar France*. Lincoln: University of Nebraska Press, 1996.

Hippolyte, Jean-Louis. *Fuzzy Fiction*. Lincoln: University of Nebraska Press, 2006.

Hirsch, Marianne. "Collateral Damage." *PMLA* 119, no. 5 (October 2004): 1209–15.

Hopkins, David. *After Modern Art: 1945–2000*. Oxford: Oxford University Press, 2000.

Irving, Clifford. *Fake! The Story of Elmyr de Hory, the Greatest Art Forger of Our Time*. New York: McGraw-Hill, 1969.

Jacobs, Didier. "Je vais vous demander d'acheter un livre." *Le Nouvel Observateur*, April 23, 2009.

Jameson, Fredric. "Postmodernism and Consumer Society." In *The Anti-Aesthetic: Essays on Postmodern Culture*, edited by Hal Foster, 111–25. Seattle: Bay, 1983.

———. *Postmodernism: Or, the Cultural Logic of Late Capitalism*. Durham NC: Duke University Press, 1991.

Jay, Martin. *Downcast Eyes: The Denigration of Vision in Twentieth-Century French Thought*. Berkeley: University of California Press, 1993.

Jean, Raymond. *Transports*. Paris: J'ai lu, 1990.

Jefferson, Ann. *Biography and the Question of Literature in France*. Oxford: Oxford University Press, 2007.

Jensen, Robert. *Marketing Modernism in Fin-de-Siècle Europe*. Princeton: Princeton University Press, 1994.

Jiminez, Marc. *Regards sur l'image*. Paris: Klincksieck, 2009.

Joselit, David. *Infinite Regress: Marcel Duchamp, 1910–1941*. Cambridge MA: MIT Press, 1998.

Joseph, Branden W. "A Duplication Containing Duplications." In *Robert Rauschenberg*, edited by Branden Joseph, 133–60. Cambridge MA: MIT Press, 2002.

Judovitz, Dalia. "Art and Economics: Duchamp's Postmodern Returns." *Criticism* 35, no. 2 (Spring 1993): 193–218.

———. *Unpacking Duchamp: Art in Transit*. Berkeley: University of California Press, 1995.

Kimmelman, Michael. "At Louvre, Many Stop to Snap, but Few Stay to Focus." *New York Times*, August 3, 2009.

Kipling, Rudyard. *Rudyard Kipling: The Complete Verse*. Edited by James Fenwick. London: Kyle Cathie, 1995.

Kofman, Sarah. *Camera Obscura of Ideology*. Translated by Will Straw. Ithaca NY: Cornell University Press, 1999.

Koos, Leonard. "Abysmal Play: Simulating Forgery in Georges Perec's *Un cabinet d'amateur*." *Romance Notes* 36, no. 1 (Fall 1995): 75–82.

Krauss, Rosalind. "Rauschenberg and the Materialized Image." In *Robert Rauschenberg*, edited by Branden W. Joseph, 39–56. Cambridge MA: MIT Press, 2002.

———. "Sculpture in the Expanded Field." In *The Anti-Aesthetic*, edited by Hal Foster, 31–42. Seattle: Bay Press, 1983.

———. *"A Voyage on the North Sea": Art in the Age of the Post-Medium Condition*. New York: Thames and Hudson, 1999.

Krieger, Murray. *Ekphrasis: The Illusion of the Natural Sign*. Baltimore: Johns Hopkins University Press, 1992.

Kwon, Miwon. *One Place After Another: Site-Specific Art and Locational Identity*. Cambridge MA: MIT Press, 2004.

Landesman, Peter. "A Crisis of Fakes: The Getty Forgeries." *New York Times Magazine* (March 18, 2001).

Lessing, G. E. *Laocoön: An Essay on the Limits of Painting and Poetry, 1776*. Edited and translated by Edward Allen McCormick. Baltimore: Johns Hopkins University Press, 1984.

Levine, Sherrie. "Interview with Jeanne Siegel." By Jeanne Siegel. *Arts Magazine* 59 (Summer 1985): 141–44.

———. "Statement." *Style* (March 1982), 48. Reprinted in *Art in Theory: 1900–2000. An Anthology of Changing Ideas*, edited by Charles Harrison and Paul Wood, 1038–39. Oxford: Blackwell, 2003.

Lopez, Jonathan. *The Man Who Made Vermeers: Unvarnishing the Legend of Master Forger Han van Meegeren*. Orlando FL: Harcourt, 2008.

Lotringer, Sylvère. "Cryptique." In *Claude Simon: Analyse, théorie. Actes du Colloque tenu au Centre Cultural International*

*de Cerisy-la-Salle du 1e au 8 juillet, 1974*, edited by Jean Ricardou, 313–33. Paris: 10/18, 1975.
Loubère, J. A. E. *The Novels of Claude Simon*. Ithaca NY: Cornell University Press, 1975.
Louvel, Liliane. *L'œil du texte: Texte et image dans la littérature de langue anglaise*. Toulouse: Presses Universitaires du Mirail, 1998.
Marin, Louis. *Détruire la peinture*. Paris: Galilée, 1977.
———. "Representation and Simulacrum." In *On Representation*, translated by Catherine Porter, 309–19. Stanford: Stanford University Press, 2001.
Massumi, Brian. "Realer than Real: The Simulacrum According to Deleuze and Guattari." http://www.brianmassumi.com/english/essays.html. Accessed January 2010. Originally published in *Copyright* 1 (1987): 90–97.
Mazzorato, Wilfrid. "*Citizen Kane*, un film d'Orson Welles dans les textes de Georges Perec." *Le cabinet d'amateur: Revue d'études perecquiennes* 7–8 (December 1998): 217–33.
McShine, Kynaston, ed. *Andy Warhol: A Retrospective*. New York: Museum of Modern Art, 1986.
Melikian, Souren. "An Art Market Suddenly at Dizzying Heights." *New York Times*, February 4, 2010.
Meltzer, Françoise. *Salome and the Dance of Writing: Portraits of Mimesis in Literature*. Chicago: University of Chicago Press, 1987.
Merleau-Ponty, Maurice. *L'œil et l'esprit*. Paris: Gallimard, 1961.
Metz, Christian. *Le signifiant imaginaire: Psychanalyse et cinéma*. Paris: 10/18, 1977.
Michon, Pierre. *Masters and Servants*. Translated by Wyatt Alexander Mason. San Francisco: Mercury, 1997.
———. *Les onze*. Lagrasse, France: Verdier, 2009.
———. *Le roi vient quand il veut: Propos sur la littérature*. Paris: Albin Michel, 2007.
———. *Vie de Joseph Roulin*. Lagrasse: Verdier, 1988.
Miller, John. "Interview with Mike Kelley." *Bomb* 38 (Winter 1992), unpaginated. http://bombsite.com/issues/38/articles/1502. Accessed March 17, 2010.

Milman, Miriam. *Le trompe-l'œil*. Geneva: Albert Skira, 1982.
Mirzoeff, Nicholas. *An Introduction to Visual Culture*. New York: Routledge, 1999.
Mitchell, W. J. T. *Iconology: Image, Text, Ideology*. Chicago: University of Chicago Press, 1986.
———. "Interdisciplinarity and Visual Culture." *Art Bulletin* 77, no. 4 (December 1995): 540–44.
———. *Picture Theory: Essays on Verbal and Visual Representation*. Chicago: University of Chicago Press, 1994.
Montfrans, Manet van. *Georges Perec: La contrainte du réel*. Amsterdam: Rodopi, 1999.
Moses, Gavriel. *The Nickel Was for the Movies: Film in the Novel from Pirandello to Puig*. Berkeley: University of California Press, 1995.
Motte, Warren. "Jean-Philippe Toussaint's TV Guide." In *Fables of the Novel: French Fiction Since 1990*, 177–94. Normal IL: Dalkey Archive, 2003.
Mougin, Pascal. *L'effet d'image: Essai sur Claude Simon*. Paris: L'Harmattan, 1997.
Muir, Peter. "Signs of a Beginning: *October* and the *Pictures* Exhibition." *Word & Image* 20, no. 1 (2004): 52–62.
Nabokov, Vladimir. *Despair*. New York: Vintage, 1965.
Nancy, Jean-Luc. *Au fond des images*. Paris: Galilée, 2003.
Naumann, Francis M. *Marcel Duchamp: The Art of Making Art in the Age of Mechanical Reproduction*. New York: Harry N. Abrams, 1999.
Neumann, Guy. *Échos et correspondances dans* Triptyque *et* Leçon des choses *de Claude Simon*. Lausanne: L'Age d'Homme, 1983.
Nietzsche, Friedrich. *Beyond Good and Evil*. Edited by Rolf-Peter Hortsmann and Judith Norman. Cambridge: Cambridge University Press, 2002.
Ortel, Philippe. *La littérature à l'ère de la photographie*. Nîmes: Jacqueline Chambon, 2002.
Owens, Craig. "Sherrie Levine at A&M Artworks." In *Beyond Recognition: Representation, Power, and Culture*, edited

by Scott Bryson, Barbara Kruger, Lynne Tillman, and Jane Weinstock, 114–16. Berkeley: University of California Press, 1992.

Patt, Lise, ed. *Searching for Sebald: Photography After W. G. Sebald*. Los Angeles: Institute of Cultural Inquiry, 2007.

Paz, Octavio. *Marcel Duchamp: Appearance Stripped Bare*. Translated by R. Phillips and D. Gardner. New York: Viking, 1978.

Perec, Georges. "Ceci n'est pas un mur." In Georges Perec and Cuchi White, *L'œil ébloui,* unpaginated. Paris: Éditions du Chêne, 1981.

———. *A Gallery Portrait*. In *Three by Perec*, translated by Ian Monk, 123–89. Boston: David R. Godine, 2004.

———. *Georges Perec: Entretiens et conférences*. 2 vols. Edited by Dominique Bertelli and Mireille Ribière. Nantes: Joseph K., 2003.

———. "Notes sur ce que je cherche." In *Penser/Classer*, 9–12. Paris: Hachette, 1985.

———. "Pour une littérature réaliste." In *L. G.: Une aventure des années soixante*, 47–66. Paris: Seuil, 1992.

———. "Species of Spaces." *Species of Spaces and Other Pieces*. Translated by John Sturrock. New York: Penguin, 1997.

———. *Un cabinet d'amateur: Histoire d'un tableau*. Paris: André Baland, 1979.

Perec, Georges and Claude Burgelin. "Le nouveau roman et le refus du réel." In *L. G.: Une aventure des années soixante*, 25–45. Paris: Seuil, 1992.

Perloff, Marjorie. *Radical Artifice: Writing Poetry in the Age of Media*. Chicago: University of Chicago Press, 1991.

Peucker, Brigitte. *Incorporating Images: Film and the Rival Arts*. Princeton: Princeton University Press, 1995.

Plato. *The Republic*. Translated by R. E. Allen. New Haven: Yale University Press, 2006.

Pliny the Elder. *L'histoire naturelle*. Edited by Hubert Zehnacker. Translated by Émile Littré. Paris: Gallimard, 1999.

Pô, Guillaume. "Perec et Boltanski, de la rue Vilin à la rue de

Vaugirard." In *Le cabinet d'amateur: Revue d'études perecquiennes* 7–8, 75–79. Toulouse: Presses Universitaires du Mirail, 1998.

Poster, Mark. *Cultural History and Postmodernity: Disciplinary Readings and Challenges*. New York: Columbia University Press, 1997.

Pouilloux, Jean-Yves. "Une prose de voyant." *Critique* 534 (1991): 866–73.

Prendergast, Christopher. *The Order of Mimesis: Balzac, Stendhal, Nerval, Flaubert*. Cambridge: Cambridge University Press, 1986.

Prince, Gerald. "The Disnarrated." *Style* 22, no. 1 (Spring 1988): 1–8.

Pugh, Anthony Cheal. "Interview with Claude Simon: Autobiography, the Novel, Politics." Translated by Anthony Pugh. *Review of Contemporary Fiction* 5, no. 1 (Spring 1985): 4–13.

Rancière, Jacques. *Le destin des images*. Paris: La fabrique des images, 2003.

Ravoux, Adeline. "Souvenirs sur le séjour de Vincent van Gogh à Auvers-sur-Oise." *Les cahiers de Vincent* 1 (1957): 7–17.

Ricardou, Jean, ed. *Claude Simon: Analyse, théorie. Actes du Colloque tenu au Centre Cultural International de Cerisy-la-Salle du 1e au 8 juillet, 1974*. Paris: 10/18, 1975.

Robertson, Duncan. *The Medieval Saints' Lives: Spiritual Renewal and Old French Literature*. Lexington KY: French Forum, 1995.

Rodowick, D. N. *Reading the Figural, or, Philosophy After the New Media*. Durham NC: Duke University Press, 2001.

Rosienski-Pellerin, Sylvie. *PERECgrinations ludiques: Étude de quelques mécanismes du jeu dans l'œuvre romanesque de Georges Perec*. Toronto: Éditions du Gref, 1995.

Saïd, Edward. *The World, the Text, and the Critic*. Cambridge MA: Harvard University Press, 1983.

Salvayre, Lydie. *Contre*. Paris: Éditions Verticales, 2002.

Samoyault, Tiphaine. "Le collectionneur." In *Le cabinet d'amateur: Revue d'études perecquiennes* 6, 83–100. Toulouse: Presses Universitaires du Mirail, 1997.

Samuels, Maurice. "Aesthetic Theories." In *The Columbia History of Twentieth-Century French Thought*, edited by Lawrence Kritzman, 134–36. New York: Columbia University Press, 2006.

———. *The Spectacular Past: Popular History and the Novel in Nineteenth-Century France*. Ithaca NY: Cornell University Press, 2004.

Sarkonak, Ralph. "Comment noyer le poisson, ou le non-dit dans *Triptyque*." *Sofistikê* 1 (2009): 37–60.

Scarpetta, Guy. *L'impureté*. Paris: Grasset, 1985.

Schwartz, Hillel. *The Culture of the Copy: Striking Likenesses, Unreasonable Facsimiles*. New York: Zone, 1996.

Schwartz, Vanessa. *Spectacular Realities: Early Mass Culture in Fin-de-Siècle Paris*. Berkeley: University of California Press, 1998.

Shaffer, Anthony. *Sleuth*. London: Mario Boyers, 1973.

Sherzer, Dina. *Representation in Contemporary French Fiction*. Lincoln: University of Nebraska Press, 1986.

Simon, Claude. *Album d'un amateur*. Remagen-Rolandseck: Rommerskirchen, 1988.

———. *Les corps conducteurs*. Paris: Minuit, 1971.

———. *Discours de Stockholm*. Paris: Minuit, 1986.

———. "La fiction mot à mot." In *Nouveau roman: Hier, aujourd'hui*, vol. 2, edited by Jean Ricardou and Françoise Van Rossum-Guyon, 73–97. Paris: 10/18, 1982.

———. *Orion aveugle*. Geneva: Albert Skira, 1970.

———. "Parenthèse." *Revue de la Bibliothèque Nationale* 15 (Spring 1985): 2–7.

———. *Photographies: 1937–1970*. Paris: Maeght, 1992.

———. *La route des Flandres*. Paris: Minuit, 1960.

———. *Triptyque*. Paris: Minuit, 1973.

———. *Triptych*. Translated by Helen Lane. New York: Viking, 1976.

Simon, Claude, and Jean Dubuffet. *Correspondance avec Jean Dubuffet, 1970–1984*. Paris: L'Échoppe, 1994.

Simon, Claude, and Jacqueline Piatier. "Entretien avec Jacqueline

Piatier: Rendre la perception confuse, multiple et simultanée du monde." *Le monde des livres*, April 26, 1967, v.

Singerman, Howard. "Seeing Sherrie Levine." *October* 67 (Winter 1994): 78–107.

Solomon-Godeau, Abigail. "Remote Control: Abigail Solomon-Godeau's Dispatches from the Image Wars." *Artforum* 42, no. 10 (Summer 2004): 61–64.

Sontag, Susan. "Interview with Gérard Lefort." *Libération*, October 11–12, 2003.

Stafford, Barbara. *Artful Science: Enlightenment Entertainment and the Eclipse of Visual Education*. Cambridge MA: MIT Press, 1994.

———. *Good Looking: Essays on the Virtue of Images*. Cambridge MA: MIT Press, 1996.

Stephens, Mitchell. *The Rise of the Image, The Fall of the Word*. Oxford: Oxford University Press, 1998.

Stern, Lesley. "*Emma* in Los Angeles: Remaking the Book and the City." In *Film Adaptation*, edited by James Naremore, 221–38. New Brunswick NJ: Rutgers University Press, 2000.

Sykes, Stuart. *Les romans de Claude Simon*. Paris: Minuit, 1979.

Thélot, Jérôme. *Les inventions littéraires de la photographie*. Paris: Presses Universitaires de France, 2003.

Thompson, Dom. *The $12 Million Stuffed Shark: The Curious Economics of Contemporary Art*. New York: Palgrave Macmillan, 2008.

Tilborgh, Louis van and Ella Hendriks. "The Tokyo *Sunflowers*: A genuine repetition by Van Gogh or a Schuffenecker forgery?" *Van Gogh Museum Journal* 6 (2001): 17–43.

YNS-Sofres. Study for *La croix*. "Les Français et la lecture." March 3, 2008. http://www.tns-sofres.com/points-de-vue. Accessed June 15, 2010.

Torgovnick, Marianna. *The Visual Arts, Pictorialism, and the Novel: James, Lawrence, and Woolf*. Princeton: Princeton University Press, 1985.

Tournier, Michel. *La goutte d'or*. Paris: Gallimard, 1988.

Toussaint, Jean-Philippe. *La télévision*. Paris: Minuit, 1996.

———. *Television*. Translated by Jordan Stump. Normal IL: Dalkey Archive, 1997.
Varnedoe, Kirk. "Joseph Roulin." *MoMA* 4, no. 2 (2001): 10–13.
Velthuis, Olav. *Imaginary Economics: Contemporary Artists and the World of Big Money*. Rotterdam: NAi, 2005.
———. *Talking Prices: Symbolic Meanings of Prices on the Market for Contemporary Art*. Princeton: Princeton University Press, 2005.
Viart, Dominique. "Pierre Michon: un art de la figure." In *Pierre Michon entre pinacothèque et bibliothèque*, edited by Ivan Farron and Karl Kürtös, 15–33. Bern: Peter Lang, 2003.
———. "What Makes People Write?" *Sites/Contemporary French and Francophone Studies* 3, no. 1 (1999): 17–20.
Vidal, Gore. "French Letters: Theories of the New Novel." In *The Selected Essays of Gore Vidal*, edited by Jay Parini, 47–72. New York: Random House, 2008.
Viel, Tanguy. "Cher Marcel Duchamp." In *Chauffe, Marcel!*, 15–20. Fonds Régional d'Art Contemporain. Paris: Isthme, 2006.
———. *Cinéma*. Paris: Minuit, 1999.
———. "La dernière conférence de Marcel Duchamp." http://www.remue.net/cont/viel.html. Accessed March 2010.
———. *Hitchcock, par exemple*. Paris: Naïve, 2010.
———. "Idées en pente." http://www.remue.net/cont/viel.html. Accessed March 2010.
———. *Maladie*. Paris: Les amis d'Inventaire/Invention, 2002.
Viel, Tanguy and H. Aubron. "Éléments pour une écriture cinéphile." *Vertigo* 19 (October 1999): 149–54.
Virilio, Paul. *The Vision Machine*. Translated by Julie Rose. Indianapolis: Indiana University Press/British Film Institute, 1994.
———. "Interview with Jérôme Sans." Translated by Henry Martin. In *Virilio Live: Selected Interviews*, edited by John Armitage, 113–20. London: Sage, 2001.
Vouilloux, Bernard. *La peinture dans le texte: xviii–xx siècles*. Paris: CNRS, 1994.
Wagner, Peter. "Ekphrasis, Iconotexts, and Intermediality—the State(s) of the Art(s)." In *Icons-Texts-Iconotexts: Essays on*

*Ekphrasis and Intermediality*, edited by Peter Wagner, 47–72. New York: Walter de Gruyter, 1996.
Wallis, Brian. "What's Wrong with This Picture? An Introduction." In *Art After Modernism: Rethinking Representation*, edited by Brian Wallis, xi–xviii. New York: New Museum of Contemporary Art, 1984.
Weber, Bruce. "Fewer Noses Stuck in Books in America, Survey Finds." *New York Times*, July 8, 2004.
Wilde, Oscar. *The Artist as Critic: Critical Writings of Oscar Wilde*. Edited by Richard Ellmann. Chicago: University of Chicago Press, 1982.
Willemen, Paul. *Looks and Frictions: Essays in Cultural Studies and Film Theory*. Bloomington: Indiana University Press/British Film Institute, 1994.

# Index

*Page numbers in italic indicate illustrations*

# In the Stages Series

*The Rushdie Letters: Freedom to Speak, Freedom to Write*
Edited by Steve MacDonogh in association with Article 19

*Mimologics*
By Gérard Genette
Edited and translated by Thaïs Morgan

*Playtexts: Ludics in Contemporary Literature*
By Warren Motte

*New Novel, New Wave, New Politics: Fiction and the Representation of History in Postwar France*
By Lynn A. Higgins

*Art for Art's Sake and Literary Life: How Politics and Markets Helped Shape the Ideology and Culture of Aestheticism, 1790–1990*
By Gene H. Bell-Villada

*Semiotic Investigations: Towards an Effective Semiotics*
By Alec McHoul

*Rue Ordener, Rue Labat*
By Sarah Kofman
Translated by Ann Smock

*Palimpsests: Literature in the Second Degree*
By Gérard Genette
Translated by Channa Newman and Claude Doubinsky

*The Mirror of Ideas*
By Michel Tournier
Translated by Jonathan F. Krell

*Fascism's Return: Scandal, Revision, and Ideology since 1980*
Edited by Richard J. Golsan

*Jacob, Menahem, and Mimoun: A Family Epic*
By Marcel Bénabou
Translated by Steven Rendall

*Naming and Unnaming: On Raymond Queneau*
By Jordan Stump

*Small Worlds: Minimalism in Contemporary French Literature*
By Warren Motte

*Loiterature*
By Ross Chambers

*The Derrida Reader: Writing Performances*
Edited by Julian Wolfreys

*Rhetorical Narratology*
By Michael Kearns

*Speaking of Crime: Narratives of Prisoners*
By Patricia E. O'Connor

*Dump This Book While You Still Can!*
By Marcel Bénabou
Translated by Steven Rendall

*Listening In: Music, Mind, and the Modernist Narrative*
By Eric Prieto

*Essays in Aesthetics*
By Gérard Genette
Translated by Dorrit Cohn

*Fuzzy Fiction*
By Jean-Louis Hippolyte

*In Praise of Flattery*
By Willis Goth Regier

*Jail Sentences: Representing Prison in Twentieth-Century French Fiction*
By Andrew Sobanet

*Why Fiction?*
By Jean-Marie Schaeffer
Translated by Dorrit Cohn

*Quotology*
By Willis Goth Regier

*The Other Book: Bewilderments of Fiction*
By Jordan Stump

*Pictures into Words: Images in Contemporary French Fiction*
By Ari J. Blatt